ADVANCE PRAISE FOR

Très Green, Très Clean, Très ~~Chic~~

D0508375

"Rebecca Leffler shares her savoir faire for keeping healthy, with French-inspired beauty tips along with tasty salads, soups, ~~dips~~, and tonics—*à votre santé!*"

—**David Lebovitz,** author of *My Paris Kitchen*

"Rebecca manages the rare feat of bringing together glamour, a playful tone, and a good appetite. Like a good friend, she shares the best of her French and American influences through tips and delicious recipes that are sure to inspire a fresh and healthy new you."

—**Clotilde Dusoulier,** author of *The French Market Cookbook* and *Edible French*

"Rebecca Leffler is a bright light in the world of wellness—she has a lot of fun all while helping you eat and live healthier and cleaner. This book is a treat!"

—**Drew Ramsey, MD,** author of *Fifty Shades of Kale*

"If you've ever assumed that healthy eating means bland, "crunchy," or flavorless food, think again. Rebecca Leffler has set out to prove that green cuisine—food that's wholesome, unprocessed, and veggie-centric—can be sophisticated, fun, and—above all else— *très* chic. With her colorful, creative recipes, and cheery voice, Leffler marries the art of living fashionably with the art of living well."

—**Gena Hamshaw,** certified clinical nutritionist and author of *Choosing Raw*

"A fantastic combination of delicious recipes, beauty tips, and yoga exercises for any time of the year."

—**Rachel Khoo,** author of *The Little Paris Kitchen* and *My Little French Kitchen*

"Rebecca's Leffler's book *Très Green, Très Clean, Très Chic* is witty, and full of delicious recipes, it's true. But she has created so much more than a cookbook: this is truly a green, healthy, and happy lifestyle guide with fabulous beauty tips, energizing yoga postures, and even playlists to make your days shine! Her sense of humor and passion for all things wholesome will surely inspire you to put a green, French twist on just about everything. *C'est magnifique!*"

—**Sarah Britton,** author of *My New Roots*

"This is the instruction manual for the 'It Girl' who wants to live a green and glamorous life. *Très Green, Très Clean, Très Chic* is sassy and witty, and packed with beautifully designed meals that will keep a girl energized, radiant, and ready to strut her stuff! Rebecca Leffler's book is this generation's *French Women Don't Get Fat.*"

—**Dana James, MS, CNS, CDN, BANT, AADP,** founder and director of Food Coach NYC

"Rebecca Leffler's haute approach to green cuisine and everything in between makes *Très Green, Très Clean, Très Chic* a must-have for anyone who wants to embody the eco-friendly, green lifestyle. Her tasty and health-affirming recipes work wonders on the skin and promote optimal wellbeing. Nestled in colorful pages are hip lifestyle tips that speak to Rebecca's expertise, style, and passion. It's a great primer for anyone who wants to live a green and glamorous life!"

—**Latham Thomas,** maternity wellness expert and author of *Mama Glow: A Hip Guide to Your Fabulous Abundant Pregnancy*; www.mamaglow.com

THE EXPERIMENT

BECAUSE EVERY BOOK IS A TEST OF NEW IDEAS

TRÈS GREEN, TRÈS CLEAN, TRÈS CHIC

Eat (and Live!) the New French Way

WITH PLANT-BASED, GLUTEN-FREE RECIPES FOR EVERY SEASON

Rebecca Leffler

Photographs by Sandra Mahut

THE EXPERIMENT
NEW YORK

The Experiment, LLC
220 East 23rd Street, Suite 301
New York, NY 10010-4674
www.theexperimentpublishing.com

This book contains the opinions and ideas of its author. It is intended to provide helpful and informative material on the subjects addressed in the book. It is sold with the understanding that the author and publisher are not engaged in rendering medical, health, or any other kind of personal professional services in the book. The author and publisher specifically disclaim all responsibility for any liability, loss, or risk—personal or otherwise—that is incurred as a consequence, directly or indirectly, of the use and application of any of the contents of this book.

The Experiment's books are available at special discounts when purchased in bulk for premiums and sales promotions as well as for fund-raising or educational use. For details, contact us at info@theexperimentpublishing.com.

Library of Congress Cataloging-in-Publication Data
Leffler, Rebecca, author.
 [Green, glam & gourmande. English]
 Très green, très clean, très chic : eat (and live) the new French way with plant-based, gluten-free recipes for every season / Rebecca Leffler ; photographs by Sandra Mahut.
    pages cm
 Includes index.
 ISBN 978-1-61519-251-9 (pbk.) -- ISBN 978-1-61519-252-6 (ebook)
 1. Vegan cooking--France. 2. Seasonal cooking--France. 3. Cooking, French. 4. Gluten-free diet--Recipes. 5. Gluten-free foods. I. Title.
 TX837.L4413 2014
 641.5944--dc23
                    2014040394

ISBN 978-1-61519-251-9
Ebook ISBN 978-1-61519-252-6

Cover design by Anna Goldstein
Cover photographs by Sandra Mahut
Author photograph by Ola Rindal
Text design by Pauline Neuwirth, Neuwirth & Associates, Inc.

Manufactured in China
Distributed by Workman Publishing Company, Inc.
Distributed simultaneously in Canada by Thomas Allen & Son Ltd.

First printing February 2015
10 9 8 7 6 5 4 3 2 1

"Let food be thy medicine and medicine be thy food."
Hippocrates

"Eat food. Not too much. Mostly plants."
Michael Pollan

"OK, as long as it's très *chic and* très *delicious."*
Rebecca Leffler

Contents

Fall

Winter

INTRO

Santé! Cheers to your health!

Santé! In French, *santé* means "cheers," but it's also the word for "health." While it may seem ironic to yell about health in the midst of drinking wine (likely while eating bread, cheese, meat, and pastry), good health and enjoying *la vie* aren't mutually exclusive. France may be known for its exquisite pastries and cream sauces, but in fact there is a lot to learn about health from the French way of eating. The French typically eat in moderation and, instead of depriving themselves, enjoy small portions of things like butter, chocolate, and crème.

Seasonal eating is the norm all over the country. I remember searching desperately for an apple tarte Tatin in the summertime to no avail, and asking for blueberries at the farmers market in February, much to the local farmers' chagrin: *Blueberries? In February? Sacre bleu!* they said with a chuckle.

In France, mealtime is sacred. It's a time when friends and family come together to enjoy food, drinks, and each other's company. Yes, I do mean *enjoy*, without counting calories or worrying about sugar content. Remember the last time you did that? I've learned never to make any plans for "after dinner" in France, since dinners spent with friends typically last for hours on end. They eat slowly and savor every bite.

And while we like to mock Europeans' typical "long lunch," taking time to relax and fully chew our food is essential to digestion and is eventually more productive than grabbing a sandwich and chowing down at one's desk. Sure, we don't always have the time for this, but even simply turning off our cell phones while we eat a quick lunch on the go can make all the difference.

But it's not just the rest of the world that has something to learn from the French; the French are learning new ways to eat, too. That's what this book is all about—so read on!

VIVE LA VÉGOLUTION!

We're in the midst of a *végolution* across the globe. *Au revoir* to the old regime of processed foods and *bonjour* to a new Green Republic. *Oui oui,* "green" indeed. Don't be scared. Going green doesn't have to mean moving to a farm, adopting a pet goat, and giving up all worldly possessions. Goats are cute, but come *on*—we live in the twenty-first century, many of us in urban environments. It would be impossible to be 100 percent "green" just like it isn't realistic to plan to eat a perfect diet 100 percent of the time.

In fact, the "perfect" diet doesn't exist. What is perfection for one person may be the worst possible diet for someone else. The "perfect" diet depends on our individual body types, the pace of our daily lives, the season, and where we're living. A seventy-year-old Minnesotan won't have the same diet as a teenager in Mexico, and a thirty-year-old male marathon runner has different dietary needs from a sixty-year-old woman (even if she runs marathons, too!).

But some things are more universal than others. From Hollywood to NYC, green is the new black—it's a *must-have* for leading a happy and healthy life. Celebrities are being photographed carrying *the* new "it" accessory: a giant jar of green smoothie. Even Beyoncé and Jay-Z were momentarily vegan. *Le green, c'est chic!* And Kermit the Frog was ahead of his time: Today, it's also *easy* being green, even if you aren't a millionaire or celebrity or famous frog.

Having to choose between pleasure and health is *so* last season. And "salad" doesn't have to mean a sad pile of lettuce on a plate. With just a few lifestyle changes, a carrot can become sexy, a sweet potato breathtaking, and an avocado a work of art. Changing your way of eating doesn't mean depriving yourself. Counting calories. Worrying all the time. Depressing, isn't it? And totally counterproductive.

So let's get rid of this "no" mentality. Instead, let's say *OUI. Oui* to more color, more flavor, more variety, more vegetables, more grains, more seeds, more legumes, more nuts and fruits, and more respect for each food. *Oui* to taking more time to savor every morsel, to meditate, to enjoy . . .

In French, the word for "vegan" is *végétalien.* Pronounced vay-jay-tALIEN. Yes, it sounds like a little green Martian is coming to invade your plate and your life, right? I can see you sweating profusely as you read this. "This girl is about to take away my sacred cheese and meat! Help!" Don't panic! My intentions are peaceful.

All of the recipes in this book—even the cakes—are technically "v-v-v-egan" (OK, there, I said it), gluten-free, soy-free (unless you opt for tamari or soy-based miso), and refined-sugar-free. However, I'm not trying to convert anyone to an exclusively vegetarian, vegan, sugar-free, soy-free, gluten-free diet, and certainly not a *taste*-free one! In fact, let's throw all labels out the door, shall we?

Unless you have allergies or other food-related health issues, the idea isn't necessarily to eat a specific way 100 percent of the time. Instead, try to incorporate *more* wonderful, healthy plant-based foods into your life and, consequently, eat *less* processed food and artery-clogging fare. Start eating chickpea pizza, *Love*sagna, and creamy "cheesecake" made from nuts and, over time, you'll want *less* of the other stuff, I promise. Plus, these recipes are notably *without* many ingredients, but if said ingredients are near and dear to your heart, I invite you to enjoy them *with* these things.

Not everyone needs to stop eating gluten, but many people feel better if they do—and just about everyone is better off without the highly refined carbs found in most wheat products! The same goes for soy, refined sugar, alcohol, and other foods you might be sensitive to. Listen to *your* body.

A whole-foods, plant-based diet respects the body and gives it everything it needs. You just need to learn how to do it. Warning: Side effects may include enjoying it, feeling more energized, and looking fabulous.

This isn't simply a cookbook. *Au contraire!* You'll find positive playlists, beauty tips, and even yoga poses. "Yoga poses? In a cookbook?" Yes, because haven't you heard? Body and mind are intertwined. Eating

healthy foods is important, *bien sûr*, but it's all part of a healthy *lifestyle*. We also need to take pleasure in our food, respect our digestion, and eliminate stress (or at least, more realistically, do the best we can to decrease it). Yoga works on our feelings, our movement, our breathing, our concentration, our determination, and our ability to release tension. So if you happen to stumble upon a yoga posture or *deux* among the recipes, don't hesitate to test them out, even in your kitchen while that pot is simmering!

Oh, and feel free to sing and dance as well—I've included positive playlists in every chapter to put you in the mood for food! The energy you put into what you're eating really affects its taste and the ability of your body to absorb its goodness. I'm not telling you to sing to your food (though you may be inclined to serenade your chocolate mousse; it's *that* good)—I just want you to *enjoy* the process.

Speaking of rhythm, listening to your body—and mind!—means paying attention to the rhythm of the seasons, so I've divided this book into the four seasons. Depending on the temperature or the brightness outside, our bodies want and need different things. So say *oui* to the freedom of bodily expression. Listen to your body: it will reward you.

So let's raise a glass (of green juice!). Santé! To your health!

The Pantry:
Must-Have Basics

A kitchen is like a closet: You need to fill it appropriately
to prepare for any situation.

As Julia Child said, "You don't have to cook fancy or complicated
masterpieces—just good food from fresh ingredients."

INGREDIENTS YOU CAN'T LIVE WITHOUT

(Well, you can, but why would you want to?)

FRESH PRODUCE

The availability, price, flavor, and carbon footprint of produce all depend on the season. The following list is adaptable based on what you find at the store or market, even if today, thanks to globalization, most of these items—even the organic ones!—are available all year long. Of course, if you're in the United States, an American tomato in the summer is likely cheaper and more flavorful, ubiquitous, and farmer-friendly than a coconut that travels all the way from Thailand in the dead of winter, but you also need to listen to your body. If your body wants an avocado in wintertime (mine usually does!), then even if you don't live in California or Spain, go on, eat it!

Your food fashion essentials for all seasons:

Greens! (kale, spinach, chard, collards, dandelion, arugula . . .) • Avocados • Broccoli • Carrots • Celery • Cauliflower • Sweet potatoes • Onions • Garlic • Fresh or dried herbs (parsley, cilantro, basil, rosemary, thyme, chives, mint, dill . . .) • Bananas • Apples • Lemons • Berries (strawberries, blueberries . . . fresh during berry season, but frozen organic are also great)

If possible, organic produce is usually the better option, but I know that it is typically more expensive and harder to find. So *voilà*: a list of the "Dirty Dozen," the foods that it's best to buy organic, and a list of the "cleanest," of which it's OK to buy conventional versions.

The Dirty Dozen Plus* (packed with pesticides)

Apples • Celery • Strawberries • Grapes • Peaches • Imported nectarines • Spinach • Sweet bell peppers • Cherry tomatoes • Imported snap peas • Cucumbers • Potatoes • Kale/collard greens • Hot peppers

The Clean Fifteen* (less pesticide-ridden)

Avocados • Sweet corn • Pineapple • Cabbage • Peas (frozen) • Onions • Asparagus • Papaya • Kiwi • Eggplant • Sweet potatoes • Mangoes • Grapefruit • Cantaloupe • Cauliflower

"To peel or not to peel . . . that is the question."

Occasionally in these recipes, you'll notice that I recommend using fruit and vegetables without peeling them. It's totally fine . . . and healthy! Have you noticed that your skin is simply *magnifique* since you've started to pay attention to your lifestyle choices? It's the same for plants! They have magnificent skin, rich in fiber, antioxidants, vitamins, and minerals. When we peel off the skin, we lose these nutrients. So don't throw away apple, pear, peach, or nectarine skins or lemon and orange zest. You can even eat the skins of mangoes and kiwis, but hey, even *I'm* not quite there yet.

Keep the skins on when you can, especially if you buy organic and wash thoroughly—very thoroughly!—before you eat them. Organic is important here because most fruit and vegetable skins are rich in nutrients, but also rich in . . . pesticides! (Remember Snow White's poisoned apple? Oh yes, it was definitely not organic. She should have tried a pesticide-free variety and lived happily ever after from the start.) If you can't buy organic fruit, no problem—just peel it.

And . . . don't be scared! The skin of organic fruits and veggies is often quite ugly, but remember you can't judge a book by its cover. The beautiful apples you see in the supermarket? They are often covered with wax! Beware!

SHELF-STABLE INGREDIENTS

Grains (and "pseudograins," seeds of other plants in disguise)

White quinoa • Red, black, or multicolored quinoa • Brown rice • Wild rice • Millet • Amaranth • Buckwheat

Pasta

Mung bean noodles • 100% buckwheat soba noodles • Other gluten-free pasta (usually brown rice or quinoa based)

Legumes

Red lentils • Green lentils (preferably du Puy or French) • Chickpeas • White beans • Black beans • Mung beans

Nuts and dried fruits

Almonds • Walnuts • Cashews • Hazelnuts • Macadamia nuts • Brazil nuts • Pecans • Dates (preferably Medjool) • Raisins • Sun-dried tomatoes • Coconut flakes

Nut and seed butters

Almond butter • Hazelnut butter • Tahini • Coconut butter (or Coconut Manna)

Seeds

Sesame seeds • Hemp seeds • Chia seeds • Sunflower seeds • Flaxseeds • Pumpkin seeds

Superfoods (see page 25)

Raw cacao powder • Mesquite powder • Carob powder • Spirulina powder • Maca powder (opt for gelatinized maca, as it is more potent and easier to digest) • Goji berries • Lucuma powder • Açaí powder or frozen açaí • Bee pollen (for "bee-gans" only) • Aloe vera • Mulberries • Goldenberries

Oils and vinegar

Coconut oil (extra virgin, unrefined, and cold-pressed) • Apple cider vinegar • Olive oil (extra virgin and cold-pressed) • Pumpkin seed oil • Sesame oil (plain and toasted) • Walnut oil • Hemp oil • Hazelnut oil • Truffle oil (if you feel fancy!) • Avocado oil

Spices and herbs

Vanilla† • Cinnamon • Turmeric • Black pepper • Cayenne pepper • Cumin • Coriander • Curry powder • Oregano • Nutmeg • Cloves • Cardamom • Herbes de Provence blend • Thyme

Plant-based milks (if you don't make your own! See page 1 if you want to.)

Almond milk • Hazelnut milk • Hemp milk • Oat and/or rice milk • Coconut milk

Condiments

Miso paste (preferably sweet white or chickpea miso) • Coconut aminos or tamari • Nori sheets • Dulse • Other seaweed (fresh or dried): wakame, arame, hijiki, kelp, sea lettuce, kombu • Nutritional yeast • Salt (Himalayan pink salt, if possible, or sea salt) • Olives (non-vinegar-based if possible) • Dijon mustard (preferably apple cider vinegar–based) • Sauerkraut (unpasteurized!)

---

*based on 2014 EWG (Environmental Working Group) data

† Try to use vanilla bean or powder when possible. If you can't find it, vanilla extract works in most recipes, but try to opt for an alcohol-free variety.

Baking basics

Buckwheat flour • Chickpea flour • Brown rice flour • Coconut flour • Quinoa flour • Almond flour (for homemade, see page 14) • Baking powder • Arrowroot powder • Sorghum, millet, or all-purpose gluten-free flour

Teas, herbal blends, and essential oils

Matcha powder • Green tea • Herbal teas (fresh chamomile, mint, fennel, licorice, lemon verbena, or prepared tea bags) • Peppermint essential oil

Sweeteners

Coconut sugar • Coconut nectar • Maple syrup • Honey (raw and preferably local—for "bee-gans" only) • Stevia • Yacon syrup

Useful kitchen tools for green cooking

Refrigerator • Freezer • Oven • A powerful blender (the "it" blender is the Vitamix; in select recipes a personal or mini-blender works, too) • Steamer (Gaggenau's built-in steamer is the best of le best, but a pot with a steamer addition also works) • Food processor • Tea kettle • Good cutting boards • Microplane zester • Glass jars • Circular metal mold • Optional: dehydrator, mandoline, juicer, nut milk bag, toaster oven, slow-cooker, spiralizer

Spice up your life!

The health benefits of spices

The French have a word for something that never goes out of style: *indémodable*. Well, spices are every kitchen's *indémodable* accessory. Spices make any meal smell good, taste good, and look good . . . without adding any fat, calories, salt, or sugar. With just a spice or *deux*, a dish can be completely transformed! Not to mention that they are packed with nutritional benefits to boot. Cloves help get rid of bad breath, make teeth healthier, ease digestion, fight inflammation, and soothe a headache or sore throat. Nutmeg calms the stomach, detoxifies the liver, makes the skin glow, and is a natural remedy for anxiety and depression. Cardamom fights bloating, warms the entire body, and is very detoxifying. And that's only the beginning! Make sure to give spices center stage in your kitchen. (That's right, the newest member of the Spice Girls is Healthy Spice!)

Himalayan salt

Stop the assault on salt!

Now, I'm sure everyone has been telling you throughout your life to avoid salt, *oui*? They're not altogether wrong. Too much salt isn't good for you, and table salt is dried at such a high heat that its natural structure is completely altered and void of any nutrients, except added iodine. Himalayan salt, however, is a pretty-in-pink natural salt mined in the Himalayan mountains and revered for centuries for its healing properties. Himalayan salt is rich in minerals and iodine and has less sodium than table salt. This is salt in its most natural form, and it helps to create a balance of electrolytes in the body, increase hydration (oh yes, you read correctly), balance the pH of the entire body, strengthen bones, and help you detoxify and better absorb nutrients. So don't throw this incredible ingredient away: Cook with it, sprinkle it (I said *sprinkle*—moderation, my friends!) over salads, and add it to soups to season.

MY BEST FRIEND FOODS

Just like in life, we all have our best friends in the kitchen. Meet mine! You'll see, they're all lovely. They mix well with other foods, and you can keep most of them around for a long time without getting sick of them. You'll find them in many recipes in this book, so get used to spending time together. You can always recognize your new taste "buds" by this logo: ♥

Avocado (page 87) • Lemon (page 26) • Ginger (page 93) • Sweet potato (page 152) • Almonds (page 14) • Seaweed (page 158) • Spirulina powder (page 62) • Banana (page 116) • Chia (page 39) • Hemp (page 10) • Cacao (page 71) • Quinoa (page 15) • Apples (page 112) • Greens galore (page 16) • Miso (page 8) • Coconut (page 3) • Carrots (page 68) • Turmeric (page 160)

MY BEST ENEMY FOODS

"Keep your friends close, and your enemies closer. . ." No, please don't keep enemy foods close, or in the house if you can help it, even if you indulge once in a while. Just so things are clear between us from the get-go, I'd like to warn you that you won't find any recipes in this book that include dairy, gluten, coffee, alcohol, soy (other than optional tamari and soy-based miso), white/refined sugar, meat, eggs, or fish. You are of course welcome to integrate those foods into these recipes. Nothing is off limits; just listen to your body.

Sugar, Sugar . . .

Hey, sugar!

Yes, you. I think you're sweet. So sweet, in fact, that you don't need to get any sweeter. Step away from the sugar! I know, I know, sugar is addictive. And I am a reformed sugar addict, so I'm here to be your sugar sponsor.

Let me guess. Open your pantry drawer and you've got the white stuff, baby. Grab it. Pour some sugar on me. No, don't, but please pour it into your garbage can immediately. Wow, doesn't that feel good?

Sugar is the new enemy of the state. Everywhere you turn, doctors and nutritionists (and your best friend, am I right?) are waging war against sugar. Look—they're all right. Sugar is BAD to the bone (literally—too much will make your bones brittle).

That said, part of a sweet life is . . . pleasure! So if, once in a while, a tiny spoonful of sugar makes its way onto your plate, enjoy the moment and let your saccharine sister sing and dance her way through your body. Just be sure to get rid of this unwanted houseguest when you're done with her and detox!

As you know, I am a big fan of consuming nutrient-rich fruits, plus adding just a spoonful of coconut sugar or maple syrup to help the food-as-medicine go down. That said, even natural sugar is something to be enjoyed in moderation, so don't go becoming a fruitarian (yes, that's a real thing).

EGGCELLENT EGG REPLACERS

Don't be chicken: try these easy replacements for eggs in cooking and baking.

SAVORY	SWEET
1 tablespoon agar-agar + 2 tablespoons room-temperature water	1 tablespoon potato or tapioca starch + 2 tablespoons water (to bind ingredients in a cupcake or bread, for example)
♥ 1 tablespoon chia seeds + 3 tablespoons room-temperature water	♥ ½ large mashed banana (for a soft or moist consistency plus sweetness)
1 tablespoon ground flaxseeds + 3 tablespoons room-temperature water	♥ ¼ cup (50 ml) applesauce or pumpkin puree (for moist cake)
1 tablespoon arrowroot powder + 2 tablespoons room-temperature water	2 tablespoons nut butter or tahini

SIX RULES FOR HEALTHY EATING

Leo Galland, MD

Author of The Fat Resistance Diet, *Director of the Foundation for Integrated Medicine*

Good nutrition is the foundation of a healthy lifestyle. These six principles for healthy eating are supported by hundreds of scientific studies. They help your body combat inflammation and resist chronic degenerative diseases that promote aging and attack your heart and blood vessels, your immune system, your brain, and your digestive tract.

RULE #1: HIGH NUTRIENT DENSITY

Put simply, this means that you get the most nutritional value for the calories you consume. Food should be rich in one or more of the dietary elements you need to stay healthy, heal inflammation, and maintain a permanently healthy weight, like vitamins, minerals, phytonutrients, fiber, and omega-3 fatty acids. You won't see any junk food or empty calories in this book. You won't find any added sugar, artificial sweeteners, or processed fats and oils in any of the recipes.

RULE #2: NO TRANS FATS

Trans fats are created by modification through hydrogenation (the addition of hydrogen) of the polyunsaturated fats found in vegetable oils and fish oils. Most trans fats are created by industrial hydrogenation, but cattle naturally hydrogenate the fatty acids they eat, creating trans fats that enter their flesh and their milk. Trans fats can be found in margarine and in the hydrogenated vegetable oils used in most packaged and processed foods and baked goods. Trans fats serve no nutritional purpose and are extremely bad for your health. Healthy vegetarian meals steer you clear of them.

RULE #3: ABUNDANT OMEGA-3 CONTENT

Omega-3 fats are essential to the healthy functioning of body and brain. Omega-3s help heal inflammation as well as promote a wide range of cellular activities. They improve or prevent depression, Alzheimer's disease, cardiac arrhythmias, and a number of other disorders. Plant sources of omega-3s include ground flaxseeds, walnuts, beans (such as navy and kidney), and leafy greens.

RULE #4: LOTS OF FIBER— AT LEAST 20 TO 30 GRAMS PER DAY

Numerous studies have shown that high-fiber diets have an anti-inflammatory effect. For example, a study conducted at the Medical University of South Carolina, published in 2003 in the *American Journal of Cardiology*, found that, among nearly 5,000 adults who represented a cross-section of the US population, higher consumption of dietary fiber was correlated with lower levels of C-reactive protein (CRP), a key indicator of inflammation. In other studies, high fiber intake was associated with protection against heart disease, stroke, and certain kinds of cancer.

High-fiber foods aren't only healthy; they're also bulky and filling. Studies have shown that higher fiber intakes are associated with more satisfaction after a meal and better appetite control, helping to facilitate weight loss.

RULE #5: AT LEAST 9 SERVINGS OF VEGETABLES AND FRUITS EACH DAY

Vegetables and fruits are an excellent source of fiber and antioxidants, including the flavonoids and carotenoids that give fruits and vegetables their intense flavors and bright colors. Many flavonoids have anti-inflammatory effects that have been demonstrated in scientific studies and are associated with a decreased risk of heart disease and stroke. The human diet potentially includes some 400 separate flavonoids—but most Westerners eat only a tiny fraction of these enticing nutrients.

To give you a rough idea of how impoverished most of our diets tend to be, traditional Asian cuisines supply 4 to 5 grams of flavonoids per day, from tea, spices, herbs, and vegetables; the typical Western diet supplies only about 1 gram per day, mostly from onions and apples.

The deepest red and blue flavonoids belong to a subgroup called anthocyanins, found in the jewel-like colors of blueberries, cherries, and pomegranate seeds.

Carotenoids are abundant in carrots, tomatoes, and other yellow, red, and orange foods, as well as spinach. Carotenoids have antioxidant and anti-inflammatory effects, and their consumption is associated with a decreased risk of cancer and heart disease. The best known is beta-carotene, which helps the body make vitamin A. Lutein, found in spinach, has been shown to protect the retina of the eyes from a condition called macular degeneration, which can lead to blindness. Lycopene, found in tomatoes, decreases the incidence of ovarian cancer and prostate cancer.

It's easier for the body to absorb carotenoids if they're consumed with a little oil or fat. For a large bowl of salad, for example, a teaspoon of oil is needed for maximum absorption.

For fighting inflammation, the more colorful your diet, the better.

RULE #6: SPICE YOUR FOOD

Herbs and spices have been shown to contain potent anti-inflammatory compounds—not only in research studies, but among real people eating real food. I recommend them not only for their anti-inflammatory effects but also for the great taste they impart to food. Use spices from this list generously every day: basil, cardamom, cilantro, cinnamon, cloves, cumin, garlic, ginger, onion, parsley, and turmeric.

A Très Green Makeunder

by Rose-Marie Swift

Rose-Marie Swift is the epitome of green and glam beauty. She's been a makeup artist for more than 20 years and is the glow-to girl for Gisele Bunchen, Miranda Kerr, Zoe Saldana, and so many other celebeauties. She's worked with some of the top photographers in the world (Hedi Slimane, Patrick Demarchelier, Mario Sorrenti . . .) and collaborated with top magazines (*Elle, Vogue, W, Marie Claire* . . .) and brands (Louis Vuitton, Ralph Lauren, Victoria's Secret . . .). When she discovered just how much cosmetic products can contribute to serious health issues—including her own!—Rose-Marie set out to quite literally change the face of cosmetics. Her RMS Beauty line of makeup is free of toxic chemicals and filled with unrefined, organic, healing ingredients (most of which are so natural you could—almost!—eat them).

I asked this beauty guru to share her inside secrets to glowing skin.

"Your skin is a living organism. It breathes, interacts, and absorbs information from everything it encounters. It's in constant communication with the environment. We now know that whatever we put on the skin is absorbed into the bloodstream. So feed yourself—and your skin!—well."

Xoxo, Rose-Marie

Healthy Skin Do's and Don'ts à la Rose-Marie

DO . . .

Eat well: I am a firm believer that your skin is a mirror to your gut, and that a healthy diet does more for your skin health than a bottle of the most expensive synthetic and genetically engineered "hope in a jar." Eat healthy food, eat wisely, and don't underestimate the power of clean water, fresh organic fruits and vegetables, probiotics, digestive enzymes, and exercise. Living a healthy life is what gives us beautiful, healthy, glowing skin.

Drink Rose-Marie's skinsational green juice: cucumber, celery, fennel, kale, Swiss chard, and an apple (optional).

Slather coconut oil all over your face: My favorite ingredient in my products has to be the raw coconut oil that I use. My line wouldn't be what it is without that key ingredient. Coconut oil contains high levels of lauric acid, which is plentiful in human breast milk and rarely found in nature. Lauric acid is antifungal, antibacterial, antiviral, and antimicrobial.

Opt for a simple, but elegant, look: My beauty philosophy will always be "less is more." In the era of YouTube and Instagram, being overly made up is alive and well, but in reality (and natural light) that amount of makeup is not a desirable look by any means. Allow your skin to breathe and choose products that work synergistically with it.

Drink lots of water: The solution to pollution is dilution—so drink lots of water to flush toxins out of the body. Our environment is full of them in this day and age. Remember, you wear your skin for the rest of your life.

Put your food on your face. You can use masks made of spirulina and use zeolite clay in the bath to help pull out toxic chemicals.

Use pure organic oils on the skin, such as jojoba and coconut. The cosmetic industry has led us to believe that oils clog the skin. This old belief is dated, and even top dermatologists are recommending oils for the skin.

DON'T . . .

Choose loose powder mineral lines. They tend to dehydrate the skin over the long term and look terribly aging on mature skin. You do not want to exaggerate fine lines and wrinkles.

Overuse products that contain an abundance of steam-distilled essential oils, as they can cause irritation to sensitive skin and can dehydrate the skin in the long term.

Use a powder brush. Opt for a cotton puff (natural, not synthetic). A puff sets the look of the skin better, while a brush simply deposits the powder onto the skin causing a powder buildup.

Forget to clean off your makeup in the evening before you go to sleep. Never go to bed with your makeup on. Those nasty synthetic chemicals and alcohols will ruin your skin, dry out your eyelashes and the delicate skin around your eyes, and cause premature aging. Do not get into that habit.

The Basics: A Vegucation

"Once you have mastered a technique, you barely have to look at a recipe again."

—Julia Child

Hey, fancy-pants, before you dress for green kitchen success, make sure you have mastered the basics of healthy cooking. Think of these as the skinny jeans of green eating. If you try to twist, turn, squeeze, crunch, and scream your way into them, you'll only injure yourself (and your ego). If you wait until you and your body are ready for them, they'll slide on easily. (This is also a wonderful metaphor since, odds are, once you start listening to your body and eating *more* green, there may be *less* of you to jam into those jeans!)

Once you master these basic preparation techniques, the rest is easy, I promise! Plant-based cooking is all about intriguing color and flavor combinations, but we need to start with the basics. They may seem boring or simple, but they are essential for quality cuisine. So, *voilà*: my favorite classic, timeless recipes that can be reinvented season after season for your culinary haute couture collection.

Soaking and cooking times and tips can be found on pages 14 and 18.

LAIT DE PLANTS: HOMEMADE PLANT-BASED MILKS

For smoothies, milkshakes, warm drinks, tea lattés, soups, grains, granola, porridge, oatmeal, pudding, or simply "naked" in a glass!

Wipe away that milk mustache. White dairy foam may have been a fashionable facial accessory in the past, but the fact is that milk does *not* do a body good. Don't have a cow—there are so many alternatives to classic dairy milk that you'll never feel deprived.

So why do we need an alternative?

Cow's milk is a wonderful thing … for baby cows. For humans, however, not so much. For the first few formative years, children can benefit from milk's nutrient content, but after that … forget it! Or at least try to minimize dairy consumption. Dairy is very difficult for human bodies to digest and metabolize, so the less we ingest, the better off we are.

Many people don't produce enough lactase, the enzyme that digests milk sugar, so the sugar ferments in the gut, causing unpleasant symptoms that can manifest in digestive, skin, and other inflammatory conditions. According to *The China Study,* casein—the main protein in dairy—has been linked to cancer. And what about the famous calcium? In fact, countries that consume the most dairy have the highest osteoporosis rates. Dairy is highly acidic, so our bodies tend to draw calcium from our bones to neutralize that acidity. Plant-based calcium (from leafy greens, almonds, sesame seeds, broccoli, whole grains, and beans, for example) has been scientifically proven to be more absorbable by the body than the calcium in dairy.

As for dampening your morning bowl of cereal, thickening your main courses, or creating creamy sauces or desserts, have no fear: Plant-based milks are here! Nowadays, there are entire shelves devoted to them in most grocery stores. However, most of these are unfortunately packed with artificial sweeteners and additives. It's so easy to make your own instead! Don't worry, no farm needed. Plant-based milk isn't, in fact, milk; it's a liquid made from nuts, seeds, or grains that *looks* like dairy milk, thanks to a white color and creamy texture, but that tastes far better and is much easier to digest.

Almond milk may be the most ubiquitous of *lait de* plants, but any seed, nut, or grain can be miraculously transformed into "milk." Sure, some taste better than others, and they all feature different nutritional profiles, but the possibilities are endless . . . and delicious. Store your *lait de* plants in the fridge in a glass jar for just a few days.

Basic Lait de Nuts (almond milk, hazelnut milk, walnut milk . . .)

MAKES 1 SERVING

♥ ¼ CUP (50 G) ALMONDS, HAZELNUTS, PECANS, BRAZIL NUTS, WALNUTS, CASHEWS, ETC.
1 MEDJOOL DATE
1 CUP (250 ML) WATER OR COCONUT WATER
A PINCH OF SALT
¼ TEASPOON VANILLA POWDER OR EXTRACT

Soak the nuts according to the directions on page 14. Soak the date in hot water, then peel it and remove the pit. Rinse the nuts in a sieve, then add to a blender with the water and vanilla and blend until it takes on a "milky" appearance and texture. Strain through a sieve or nut milk bag for a thinner consistency or leave thick and creamy.

For a très quick lait de nuts, simply blend 2 tablespoons of nut butter (homemade or store-bought) with 1 cup of coconut water or water, then add whatever sweetener and spices you like. Magic milk!

"Totally Nuts" Lait de Nuts

MAKES 1 SERVING

1 TABLESPOON WALNUTS
♥ 1 TABLESPOON ALMONDS
1 TABLESPOON BRAZIL NUTS
1 TABLESPOON PECANS
1 MEDJOOL DATE
1 CUP (250 ML) WATER OR COCONUT WATER
A PINCH OF SALT
¼ TEASPOON VANILLA POWDER OR EXTRACT

Soak the nuts according to the directions on page 14. You can soak each variety of nuts separately or soak all together. (Note: The nuts all have different "soaking times," but you just want them to be soft enough to blend, so it's OK if they haven't taken a bath for the "official" amount of time.) Either way, make sure to rinse them very well first. Soak the date in hot water, then peel it and remove the pit. Rinse the nuts in a sieve, then add to a blender with the water and vanilla and blend until it takes on a "milky" appearance and texture. Strain through a sieve or nut milk bag for a thinner consistency, or leave thick and creamy.

Hippie-Chic Hemp Milk

Hemp milk is so easy to make—just blend and drink. It also happens to be *très* nutrient-dense (think protein, omega-3s, vitamins, calcium, iron, and more!). I can't hemp falling in love with this easy, breezy beverage.

MAKES 1 SERVING

♥ 3 TABLESPOONS HULLED HEMP SEEDS
1 CUP (250 ML) WATER OR COCONUT WATER
1 MEDJOOL DATE, SOAKED, PEELED, AND PITTED
A PINCH OF SALT
¼ TEASPOON VANILLA POWDER OR EXTRACT

Blend all ingredients in a high-speed blender. *Voilà!*

Lait de Coconut, Two Ways

LAIT DE COCONUT: PART UN

The 100 percent coconut version.

MAKES 1 SERVING

♥ 1 YOUNG THAI COCONUT

Using a sharp knife, *carefully* jab the tip of the coconut until you find the softest point. (Please don't hurt yourself! Coconut milk is so good, but *so* not worth a trip to the hospital.) Pierce through the shell, then move the knife around a bit to make a small hole. Pour the coconut water out into a glass. Tap the outer edge of the coconut with a hammer until it's cracked enough that you can open it easily with your hands (again, be careful!). Scoop the white "meat" of the coconut from the sides of the shell and place into a blender with the coconut water. Blend until silky smooth. No need to strain, but feel free to add more water if you prefer a thinner consistency.

LAIT DE COCONUT: PART DEUX

The "I-don't-feel-like-cracking-open-a-coconut" version.

MAKES 1 SERVING

♥ ¼ CUP (50 G) COCONUT FLAKES OR 3 TABLESPOONS COCONUT BUTTER (*NOT* OIL!)

1 CUP (250 ML) WATER

1 MEDJOOL DATE, SOAKED, PEELED, AND PITTED

A PINCH OF SALT

¼ TEASPOON VANILLA POWDER OR EXTRACT

Add all ingredients to a high-speed blender and mix until it turns into "milk"! (This may take longer than typical nut milks, as coconut flakes are quite hard.) Strain through a nut milk bag or sieve, or drink as is.

COCONUT

The other other other white meat

Your coconut water and meat should be WHITE. If it is pink, the phenolic-antioxidant compounds in the coconuts have reacted with oxygen. These compounds are the same ones that can turn wine, champagne, or beer pink or brown if they're not treated with chemicals. You of course won't die if you use pink meat or drink pink water, but it *can* be a sign of mold or bacteria, so I say coconuts are *not* pretty in pink. Opt for white meat and water if you can.

MILK MONEY

Lait de plants is a foundation for plant-based cooking. If you prefer to buy nut, rice, hemp, or oat milk to speed things up, you have my permission! Make sure to buy unsweetened versions, preferably without carrageenan (an additive derived from red algae that is commonly used as a food thickener or stabilizer). A general rule: if you can neither pronounce nor identify the additives on the ingredients list, don't buy it!

♥ BEST FRIEND FOOD

Coconut

Coconut is a detox food extraordinaire. It boosts the immune system, eases digestion, and is rich in antioxidants, fiber, protein, and healthy fats. It hydrates and energizes the entire body, keeps the skin glowing, and helps blood circulation.

Let's be honest here: It's better to be young. Youth means more flexibility, more energy, flawless skin . . . well, it's the same for coconuts. Young coconuts have meat that is more tender and easy to blend into creamy culinary concoctions. They also have a much higher water content than their elders do—and the water is packed with potassium and electrolytes. If you don't live in Thailand or Hawaii, look for this luxury item at Asian markets or buy frozen meat and water.

BEAUTY RECIPE

Coconut hair treatment

This 100 percent natural hair and scalp treatment is so nourishing for your hair and can prevent dandruff since it's *très* moisturizing. Shower yourself with this miracle mélange!

♥ 1 GLASS OF *LAIT DE* COCONUT (PAGE 2) OR BPA-FREE CANNED COCONUT MILK

1 TABLESPOON ALMOND OIL OR OLIVE OIL

A FEW DROPS OF ESSENTIAL OIL OF CHOICE (PEPPERMINT, LAVENDER . . .)

Pour the ingredients into a glass bottle or mason jar and cover. Shake well until everything is mixed together. Massage into your scalp onto damp hair just after a shower. Massage well so that the mixture covers your entire scalp. Let it sit for around 30 minutes, then rinse well with water.

PROTEIN!

"Protein! Protein! You need to eat enough protein! Where do you get your protein?"

Does any of this sound familiar to you? Perhaps you've threatened your friends or family with a desire to "eat more plants." Is this typically the response?

In many ways, they're right. Protein is necessary for the proper functioning of our hormones, our muscles, our skin, the enzymes that aid digestion, and our immune systems.

Amino acids are the building blocks that come together to form protein in the body (sort of like Legos).

Amino acids and proteins are the foundations of life! The essential amino acids are those that can't be made by the body so need to be brought in by eating. And yes, you can get them all from eating "only" plants! However, when we don't eat animal protein, we do need to be extra careful to make sure we are getting enough protein from plant-based sources. Think nuts, nut butters, seeds, quinoa, lentils, beans, peas, and greens, like kale, broccoli, and spinach.

COCONUT YOGURT

Yogurt, wassup? This yogurt is creamy and tart, but totally dairy free, with all of the benefits of probiotics to boot. It's perfect—or shall I say *parfait?*—for breakfast with granola and fruit, in a smoothie, on top of a dessert, or as a snack anytime. The fermented probiotics make it tart, but if you don't have time, you can cheat and use lemon or lime juice. It won't offer the benefits of probiotics, but it is still hydrating, creamy, and delectable! Here are a few different versions of coconut yogurt: a fancy *haute couture* version using a young Thai coconut, a ready-to-eat version using frozen coconut meat and water, and a "thrift store" version using canned coconut milk.

La Haute Yogurture

MAKES 1 BOWL

♥ 1 YOUNG THAI COCONUT
½ TEASPOON VANILLA POWDER OR EXTRACT
1 PROBIOTIC CAPSULE OR 1 TABLESPOON LEMON JUICE

Ready-to-eat yogurt

MAKES 1 BOWL

♥ ½ CUP (100 G) FROZEN COCONUT MEAT
½ TEASPOON VANILLA POWDER OR EXTRACT
¾ CUP (150 ML) COCONUT WATER
1 PROBIOTIC CAPSULE OR 1 TABLESPOON LEMON JUICE

Thrift-store yogurt

MAKES 2 BOWLS

♥ ONE 13.5-OUNCE (400 ML) BPA-FREE CAN FULL-FAT COCONUT MILK, REFRIGERATED OVERNIGHT UPSIDE-DOWN
½ TEASPOON VANILLA POWDER OR EXTRACT
1 PROBIOTIC CAPSULE OR 2 TABLESPOONS LEMON JUICE

FOR *HAUTE* YOGURT:

Place the coconut onto a sturdy cutting board. Jab it on top in the center (carefully) until you hit its soft spot and form a hole. Turn the knife around to widen the hole. Pour the coconut water into a glass or bowl. With a hammer, gently tap the center of the coconut, then continue to tap, gradually tapping harder and harder until the coconut cracks. Keep tapping around the outside of the coconut until you can easily break it in half with your hands. (Again, be careful!) Open the coconut. Scoop out the "meat" with a spoon.

FOR READY-TO-EAT YOGURT:

Defrost the coconut meat (leave out on the counter for a few hours, place in the fridge overnight, or if you're really in a hurry, place the bag into a bowl of hot water).

FOR THRIFT-STORE YOGURT:

Open the top of the can of coconut milk. Don't shake it! The "cream" should have risen to the top. Using a spoon, scoop this thick cream into a bowl. Reserve the liquid in the bottom of the can.

FOR ALL YOGURTS:

Blend the coconut meat or milk in a high-speed blender with the vanilla powder until smooth and creamy. Add coconut water to taste for a thinner yogurt. (Keep in mind it will also thicken in the refrigerator.)

NEXT, YOU CAN EITHER:

Open the probiotic capsule and pour the powder into the blender. Discard the capsule. Blend again. Pour into a bowl, cover with cheesecloth, and let sit on your counter for 8 to 12 hours. Place in the refrigerator.

OR:

Add lemon juice, blend, and . . . your tangy treat is ready to eat!

Top your coconut yogurt with some Granolove (page 36), seasonal fruits, mashed banana, and/or nuts, seeds, or dried fruit. You can also use your yogurt as a topping for desserts (like Apple Tarte Tatin, page 168, or Peach Crumble, page 110), an extra-creamy smoothie addition, or—if you make it without the vanilla—a savory topping for soups or curries!

LE FAUX-MAGE:
NUT CHEESE, THREE WAYS

Add to grains (quinoa, buckwheat, millet, brown rice), gluten-free pasta, spiralized vegetables, salads, sandwiches, wraps, pizza, and lasagna, or spread on crackers or toast.

I'm not going to tell you that my faux-mage has the same taste as real *fromage*, or cheese. But holy cow, it's so good! Please think of faux-mage as its own magnificent masterpiece . . . that happens to replace cheese in pretty much any recipe you can think of. This faux-mage is like cheese's little plant-based cousin—salty, creamy, and tasty, but also digestion-friendly!

Naturally rich, creamy macadamia nuts and pine nuts add incredible texture reminiscent of mozzarella or goat cheese. These nuts can be expensive or hard to find, however, so feel free to substitute cashews, soaked and peeled almonds, or your personal nuts *du jour!* Seeds, like pumpkin and sunflower seeds, work too.

Store faux-mage for 4 to 5 days in the refrigerator.

MACADAMIA NUTS

The good fats!

Macadamia nuts contain "good fats." Oh yes, I did indeed just use the words "good" and "fats" in the same sentence. I'm talking about monounsaturated fatty acids that fight cardiovascular disease and diabetes and lower cholesterol. Macadamias also contain fiber, antioxidants, vitamins B and E, manganese, potassium, magnesium, calcium, phosphorous, and zinc. However, because macadamia nuts are approximately 70 percent fat, they are very caloric, so enjoy in moderation.

Faux-mage au Naturel (Plain)

MAKES 1 SERVING

¼ CUP (50 G) MACADAMIA NUTS (OR PINE NUTS, ALMONDS, CASHEWS . . .)

♥ 1 TEASPOON LEMON JUICE

½ TEASPOON APPLE CIDER VINEGAR

1 TABLESPOON OLIVE OIL

A PINCH (OR TWO!) OF SALT

1 TABLESPOON NUTRITIONAL YEAST (OPTIONAL, FOR A "CHEESY" FLAVOR)

Soak the nuts according to the directions on page 14 to soften them, then drain.

Blend all ingredients in a high-speed blender or food processor until smooth.

Herbed Faux-mage

MAKES 1 SERVING

¼ CUP (50 G) MACADAMIA NUTS (OR PINE NUTS, ALMONDS, CASHEWS . . .)

♥ 1 TEASPOON LEMON JUICE

½ TEASPOON APPLE CIDER VINEGAR

1 TABLESPOON OLIVE OIL

A PINCH (OR TWO!) OF SALT

1 TABLESPOON CHOPPED FRESH CHIVES

1 TABLESPOON CHOPPED FRESH BASIL

1 TABLESPOON CHOPPED FRESH PARSLEY

1 TABLESPOON NUTRITIONAL YEAST (OPTIONAL, FOR A "CHEESY" FLAVOR)

Soak the nuts according to the directions on page 14 to soften them, then drain.

Blend all ingredients in a high-speed blender or food processor until smooth.

Miso Faux-mage

MAKES 1 SERVING

¼ CUP (50 G) MACADAMIA NUTS (OR PINE NUTS, ALMONDS, CASHEWS . . .)

♥ 1 TEASPOON LEMON JUICE

♥ 1 TEASPOON WHITE MISO PASTE

Soak the nuts according to the directions on page 14 to soften them, then drain. Blend all ingredients in a high-speed blender or food processor until smooth.

PROBIOTICS

Beautiful bacteria

Mesdames and *messieurs*—ladies and gentlemen—for dinner this evening, I will be serving a big bowl of . . . bacteria! Sound good? OK, so I realize that the idea of eating a hearty portion of microscopic critters traditionally known for attacking our bodies isn't very appetizing. But I'm referring to the *good* bacteria, those hidden treasures we call probiotics.

Bugs are suddenly in fashion. Doctors everywhere are hailing the benefits of magnificent microbes and talking about the gut microbiome—the billions of bacteria in our intestinal flora that directly influence our immune systems. Oh yes, billions of bacteria do indeed live in our bellies. These bacteria, however, aren't the enemy—they're our friends! Think of them as an intestinal police force that aids digestion and strengthens our nervous and respiratory systems. You don't need a pill to take advantage of the power of probiotics. Just eat more fermented foods! Say *oui* to miso, sauerkraut, pickles, and coconut yogurt.

VEGGIE CRÈME DE LA CRÈME

For grains, pasta, cooked or raw vegetables, salads, soups, tacos . . .

The French love to put crème fraîche on anything and everything. Luckily, Veggie Crème de la Crème offers all of the creaminess and soft, velvety texture of crème fraîche without the dairy.

Cashew Crème de la Crème

MAKES 1 SERVING

2 TABLESPOONS CASHEWS
2 TABLESPOONS WATER
1 TEASPOON APPLE CIDER VINEGAR
♥ 1 TEASPOON LEMON JUICE

Soak the cashews for at least 30 minutes and up to 12 hours (overnight) to soften them, then drain.

Place all ingredients into a blender or food processor and blend. Gradually add water until the crème becomes smooth yet still very thick.

Macadamia Crème de la Crème

MAKES 1 SERVING

2 TABLESPOONS MACADAMIA NUTS
2 TABLESPOONS WATER
1 TEASPOON APPLE CIDER VINEGAR
♥ 1 TEASPOON LEMON JUICE

Soak the macadamia nuts for at least 30 minutes and up to 12 hours (overnight) to soften them, then drain.

Place all ingredients into a blender or food processor and blend. Gradually add water until the crème becomes smooth yet still very thick.

Note: You can keep these crèmes to use them again later, but they will naturally thicken in the refrigerator. Before using, add more water or lemon juice to thin them out a bit.

BETTER BUTTERS

For grains, cooked veggies, and sweet potato purée, or spread on pancakes, scones, muffins, toast, or crackers.

Store in a glass container in the refrigerator. Both will last for weeks (if you can keep your hands off them, that is!).

Miso Butter

This plant-based butter is salty and flavorful, not to mention packed with probiotics and healthy fats.

MAKES 2 SERVINGS

♥ 2 TABLESPOONS COCONUT OIL
♥ 2 TEASPOONS WHITE MISO PASTE

Mix the coconut oil and the miso paste with a spoon to form a thick paste. Form into the shape of your choice. If the coconut oil is liquid, this will harden in the refrigerator to form a more butterlike spread. If it's still solid when you mix it, you can eat it right away.

Sweet Butter

This easy and creamy "butter" is a sweet addition to breakfasts or desserts. Kids love it!

MAKES 2 SERVINGS

♥ 2 TABLESPOONS ALMOND BUTTER, HOMEMADE (SEE PAGE 14) OR STORE-BOUGHT
♥ 1 TABLESPOON COCONUT OIL
1 TEASPOON MAPLE SYRUP OR COCONUT SUGAR
⅛ TEASPOON VANILLA POWDER OR EXTRACT

Mix the ingredients together with a spoon to form a thick paste.

TASTY TOPPINGS

For grains, pasta, vegetables, salads, soups, lasagna, pizza, etc....

Hemp Sprinkle

♥ 2 TABLESPOONS HEMP SEEDS
  2 TEASPOONS NUTRITIONAL YEAST
  A PINCH OF SALT

Stir together all ingredients. If desired, process in a blender for a finer consistency.

Almond Crumble

♥ ¼ CUP (50 G) ALMONDS
  1 GARLIC CLOVE
  A PINCH OF SALT

Toast the almonds for a few minutes until browned (but not burned!) for 1 to 2 minutes in a saucepan over medium heat or around 5 minutes in the oven at 400°F (200°C). Peel and chop the garlic. Add all ingredients to a dry-blade blender or food processor and pulse a few times, until coarsely ground.

NUTRITIONAL YEAST

Your flakiest friend

The name "nutritional yeast" sounds like the opposite of glam, *oui*? But what's in a name? That which we call nutritional yeast by any other name would smell as . . . cheesy! Oh yes, these unfortunately named yet infinitely healthy yellow flakes add a cheesy flavor to so many recipes! (Note the word choice, chees-*y*. This is not cheese. But it does provide an incredible replacement.)

Nutritional yeast isn't the same thing as baking yeast, active dry yeast, or brewer's yeast. It's an *inactive* yeast that is alcohol free and, in moderate amounts, won't aggravate a Candida overgrowth. It's grown on beets and dehydrated.

It's a great source of B vitamins, even the elusive B12 (albeit in small quantities, and only if fortified). B vitamins are so important for strengthening hair, nails, and pretty much every system in the body. Nutritional yeast contains all eighteen amino acids, so it's also a great vegan, gluten-free, soy-free, sugar-free protein source.

However, surgeon *green*eral's warning: This tastes so good that you may be tempted to eat large quantities of it. Careful! It can cause gas if you have a sensitive stomach. Start slowly and work your way up to 1 to 2 tablespoons maximum per portion.

Gomasi-oh-là-là!

Gomasio is a very useful condiment that can replace salt in so many recipes. Sprinkle over your food for a flavorful and nutritious boost.

Store for a few weeks in a glass container in a dry place.

MAKES 1 SERVING
  ¼ CUP (100 G) SESAME SEEDS
♥ 1 TABLESPOON SEAWEED FLAKES (DULSE OR MIXED)
  A PINCH OF SALT

Lightly toast the sesame seeds in a saucepan for 1 to 2 minutes to brown them a bit (you'll know they're done when they start smelling good—don't burn them!). Grind all ingredients together in a spice grinder or dry-blade blender.

You can also opt for a raw version, which is a bit less flavorful but richer in enzymes. Soak the seeds in water for 4 to 8 hours, then dry them in a dehydrator for 6 to 8 hours. Grind together with the other ingredients.

SEXY SESAME

Where to get your calciYUM!

Open sesame! In *One Thousand and One Nights*, this expression is the key to opening a cave complete with a hidden treasure. Sesame seeds are nature's own treasure. Popular in Asian and Mediterranean cooking, they are rich in nutrients, fiber, and minerals, made up of 20 percent protein with a high amino acid, methionine, and tryptophan content. These seeds increase circulation, strengthen the immune system, and help the liver and the kidneys detox your body. Plus, sesame may just be the sexiest seed, thanks to its high zinc content that boosts sexual health and can even increase sperm production in men.

There are so many ways to enjoy sesame seeds. Tahini is my favorite—it's an amazingly creamy base for sauces, salad dressings, or spreads. Toasted sesame seeds add an incredible flavor to any dish and are a great gluten-free, vegan substitute for bread crumbs in "breaded" dishes. Gomasio is a wonderful replacement for salt in any recipe.

DRESSINGS AND SAUCES

"Sauces are the splendor and the glory of French cooking."
—Julia Child

Traditional French cuisine is all about using fresh, seasonal ingredients and adding the perfect sauce to bring them to life. These basic sauces can transform any plate into a work of art!

Famed chef Auguste Escoffier used five "mother sauces": Hollandaise, Béchamel, "Espagnole" sauce, velouté, and tomato sauce. My adaptations of these classic concoctions may be different from their famous mothers, but they are wonderful and healthy additions to this saucy family. Plus, I've added a few of my own sauces and dressings to the mix—sorry, Monsieur Escoffier, but *le green, c'est chic*!

All sauces can be stored in the refrigerator for around 3 days. Add water or lemon juice as needed to thin them out.

Tahini Hollandaise

When in doubt . . . pour tahini sauce over anything and everything. This sauce is rich and creamy, just like Hollandaise sauce, but is easier to digest and packed with nutrients.

MAKES 1 SERVING

1 TABLESPOON TAHINI
♥ 1 TABLESPOON LEMON JUICE
1 TABLESPOON OLIVE OIL
SALT AND PEPPER TO TASTE
1 TEASPOON MINCED GARLIC (OPTIONAL)
1 TEASPOON HONEY (OPTIONAL, FOR BEE-GANS ONLY!)

Blend all ingredients in a blender or stir by hand until smooth.

For miso-ginger tahini Hollandaise: Add a piece of fresh ginger or ¼ teaspoon ground ginger, 1 teaspoon miso paste, and 1 teaspoon tamari, and substitute 1 teaspoon toasted sesame oil for the olive oil.

For a turmeric tahini Hollandaise: Add ½ teaspoon turmeric, an extra pinch of black pepper, a pinch of cayenne pepper (to taste), 1 teaspoon maple syrup, and 1 teaspoon apple cider vinegar.

Parsley Pistou

Poor parsley—no one ever thinks of it until the last minute to garnish a dish. What a shame—it merits so much more! *Voilà*: pistou, a French pesto usually made without pine nuts or Parmesan. This version lets parsley steal the spotlight for once!

MAKES 1 SERVING

1 GENEROUS HANDFUL OF FRESH PARSLEY
1 HANDFUL OF SPINACH
2 TABLESPOONS OLIVE OIL, OR MORE TO TASTE
♥ 2 TABLESPOONS LEMON JUICE, OR MORE TO TASTE
½ TEASPOON LEMON ZEST
1 TABLESPOON NUTRITIONAL YEAST (OPTIONAL)

Blend all ingredients in a food processor or blender until smooth, but not too liquid. Add more oil or lemon juice if you find it too dry. Keeps fresh in the refrigerator for a few days.

♥ BEST FRIEND FOOD

Miso: Miraculous medicine from Japan

Let me introduce you to your new best friend from Japan! (Yes, isn't it chic to have friends from all over the world?) Even though this new friend is very old—born in China around the third century AD, then adopted by Buddhist and Japanese cultures—miso is full of life: It's part of the fermented foods family, rich in "good" bacteria.

Miso is a paste made of soy, other beans (such as chickpeas), or rice and is filled with enzymes, probiotics, protein, and antiaging antioxidants. *Voilà*: the secret to the beauty and longevity of Japanese women!

Add hot water to the paste for an instant soup that stimulates digestion, warms the body, fortifies the blood, and strengthens the immune system. In Japan, it's even eaten in the morning to wake up the body, the mind, and especially the digestive system! Miso is naturally very salty, so you can mix it into any dish, dressing, or spread to replace salt and add extra flavor. Just don't overdo it: 1 teaspoon per cup of soup, for example, is sufficient.

I prefer gluten- and soy-free miso blends, such as chickpea-based varieties, but any will do. Most of the recipes in this book call for white, or *shiro,* miso, a sweeter, subtler variety than the stronger red, or *hatcho,* miso. Quick tip: To keep miso's enzymes intact, don't boil it or buy it pasteurized.

Espagnole (Brown Sauce)

One of my favorite French expressions is *Vous parlez français comme une vache espagnole,* or "You speak French like a Spanish cow," used to describe someone whose pronunciation is so poor that it barely resembles the mother tongue. This is an appropriate expression to describe my version of "espagnole" (Spanish) sauce, a rich and aromatic brown sauce. My version is so far from the original that Escoffier would likely be turning over in his grave, but it's brown and it's bursting with flavor, so as they say, *tant pis!*

MAKES 1 TO 2 SERVINGS

- ♥ 1 TABLESPOON COCONUT OIL
- ¼ CUP (60 ML) *LAIT DE* COCONUT (PAGE 2) OR BPA-FREE CANNED COCONUT MILK, OR MORE TO TASTE
- ♥ 1 TABLESPOON ALMOND BUTTER, HOMEMADE (SEE PAGE 14) OR STORE-BOUGHT
- ♥ 1 PIECE OF FRESH GINGER (TO TASTE) OR ¼ TEASPOON GROUND
- JUICE OF 1 LIME
- 1 GARLIC CLOVE, PEELED
- ½ TEASPOON TAMARI OR COCONUT AMINOS
- ♥ 1 TEASPOON MISO PASTE
- 1 DATE, SOAKED, PEELED, AND PITTED, OR ½ TEASPOON MAPLE SYRUP
- A PINCH OF CAYENNE PEPPER

Add all ingredients to a blender and blend until smooth and creamy. Add water or extra coconut milk to thin it out if preferred.

Béchamel Sauce

Béchamel is a white sauce, traditionally made with butter and flour cooked in milk. This version is still thick and creamy and can be added to plant-based pasta *au gratin* or lasagna, or poured over roasted eggplant for a veggie moussaka.

MAKES 1 TO 2 SERVINGS

- ¼ CUP (50 G) MACADAMIA NUTS, CASHEWS, OR PEELED ALMONDS
- ½ CUP (125 ML) WATER
- 1 GARLIC CLOVE, PEELED (OPTIONAL)
- 1 TABLESPOON OLIVE OIL
- ♥ 1 TABLESPOON LEMON JUICE
- ½ TEASPOON APPLE CIDER VINEGAR
- SALT AND PEPPER TO TASTE

Blend all ingredients in a blender or food processor until smooth.

Velouté

Velouté is traditionally a mix of stock, butter, and flour. Here, I keep the (vegetable-based—what else?) stock and blend it with cashews to thicken. Use it as a soup base, or thin it out with more stock and add to grains while they are cooking for a creamy *mélange.*

MAKES 1 TO 2 SERVINGS

¼ CUP (50 G) CASHEWS, SOAKED (OR ¼ CUP/60 ML CASHEW BUTTER)

½ CUP (125 ML) VEGETABLE BROTH, MADE FROM A BOUQUET GARNI (SEE PAGE 161) OR STORE-BOUGHT

½ TEASPOON APPLE CIDER VINEGAR

Blend all ingredients in a high-speed blender, or with a whisk if using cashew butter.

Sauce Tomate (Tomato Sauce)

This tomato sauce is ideal in summer, when fresh herbs and juicy tomatoes burst with natural sugars and flavors, but tomatoes are easy to find all year long, and dried herbs can replace fresh ones.

MAKES 1 SERVING

1 LARGE TOMATO

3 SUN-DRIED TOMATOES (PREFERABLY UNSALTED AND DRIED; IF THEY ARE PACKED IN OIL, REDUCE THE AMOUNT OF OLIVE OIL IN THE RECIPE TO TASTE)

1 DATE, SOAKED, PEELED, AND PITTED

1 GARLIC CLOVE

1 TABLESPOON CHOPPED FRESH BASIL (OR ¼ TEASPOON DRIED BASIL)

¼ TEASPOON OREGANO (CHOPPED FRESH OR DRIED)

1 TEASPOON APPLE CIDER VINEGAR

1 TABLESPOON OLIVE OIL

SALT AND PEPPER TO TASTE

Soak the sun-dried tomatoes in warm water for around 5 minutes, until soft. Peel and chop the garlic.

Blend all of the ingredients in a food processor or blender, but not for too long—you want this to be a bit chunky. Add some of the soaking water from the sun-dried tomatoes to thin it out, if desired.

This sauce is perfect on top of a pizza (page 106), in a lasagna (page 102), or even on its own as a summer soup. Just add water and blend!

Mustard Vinaigrette

Dijon mustard adds so much flavor to a simple vinaigrette.

MAKES 1 SERVING

1 TEASPOON DIJON MUSTARD (PREFERABLY APPLE CIDER VINEGAR–BASED)

1 TABLESPOON OLIVE OIL

½ TEASPOON APPLE CIDER VINEGAR

SALT AND PEPPER TO TASTE

½ TEASPOON MAPLE SYRUP (OPTIONAL)

Mix together all of the ingredients with a whisk or spoon.

Green Chic Sauce

This is a great way to get your green on, no matter what you're eating. This sauce is especially wonderful in spring or summer, when fresh herbs and greens are at their peak, but you can make this anytime with whatever green goodness you can get your hands on.

MAKES 1 TO 2 SERVINGS

1 HANDFUL OF ARUGULA

1 GENEROUS HANDFUL OF OTHER GREENS OF CHOICE (SPINACH, KALE, CHARD...)

2 TABLESPOONS CHOPPED FRESH CHIVES

2 TABLESPOONS CHOPPED FRESH BASIL

2 TABLESPOONS CHOPPED FRESH MINT

2 TABLESPOONS CHOPPED FRESH PARSLEY

1 TABLESPOON CHOPPED FRESH CILANTRO

1 TABLESPOON OLIVE OIL

SALT AND PEPPER TO TASTE

♥ 1 TABLESPOON LEMON JUICE

1 GARLIC CLOVE (OPTIONAL)

1 TABLESPOON NUTRITIONAL YEAST (OPTIONAL)

Peel and chop the garlic. Wash and dry the arugula and other greens. Blend all of the ingredients in a high-speed blender or food processor until smooth.

Hempesto

The natural crunch and neutral yet tasty flavor of hemp seeds allow them to complement any dish, whether salty or sweet. It's the perfect ingredient to blend into a pesto! This pesto is great as a spread on toast or crackers or as a dip for veggies, veggie chips, or fries.

MAKES 2 SERVINGS

♥ ¼ CUP (50 G) HEMP SEEDS

2 GENEROUS HANDFULS OF FRESH SEASONAL HERBS (PARSLEY, MINT, BASIL...)

1 HANDFUL OF SPINACH

1 TABLESPOON NUTRITIONAL YEAST

2 TABLESPOONS OLIVE OIL

♥ 2 TABLESPOONS LEMON JUICE

1 GARLIC CLOVE

1 TEASPOON APPLE CIDER VINEGAR

SALT AND PEPPER TO TASTE

Peel and chop the garlic. Combine all of the ingredients in a food processor or blender and blend.

♥ BEST FRIEND FOOD

Hemp

If you're hempy and you know it, clap your hands! Hemp is one of the best sources of plant protein on the planet. The protein in hemp is easily digested and quickly absorbed by the body, making it a nearly perfect food for athletes (yes, walking to and from the subway every day or lifting small children qualifies you as an "athlete").

These seeds from the *Cannabis sativa* plant (yes, a plant in the same species produces marijuana, but no, you won't get high from eating these seeds) are almost too good to be true. They are packed with vitamins (A, B1, B3, B5, D, and E) and minerals, like iron and magnesium, that most ladies are usually lacking. These vegan and gluten-free seeds provide the perfect balance of those elusive omega-3 and omega-6 polyunsaturated fatty acids that are essential for the proper functioning of the body. These essential fatty acids make hemp an energizing and anti-inflammatory wonderfood. Hemp improves digestion, sleep, and mood—it's the happiest plant around. Adding just a tablespoon or *deux* to any dish adds so much flavor, crunch, and nutrition. It's totally legal and totally healthy.

DRESSING UP YOUR DESSERTS

For cakes, fruit bowls, tarts, pancakes, crêpes, coconut yogurt (page 4), Crème de Chia (page 39), parfaits, ice creams . . .

Strawberry Coulis with Goji Berries

MAKES 1 SERVING

1 TABLESPOON GOJI BERRIES

½ CUP STRAWBERRIES (GREEN TOPS REMOVED), CHOPPED OR HALVED

♥ 1 TABLESPOON LEMON JUICE

¼ TEASPOON LEMON ZEST

½ TEASPOON MACA POWDER (OPTIONAL)

Soak the goji berries in warm water for 5 minutes. Blend all of the ingredients in a blender until smooth.

Caramel Sauce

MAKES 1 SERVING

4 MEDJOOL DATES, SOAKED, PEELED, AND PITTED

♥ ¼ CUP (50 ML) ALMOND MILK, HOMEMADE (SEE PAGE 2) OR STORE-BOUGHT

½ TEASPOON VANILLA POWDER OR EXTRACT

2 TEASPOONS MESQUITE POWDER

1 TEASPOON CAROB POWDER

♥ 2 TABLESPOONS COCONUT OIL

♥ ½ TABLESPOON LEMON JUICE

SALT

1 TABLESPOON LUCUMA POWDER (OPTIONAL)

Blend all ingredients together in a high-speed blender until smooth. You can add more liquid if desired.

Crème Anglaise

MAKES 1 SERVING

¼ CUP MACADAMIA NUTS

1 TABLESPOON MAPLE SYRUP

½ TEASPOON VANILLA POWDER OR EXTRACT

♥ 1 TABLESPOON LEMON JUICE

2 TABLESPOONS WATER

Soak the macadamia nuts in warm water for 10 minutes or in room-temperature water for 1 to 2 hours, until they soften. Drain. Blend the nuts, maple syrup, vanilla, and lemon juice in a high-speed blender. Add water gradually until the mixture is smooth and creamy, but not too liquidy. (It will thicken up in the fridge, so make it a bit thinner than you'd like if you're not eating it right away.)

GOJI BERRIES

No monk-y business!

Goji berries are a superfood extraordinaire. These sacred berries hail from the Himalayas and are a beloved food of Tibetan monks. Nicknamed the "happy berry," this beautiful pinkish-red dried superfruit of the *Lycium barbarum* plant is a natural mood booster. It's rich in nutrients like the B vitamins, vitamin C, beta-carotene, and antioxidants. It's a complete source of protein, with eighteen amino acids, including the eight essential ones. Goji berries are adaptogens, which means that they will adapt to each individual and correct imbalances in the body. Goji berries have been used for thousands of years as a medicinal food throughout Asia and are now ubiquitous in the Western world. They have a raisinlike texture and add a sweet kick to any meal. They are usually sold *very* dried out, so I always recommend soaking them in warm water to plump them up. You can also soak the berries in hot water, then drink the pink tea! Ready? Let's goji!

MESQUITE

A sweet dessert from the desert!

Not to be confused with that smoky barbecue sauce, mesquite powder is milled from a high-protein seed native to desert areas in the Americas.

It balances blood sugar since it digests slowly and doesn't cause spikes in insulin. It's high in protein, fiber, calcium, lysine, iron, potassium, zinc, and manganese. It's very gentle on the stomach and can ease intestinal discomfort. Oh, and did I mention it tastes like caramel? This is one of my favorite ingredients since it marries well with so many other foods, particularly superfoods like cacao and maca. Its neutral yet nutty taste makes it perfect for thickening and sweetening sauces or smoothies, and it's my (not-so-secret) secret to incredibly rich chocolate avocado mousse.

parsley pistou

mustard
vinigarette

sauce tomate

green chic
sauce

véloute

béchamel

tahini
hollandaise

PURÉES AND FLOURS

For many, many things!

With just one ingredient, you can make your own nut flours and nut butters at home. The DIY versions are so easy and much healthier and more cost-effective (not to mention even tastier) than the store-bought varieties, so give them a try!

Nut or Seed Butter

(almond butter, hazelnut butter, sesame butter/tahini, walnut butter, cashew butter, sunflower seed butter, pumpkin seed butter . . .)

MAKES 1 SERVING
1 CUP (100 G) NUTS OR SEEDS

Lightly toast your nuts or seeds of choice in a dry skillet over low-medium heat (2 to 3 minutes) or in a 350°F (175°C) oven (5 to 7 minutes). Let cool, then add to a food processor or high-speed blender. Blend until the nuts/seeds start to form a thick paste. Scrape the sides down with a spatula then blend again. And again. And again . . . until the mixture is smooth and creamy. If the mixture is still too thick, you can add a few drops of your favorite vegetable oil or water.

Almond Flour

(or other nut flour or oat flour)

MAKES AROUND ½ CUP (50 G) FLOUR
♥ ½ CUP (50 G) ALMONDS

Grind the almonds in a food processor until they form a fine powder. (Yes, that's all, but be careful not to grind them too long, or you'll have nut butter!)

> ♥ BEST FRIEND FOOD
>
> **Almonds**
>
> Almonds are a great source of monounsaturated fats, plant-based protein, soluble fiber, and so many vitamins and minerals. They're great for the skin (vitamin E!), fight migraines and headaches (magnesium!), and are anti-inflammatory.

SOAK COOL! GIVE YOUR NUTS, BEANS, AND GRAINS A BATH

Grains, nuts, and beans are just like us—they are in much better shape after a good bath!

Mother Nature has thought of everything. Grains, nuts, and beans are so precious to health that she has taken great efforts to protect them from growing up, turning bad, and dying young. Nuts and seeds have enzyme inhibitors that prevent the seeds from sprouting. It's good for the nuts, but it can make them hard to digest, since they not only prevent our own enzymes from breaking them down but also inhibit absorption of their vitamins and minerals. Soaking nuts releases these harmful enzymes, making them easier to digest *and* even more nutritious! Just add the nuts to a bowl, sprinkle on some salt, cover them with water, and leave, covered, on the counter (or, if it's very hot, in the refrigerator) overnight or for a few hours, depending on the nut or seed (see the chart).

Almonds and hazelnuts	12 hours
Pecans	6–8 hours
Walnuts	6–8 hours
Pumpkin seeds	4 hours
Sesame seeds	4 hours
Sunflower seeds	4 hours

Macadamia nuts, cashews, pine nuts, and hemp seeds don't need to be soaked! (But feel free to treat them to a bath if you're making a crème, nut milk, or faux-mage!)

Similarly, grains and legumes contain phytic acid, an antinutrient that prevents the body from absorbing their nutrients. Soaking makes them more digestible and frees up the nutrients so our bodies can reap all of their benefits.

Add grains, like quinoa or millet, to a bowl with some lemon juice, cover with water, cover, and let them sit on the counter overnight or for several hours. Rinse, then cook! See page 18 for specific instructions.

Do the same for beans and legumes, and for even better digestion, change the water a few times and add some kombu seaweed to the water when cooking.

Does this all sound very intimidating to you? And *OMG*, what if you are *dying* for a big bowl of hummus, but you—gasp!—*forgot* to soak your chickpeas the night before? First, you can always go the (BPA-free) canned route. Second, remain calm, take a deep breath, boil a large pot of water, add the chickpeas, and cook on high for around 2 minutes. Reduce the heat to low, add some kombu, cook for around 1 hour, then rinse and cook as directed.

♥ BEST FRIEND FOOD

Quinoa

I don't like to play favorites . . . but, between us, quinoa is my favorite grain. I mean, pseudocereal. I mean, seed. OK, so perhaps my best friend is difficult to describe. She's a relative of beets, spinach, and Swiss chard (yes, a Swiss cousin—isn't that glamorous?) but prefers to live her life like a grain and cooks just like rice and other grains. Quinoa and I are very close—we spend nearly every day together, yet I never get sick of her!

Quinoa, *je t'aime* for your high protein content, your fiber, your magnesium, your healthy carbs, your vitamins B and E, your potassium, your iron . . . you're just so well rounded! What a cosmopolitan seed.

Plus, quinoa is a great, naturally gluten-free ingredient in everything from risottos and savory cakes or burgers to breakfast porridges and desserts. It can be eaten hot or cold, for breakfast, lunch, or dinner, and in the form of a fluffy "grain," a flour, or flakes.

THE RULES OF DATING

Are you ready for your hot date tonight? Don't worry, I haven't hacked into your social calendar—I am referring to the naturally sweet and energy-dense fruit. Dates are packed with fiber, potassium, copper, manganese, magnesium, and vitamins A, B, C, and K. Here's your guide to dating with ease.

1. CHOOSING A NICE DATE

Medjool dates are typically larger, softer, and sweeter than other dates, so they're the ones to buy for making date paste, puréeing into a chocolate mousse or chia pudding, or adding to warm, savory dishes. Medjool dates taste like a sweet mix of cinnamon and honey with a caramel undertone. They have wrinkly skin and should have soft interiors. Go for organic when possible, or at least make sure your date hasn't been treated with sulfur.

2. SPEED DATING

Pour some hot water over the date and let it sit for 1 to 5 minutes (depending on how hard/dry the date is to start), until the date softens. Then, it's time to get naked! (The date, that is.) Peel off the skin and—let's pause. I know, there are lots of nutrients in the skin, but the rest of the date has nutrients too, and come on: your silky-smooth mousse depends on this! After you peel the skin and remove the pit, *voilà!* Your date is ready for you to do with it what you will.

3. WHERE TO TAKE YOUR DATE

Don't give in to routine—get creative! Blend your date (ideally in a Vitamix: your date, like you, deserves royal treatment) into a Mousse au Chocolove (page 72), a creamy nut milk (page 2), or savory dishes for just a touch of sweetness.

4. WHEN TO DATE

If you're on a hardcore detox program or you need to watch your blood sugar, you may want to have a mere fleeting fling with your date—eat only as a sweet treat on occasion. However, if you do OK with natural sugars and are looking for a nutritious way to sweeten your recipes, get energized, or increase your intake of fiber, potassium, and minerals, then definitely take a date to be your lawfully wedded sweetener.

Beauty Bowl

Welcome to the first meal of the rest of your life. This is my official go-to, "everything but the kitchen sink" recipe for a healthy and simple (but elegant!) lunch or dinner. It's a loose interpretation of the famous macrobiotic bowl, one that is very balanced in terms of protein, carbs, fiber, and nutrients. Experiment with various seasonal veggies, cooked in different ways (oven roasted, sautéed, steamed, or raw), use a variety of grains and legumes, and douse it with any basic sauces or dressings.

I call it the Beauty Bowl because (1) everything in it will make you glow from the inside out and (2) if you arrange everything nicely in your bowl (or plate), drizzle on some sauce, and add fresh herbs, microgreens, and/or nuts and seeds, this can become a work of art in just seconds! You can eat it at any temperature you like, so it's a great dish to revamp according to the season and your mood.

SERVES 1

½ CUP COOKED GRAINS (QUINOA, BUCKWHEAT, MILLET, BROWN RICE, WILD RICE . . . PICK YOUR FAVORITE OR A MIX OF A FEW DIFFERENT ONES!)

½ CUP COOKED LEGUMES (CHICKPEAS, LENTILS, BEANS . . . AGAIN, PICK YOUR FAVORITE!)

½ CUP COOKED SEASONAL VEGETABLES (ROASTED, STEAMED, SAUTÉED . . .)

♥ ½ CUP COOKED SWEET POTATO OR SQUASH (ROASTED WITH COCONUT OIL, SALT, AND PEPPER; STEAMED; BAKED; OR SAUTÉED)

1 CUP RAW SALAD GREENS

♥ ¼ CUP SEAWEED OR 2 TO 3 TABLESPOONS SAUERKRAUT

2 TO 3 TABLESPOONS SAUCE (TAHINI HOLLANDAISE, HEMPESTO . . . ANYTHING GOES! SEE PAGES 8–10)

OPTIONAL TOPPINGS:

♥ ½ AVOCADO, PITTED, PEELED, AND SLICED

1 HANDFUL OF FRESH HERBS, SPROUTS, AND/OR MICROGREENS

1 TABLESPOON NUTS OR SEEDS, RAW AND SOAKED OR TOASTED (SEE PAGE 14)

Arrange the grains, legumes, vegetables, sweet potato, greens, and seaweed in a large bowl next to each other. Add optional toppings, if using. Serve with sauce on the side, then drizzle it over everything. (Feel free to continue to pour sauce over everything throughout the meal!)

This is a great meal to make ahead for travel or to bring to the office or on a picnic. Just keep the sauce on the side and wait to cut the avocado, if using, until ready to eat it. The photo shows everything laid out bento-style, ready to go. Bring a big bowl along so you can arrange everything when you're ready—just because you're not at home doesn't mean you can't dine in style!

♥ **BEST FRIEND FOOD**

Greens galore: Solar-powered energy

In the mood for a heaping bowl of . . . sun? Oh yes, the sun is edible! OK, perhaps you may want to stay (light-years) away from the hot ball of glowing gases in the sky, but you can absolutely eat the sun's energy in the form of chlorophyll. Chlorophyll gives green vegetables and herbs that color you and I love so much. Chlorophyll allows us to take the sun's energy and diffuse it throughout our bodies so we can literally glow from the inside out. Chlorophyll purifies the blood and strengthens the immune system. It increases the amount of red blood cells in the body, helping oxygen to circulate. It aids digestion, supports the liver, and cleanses the colon. It also regulates calcium levels in the body. The greener a food, the more chlorophyll it contains—think spinach, fresh herbs, and spirulina. Adding just a little more green to whatever you're eating or drinking can have so many wonderful benefits for the body. Go green!

Cooking Grains and Legumes

Grain/legume	Amount per portion (dry)	Soak time/instructions	Water with soaking	Water without soaking	Cooking time with soaking	Cooking time without soaking	Cool time after cooking
Quinoa	¼ cup (40 g)	Overnight (8–12 hrs) in water with lemon juice	firm texture: 1 portion of water fluffy texture: 1.5x water	firm: 1.5x water fluffy: 2x water	firm: 5–10 mins fluffy: 10–15 mins	firm: 10–12 mins fluffy: 15 mins	5 mins
Millet	¼ cup (40 g)	Overnight (8–12 hrs) in water with lemon juice, then rinse, add to a pot, and toast over medium-low heat for 2–3 mins before adding water and covering	firm: 2x water fluffy: 2.5x water	firm: 2.5x water fluffy: 3x water	firm: 15 mins fluffy: 20 mins	firm: 20 mins fluffy: 25 mins	
Wild rice	¼ cup (40 g)	not necessary	n/a		n/a	45 mins–1 hr	5 mins
Buckwheat	¼ cup (40 g)	not necessary	n/a	2x water	n/a	15 mins	5 mins
Amaranth	¼ cup (40 g)	not necessary	n/a		n/a	20 mins	
Brown rice	¼ cup (40 g)	not necessary	2x water	2.5 x water	30 mins	40 mins	10 mins
Chickpeas	¼ cup (50 g)	10–12 hrs	4x water	2.5 x water	1–2 hrs		
Black beans	¼ cup (50 g)	8–12 hrs (the water will turn black—don't be scared!)	3x water		1–1½ hrs		
White beans	¼ cup (50 g)	8–12 hrs	3x water		1–1½ hrs		
Adzuki and mung beans	¼ cup (50 g)	4–6 hrs	2.5x water				
Green or French lentils	¼ cup (50 g)	4 hrs	2x water	3x water	25 mins	40 mins	
Red lentils	¼ cup (50 g)	not necessary	n/a	2x water	n/a	10 mins	
Kidney beans	¼ cup (50 g)	8–12 hrs	3x water		1½ hrs		
Split peas	¼ cup (50 g)	not necessary	n/a	3x water	n/a	45 mins–1 hr (or longer if using for soup)	

Tips for a Green, Clean, and Chic Home

By Paul Scialla, Delos Living

A healthy living space is crucial to nourishing our bodies and minds, says Paul Scialla, founder of Delos. Delos fuses medicine and science with architecture and design to completely reinvent how we live. Delos designs wellness-centric homes, offices, and even hotels. Everything from the central architecture to the finishes is built with health (and happiness!) in mind. Chez Delos, air and water filters screen for pollutants, allergens, and toxins; aromatherapy scents are infused throughout each residence; the floors help maintain good posture; and lighting is set up to help you get restful sleep and wake up easily. There are hot stone paths leading to the showers; showerheads infused with vitamin C and aloe; soy-based insulation; and, *bien sûr*, juice bars in the kitchen.

Delos's spaces are *très* good for you, but they also happen to be sleek and chic. (Sound familiar?) These spaces are environmentally friendly and contribute to a balance of mind and body for those living in them. It's the stuff green dreams are made of. Delos's Manhattan apartments sell for many millions, but Paul has shared his top tips for transforming any space into a healthy haven.

Between home, work and school, we spend more than 90 percent of our time indoors. Introducing preventative medical intentions into the very spaces in which we're spending the majority of our time is an obvious and easy solution, and it can have a profound impact on our health. Whether you're building a new home or just want to enhance your current living space, you can improve your household by adding different health and wellness features that not only act as preventative medicine for you, but also can improve the health of our society on a grand scale.
—Paul Scialla

Air purifier

Did you know that in many environments, the air quality is better outdoors than indoors? Did you also know that there are national air-quality standards ensuring a certain level of air quality outdoors, but there are no standards regulating air quality inside buildings? Remember that we spend more time indoors than we do outdoors. Consider adding an advanced HEPA-standard air purification system to your home, which will reduce allergens, toxins, and pathogens, creating better air quality for breathing.

Biophilia

Introduce elements of nature such as greenery throughout the home. Studies have shown that surrounding people with live plants and visible elements of nature has a profound impact on health, lowering long-term stress and increasing happiness. Certain plants can also filter harmful and common indoor-air volatile organic compounds and CO_2 while providing a fresh source of oxygen.

Black-out shades

Adequate sleep is essential to good health, yet people around the world are chronically sleep deprived. Adding black-out shades to your bedrooms is an easy, inexpensive way to drastically improve your sleep. By fully eliminating outdoor light, black-out shades improve sleep quality and duration.

Circadian lighting

A circadian lighting system provides optimum light exposure for different times of day, including energizing light in the morning and way-finding night lights for safe navigation and minimal sleep disruption.

Seamless kitchen countertop

Nonporous surfaces prevent the collection of food particles that encourage bacteria growth. This is very important in the kitchen, where food is prepared. Single-cast concrete surfaces have no crevices, so bacteria has nowhere to breed.

Kitchen herbarium

Herbs such as lemongrass, chives, mint, basil, and dill provide vital nutrients and antioxidants. Adding a minimal-maintenance fresh herb garden in your kitchen will give you access to a variety of them throughout the year.

Steam oven

Steam ovens permit thorough cooking by steam alone without overcooking. They also help to retain certain antioxidants and vitamins without excessively altering or damaging them.

Exhaust hood

A high-powered fan removes nitrogen dioxide and other by-products of combustion.

Lumbar-supporting floor

Cork underlay flooring flexes when walked on, reducing forces generated by impact. This flooring is soft enough to allow for underfoot comfort, yet strong enough to improve lumbar support.

Reflexology path

Pebble flooring is designed to improve blood circulation and activate and support the muscular system, and it can also help you to relax.

Well shield™

This self-cleaning photocatalytic coating applied to high-touch areas triggers oxidation, resulting in cleaner surfaces. Think: a high-tech hand-sanitizer.

Water filtration

A state-of-the-art water filtration system reduces disinfectant by-products, chlorine, pesticides, and some pharmaceutical and personal-care products for the cleanest, most purified water in your home.

Good Morning!

Start the day off right

Trés Green Juice

Crème de Chia

Granolore

Citron Pressé

Energy yoga

To start the day off on the right foot, there's nothing better than . . . starting off on the right foot. Then, the left. Then the right. Stop hitting your snooze button. You have to get up eventually, and why not do it in a way that will energize you for the rest of the day? Of course, it would be nice to have the time to do a full one-hour yoga session (complete with meditation and, while we're still dreaming, massage, facial, warm bath, serenade . . .) every day, but let's be honest: As soon as that alarm goes off, it's time to spring into action. Still, just gently moving the body and focusing on breathing for a few minutes can make such a difference in the rest of the day. Try it! Voilà: a very basic "sun salutation" to tone and revitalize the body after a night of sleep (or lack thereof!). This energizing sequence is like coffee for the body—try a cuppa Joe-ga! Feel free to do these sun salutations outside under the sun or right next to your bed on a cold, rainy day—the sun is always shining inside of you!

1. START STANDING. Place your hands in prayer position over your heart ①. Breathe in and raise your hands to the ceiling, lengthening your body as much as possible ②. As you exhale, place your fingertips on the ground (you can bend your knees if your arms don't reach!) ③.

2. WITH YOUR HANDS ON THE GROUND, take a deep breath, then bring your right leg behind you, with your left leg bent. Look forward and tilt your head back to open your heart. Keep your hands on the ground, or lift them in the air if you can balance, and lean back for a gentle backbend ④. As you exhale, bring your left leg back next to your right leg so you are in a downward dog position. Keep the palms of your hands on the ground, your head facing the floor, and your arms extended. You can bend your knees slightly ⑤. Look forward and move into a plank or push-up position parallel to the ground. Or, you can head to the ground knees first, then chest, then chin. Lower yourself gently to the floor. Breathe in as you push your hands down on the floor, and open your chest into a gentle backbend or upward dog.

3. BREATHE OUT AND HEAD BACK TO a plank or push-up position parallel to the ground. Or, you can head to the ground knees first, then chest, then chin. Lower yourself gently to the floor ⑥. Breathe in as you push your hands down on the floor, and open your chest into a gentle backbend or upward dog ⑦.

4. BREATHE OUT AND HEAD BACK to your downward dog ⑧. Breathe in and place your right foot between your hands, your left leg back ⑨. Raise your hands in the air or keep them on the floor, but open your chest and tilt your head back into a gentle backbend.

5. BREATHE OUT SLOWLY : Bring your left leg next to your right and lean over to touch your toes (you can bend your knees!). Breathe in and look forward, then bend over again and exhale—let it all go! Your worries, your fears, your grudges or anger, your anxiety about the day—let it go ⑩! Breathe in as you stand up slowly and raise your hands into the air ⑪. Exhale and bring your hands to prayer position in front of your chest ⑫. Breathe in slowly through your nose, and exhale through your mouth.

Do this cycle as many times as you can, moving more slowly on days you are more tired and trying to go through the sequence more quickly for days when you need an energy boost. Listen to your body and don't try to force anything. Anything goes! If you're tired and you try to go too quickly, you'll become even more tired, so slow down (this is a metaphor for life!), but it's also nice to challenge yourself. End the sequence with savasana, AKA corpse pose, AKA lying down on your back with your hands beside you, looking at the ceiling, and thinking about NOTHING. Savasana is a great way to stock up on all of that energy you just created and save it to use when you need it later in the day. Bonne journée!

THE GREEN BREAKFAST CLUB

In French, the term for breakfast is *le petit déjeuner*, or literally "the little lunch." In America, breakfast is *not* a meal to be taken lightly. It is often referred to as "the most important meal of the day." I definitely agree. However, "most important" doesn't mean "heavy"! *Au contraire!* Breakfast should be filling but still energizing.

This will help wake up your digestive system after a night of rest *gently*, instead of with an aggressive attack. Don't surprise your stomach, or it will be angry all day, and you certainly don't want that! Wake it up gently and give it the fuel it needs to get you through the busy day ahead. You need a lot of energy for all you have to do today, am I right? No membership card or fee needed for this exclusive breakfast club. The only requirement for entry? A smile. (Note: Breakfast for lunch or dinner is allowed!)

GREEN BREAKFAST MENU

You'll find many more breakfast options throughout the book (it is my favorite meal of the day), but *voilà*: a basic menu for every day!

Weekdays: The "I'm in a rush, let's do this quickly, please" version

I meditate—if I can; otherwise, even just a few deep breaths is a great start.

I drink hot water with lemon juice or a *Citron Pressé* (page 26).

I go shower, get dressed, take care of my children, pets, significant other, and plants . . . or simply take care of ME!

I drink a tall glass of *Très* Green Smoothie (page 29) or eat a Crème de Chia (page 39) or Miraculous Muesli (page 166). If I'm *really* rushed, I will have already prepared any of these options the night before for grab-and-go green goodness.

Weekends: The Zen version

I meditate—if I can; otherwise, even just a few deep breaths is a great start.

I drink a *Citron Pressé* (page 26) upon waking.

I wait a few minutes then drink some Aloe Vera Juice (page 27).

I read the newspaper or stretch for around 5 to 10 minutes, then I drink a *Très* Green Juice (page 29).

I hang out and relax for 15 to 30 minutes, kiss my significant other (or if I don't have one of those, I kiss myself in the mirror because I'm so worth it), I play with my children and pets, do some yoga, dance around the room . . .

I enjoy some Granolove (page 36) with *Lait de* Plants (page 1) and fruit, or a plate of Pancrêpes (page 164).

SUPERFOODS

Superfabulous!

They say a meteor landing made Clark Kent super, but *I* say he was clearly a consumer of super*foods*. Superfoods are just what they sound like. First of all, they're *foods*, not pills, supplements, or fake chemicals. Superfoods are super-packed with protein and vitamins and give us the energy we need to be superheroes every day. I don't recommend sporting a cape, necessarily, but hey, if you want to, why not?

Superfoods are concentrated in nutrients, so a little bit goes a long way. As Clark can confirm, they provide:

- Superhuman strength, thanks to protein-rich superfoods like spirulina or chlorella
- Superhuman speed, thanks to the natural energy from cacao or maca
- Invulnerability, thanks to immune-boosting açaí, aloe vera, and acerola
- X-ray vision (or at least close), thanks to goldenberries, which strengthen the optical nerve
- Superhuman intelligence, thanks to blue-green algae

I have yet to find a superfood scientifically proven to make me fly, but I'm on the case (and *too* much of maca or cacao may make you *feel* like you're flying—be warned!).

Superfoods nourish all of our organs and, when consumed over long periods of time, reinforce the immune system and correct internal imbalances.

Again, superfoods are *foods*. They grow in the soil or on trees, fresh from Mother Nature's kitchen. Oh, and naturally, their flavor is unparalleled. Try adding a teaspoon to your morning smoothie, then experiment as your taste buds adapt to the flavors. Most superfoods hail from South America, but today they can be found in supermarkets or online. Carob and mesquite add subtle caramel-like flavor; spirulina and chlorella are some of the most nutritious foods on the planet; mulberries, goji berries, and goldenberries add a sweet, chewy kick and antioxidant goodness; and cacao, well, we'll get to that on page 71.

When you wake up in the morning, think: "It's a bird, it's a plane . . . it's time to add even just one superfood to my breakfast." Cape or no cape, you'll feel like a superhero.

NOT A MORNING PERSON?

"The early bird catches the worm." It's true. Waking up early allows us to take time for ourselves in the morning—to eat well, meditate, exercise, do yoga, stretch, or simply take a deep breath. We never know what the day will bring, but we can, at the very least, make those first few minutes as fabulous as possible.

I adore the morning, and the French have an adjective to describe people like *moi: matinale*! I am *très matinale*. I wake up with—or sometimes before!—the birds. I can see you—yes you, over there, rolling your eyes and saying, "This girl is crazy, I'll *never* be a morning person or even close!" *Oui oui*, I know that there are morning people and, well, people who *really* don't want to roll out of bed.

If you're in the second category, let's try some baby steps, shall we? Set your alarm just 15 minutes earlier to have time to drink a green smoothie or eat a healthy breakfast in peace (a real one, not a coffee chugged while running down the street to get to your office on time or a granola bar for the road), and already I promise you'll feel a difference. (Going to bed fifteen minutes earlier helps, too.)

If this seems impossible, you can prepare your breakfast the night before: Put a green smoothie (page 30 or 31), Crème de Chia (page 39), or Miraculous Muesli (page 166) into the fridge and—abracadabra!—when you wake up in the morning, breakfast will be ready (even if your brain and body aren't quite there yet). Your body will have the fuel it needs to meet whatever the day brings.

RISE AND (TRULY!) SHINE: MORNING BEVERAGES

Starting with liquids helps to gradually get the digestive juices flowing. Start with a simple hot water with lemon, then move on to juice or a smoothie, and finish with a heartier breakfast.

MY MORNING MAIN SQUEEZE: LEMON

Lemon and I are very close. We wake up together every morning and spend much of the day together, too. No matter what your day has in store, start it with this lemony beverage that hydrates your body, freshens your breath, and energizes you.

Citron Pressé (Lemon Detox Drink)

MAKES 1 SERVING

- ♥ 1 SMALL LEMON
  STIMULATING SPICE BLEND (OPTIONAL):
  - A PINCH OF CAYENNE PEPPER
  - ♥ A PINCH OF TURMERIC
  - A PINCH OF CINNAMON
  - ♥ A PINCH OF GROUND GINGER OR GRATED FRESH GINGER (OR FRESH GINGER JUICE)
- 1 CUP WARM WATER (NOT BOILING)
- 1 TEASPOON SWEETENER OF CHOICE: STEVIA, MAPLE SYRUP, COCONUT SUGAR . . . (OPTIONAL)

Add the lemon juice and the spice blend (if using) to a mug. Pour warm water over the mixture. Allow to infuse, add a sweetener if desired, and sip slowly.

You can also simply mix lemon with warm water and skip the spices—that simple morning detox will do the trick.

MY OTHER MORNING LOVER: ALOE VERA

I confess. Sometimes I cheat on lemon and wake up with aloe vera. And sometimes I even go straight from one to the other. Aloe vera is one of the most healing plants in the universe (or at least on planet Earth—that's the most I can confirm to date, though the plant does look quite alien at first glance, doesn't it?).

This plant may be more often used as a beauty product than as a beverage, but it can heal the body inside and out. Aloe vera is truly a super superfood. Its leaves are bursting with nutrients, minerals, vitamins, amino acids, and active enzymes. It stimulates immune defense, eases scarring, eliminates toxins, soothes stomach cramps, improves blood clotting, soothes ulcers or inflamed intestines, and makes the skin shine. But this isn't breaking news: Cleopatra used it, and the Mayans called it the "fountain of youth." (OK, so perhaps given their predictions of the end of the world, we may not be so inclined to listen to them, but they were right about *some* things . . .) Even Hippocrates was a fan. So learn from the past: Say hello to aloe and bye-bye to health problems!

Aloe Vera Juice

MAKES 1 SERVING

¼ CUP (60 ML) ALOE VERA GEL (SEE BELOW TO MAKE YOUR OWN)

¼ CUP (60 ML) ROOM-TEMPERATURE FILTERED WATER

Pour the gel into a glass. Add the water. Stir until homogenous.

Feel free to add blended fruit or juice for extra flavor and sweetness, but this mix is best *au naturel*, on an empty stomach just after waking up. Wait a few minutes before drinking a juice or smoothie or around 15 to 30 minutes before a bigger meal.

Unbe-leaf-able Homemade Aloe Vera Juice

MAKES 6 TO 10 SERVINGS

1 MEDIUM ALOE VERA LEAF

¾ CUP (200 ML) WATER

Slice off the outer edges and inner yellow layer of the leaf, leaving only the clearly gelatinous interior—that's the gel! Put the gel into a blender with the water and blend until smooth.

This preparation will last for several days in the fridge. Alternatively, leave the leaf in the fridge and cut off small portions each day to blend with about ¼ cup (60 ml) water for your morning drink.

BEAUTY TIP

Aloe Vera Mask

MAKES 1 MASK

1 ALOE VERA LEAF

Slice off the outer edges and inner yellow layer of the aloe vera leaf (or, even better, use the leftover outer layers after you've made your morning drink). Rub the gel side of the leaf all over your face (and the rest of your skin—it's a wonderful, hydrating, and healing substance!). Let it absorb on your face for 5 to 10 minutes. Wash your face. Your skin will glow!

GREEN SMOOTHIES AND JUICES

Unless you've been living under a rock, you've surely heard about the global superstars that have everyone talking: the green smoothie and her younger, thinner, juicy sister. You've seen the smoothie photos on Instagram, you've watched the beautiful people walk around with glass jars filled with thick green liquid, and perhaps you've wondered why on earth anyone would pay ten dollars for some carrots in a cup. Or maybe you've succumbed to the craze yourself.

If not, get ready—sit down if you need to—because I'm about to change your life. From now on, you're going to drink raw vegetables in a glass. And you're going to enjoy it.

CHIC GREEN SMOOTHIE MAKING

A green smoothie is a mix of fresh fruits and vegetables blended together to form a liquid that resembles soup. Whether you call it a sweet soup or a smoothie, the bottom line is that it's a great way to start the day or tide you over on the go. The three secrets to a great green smoothie are (1) balancing fruits and veggies, (2) varying the textures, and (3) adding tiny touches of taste such as spices or superfoods.

As for the veggies, the most common are, of course, *greens* (think kale, spinach, romaine, and even dandelion greens) since they are especially rich in nutrients. They are a source of fiber, protein, minerals, vitamins, antioxidants, and chlorophyll, and they help to oxygenate the body and the skin, strengthen the immune system, and eliminate toxins. Blending raw greens breaks down their cell walls, releasing the nutrients to be predigested and thus more easily absorbed by the body. Everyone with me now: "Free the nutrients!" Chewing and digesting take energy; letting our blender do the work for us leaves us feeling lighter and more energetic.

Making a green smoothie is an art that gets better with practice. I won't lie—spinach in a blender with a cup of water tastes horrible. However, plants of all kinds add nutrition and style. Throw in some banana, creamy almond milk, spices, and superfoods and a green smoothie becomes a velvety milkshake.

Like any celebrity, the green smoothie has received its fair share of criticism. It's true that moderation is key, and what "works" for one person might be a health concern for someone else. If you're an athlete, a protein-packed smoothie might be the perfect combo, whereas if you're trying to lose weight, it may not be the smartest choice. There is also a war waging across the globe between

Team Juice and Team Smoothie. How often do you hear "Do you juice or blend?" Why does it have to be one or the other, I ask you? Why can't we all juice *and* blend?

A few suggestions for a super smoothie:

Take baby steps.

At first, swallowing a tall glass of green can surprise not only your eyes but also your taste buds and digestive system. Start slowly, with one spinach leaf, then add half a handful, then a whole handful, and so on until you settle on a quantity that pleases you—and your stomach! When it comes to changing your lifestyle, slow and steady wins the race.

Keep things simple, but elegant.

While smoothies are a great way to enjoy many different superfoods, fruits, and veggies at the same time, try to avoid the "put everything in my kitchen into one glass" smoothie recipe. (I'm guilty of this, too!) The fewer the ingredients, the more you'll be able to enjoy the flavors.

Avoid adding frozen fruits or icy cold liquids to your smoothies.

Cold inhibits digestion. While a frozen banana does add both texture and refreshment, try to keep cold smoothies to a minimum and enjoy only on warmer days.

Rotate your greens.

One of the "dangers" often associated with green smoothies is the oxalic acid in raw leafy greens like spinach and kale, a substance found on the leaves of many plants that can become poisonous or cause kidney stones, but only in extremely large doses (at least 2 kilograms a day of leafy greens; that's around 10 cups per day!). Plus, different greens have different health profiles, so by rotating them, you'll be getting the best of everything.

Spice it up!

Even if you haven't yet started to speak fluent superfood ("Maca who?"), adding spices like cinnamon, nutmeg, or cardamom will help you to digest your smoothie and add incredible flavor.

There are so many possible combinations. Here is my favorite recipe, adaptable according to season, whim, and personal taste. *Bon sip-étit!*

Très Green Smoothie

MAKES 1 SERVING

- ♥ 1 BANANA (OR ½ AVOCADO, OR ½ BANANA AND ¼ AVOCADO)
- 2-INCH (5 CM) PIECE OF CUCUMBER
- ♥ 1 APPLE, OR ½ PEAR AND ½ APPLE (OR, IN SEASON, ½ CUP SEASONAL BERRIES OR OTHER FRUIT)
- ♥ 1 SMALL PIECE OF GINGER OR A FEW PINCHES OF GINGER POWDER
- ½ CUP (125 ML) *LAIT DE* NUTS OF CHOICE (PAGE 2) OR STORE-BOUGHT NUT MILK, COCONUT WATER, OR WATER
- 1 HANDFUL OF SPINACH, ROMAINE, KALE, OR A MIXTURE OF GREENS
- ♥ ½ TEASPOON VANILLA POWDER (OPTIONAL)
- 1 MEDJOOL DATE, SOAKED AND PITTED (IF USING UNSWEETENED ALMOND MILK)
- ½ TEASPOON MATCHA POWDER (OPTIONAL, FOR AN ENERGY BOOST)
- ♥ 1 TEASPOON SPIRULINA POWDER (OPTIONAL, FOR A GREEN BOOST)

If using a date, soak it in warm water until soft, then peel and remove the pit. If you're using homemade nut milk, no extra date is needed!

Peel the banana, peel and pit the avocado (if using), and cut into small pieces. Wash or peel the apple, core, and chop into small pieces. Peel and chop the ginger.

Add the prepared banana, avocado, apple, and ginger to a high-speed blender along with the remaining ingredients and blend until smooth. If your blender isn't very powerful, start with the liquid and greens, then add the fruit, ginger, vanilla, date, and superfoods. I like my smoothies thick, but if you prefer a thinner texture, just add more liquid.

CHIC GREEN JUICING

At first, the difference between juice and smoothie isn't obvious. They're both green, liquidy, and "healthy," right?

Here's what's different: A smoothie is thick like a milkshake, and a juice is fluid like water. A smoothie is made in a blender and a juice is made in . . . you guessed it, a juicer! How "juice" originally became a verb, I can't say, but now I juice, you juice, we juice . . . everyone juices. ("Smoothie," however, is just a noun to date, but let's

change that, shall we? *Voulez-vous* smoothie *avec moi ce soir?*) Green juice has no fiber, making it even more easily absorbed by the body than a smoothie. Green juice is like an injection of vitamins directly into the bloodstream. A green smoothie is filling and can be a meal in itself, while a juice is more of an interlude between meals or a gentle morning wake-up to the digestive system. Juice still contains calories, so don't go drinking gallons and gallons a day if you're watching your weight.

Four juice-making secrets:

No need to peel anything—the juicer does all the work!

If you don't have a juicer, blend everything in a blender, then pour it through a nut milk bag, cheesecloth, or sieve into a cup.

Add fresh spices like ginger or turmeric directly to the juicer; add dry spices after juicing.

Green juice is best first thing in the morning or on an empty stomach. Wait at least 15 minutes before eating breakfast. Enjoy it later, too, though not late at night—it can be a jolt of energy!

Très Green Juice

MAKES 1 SERVING

- 1 HANDFUL OF GREENS (KALE, ROMAINE, CHARD . . .)
- 1 CUCUMBER
- ♥ 1 CARROT
- ♥ 1 SMALL PIECE OF GINGER
- ♥ 1 APPLE
- ♥ 1 LEMON
- 1 CELERY STALK

Wash all of the fruits and vegetables. Core the apple. Then follow the instructions on your juicer; all are different, just like us!

"A handful"
How to measure vegetables in green cuisine

In the smoothie and juice world, a lot of recipes call for "a handful" of greens. But whose hands are we filling? A petite woman's hands? A 300-pound football player's hands? How do I do this correctly?

First of all, forget about "correctly." There's no such thing! Let's take our lives—and our smoothies—back into our own hands (whatever size they may be!). One handful of greens is about 1 cup. But your handfuls can be as big or as small as you want. So go ahead, invite that football player over *chez vous* for a superbowl of smoothie, and get *your* green on!

Medley of Smoothies

1. *Choose your ingredients.*
2. *Clean and prepare your ingredients*
(keep the skin on fruits and vegetables when possible).
3. *Throw everything in your blender and blend.*
4. *Enjoy.*

Brown Smoothie

Green Smoothie 1

Orange Smoothie

Blue Smoothie

Blue smoothie: ½ cup (150 ml) water, 2 tablespoons hemp seeds, ½ cup blueberries, 1 teaspoon açai powder, ⅛ teaspoon vanilla powder or extract

Green smoothie #1: ¼ cup (100 ml) water, 1 tablespoon tahini, ½ banana, ⅛ teaspoon vanilla powder or extract, 1 date, ½ teaspoon matcha powder

Orange smoothie: ¾ cup (150 ml) fresh-squeezed orange juice, 2 medium carrots, 1 banana, 1 tablespoon coconut oil, 1 small piece of ginger or ground ginger to taste, ¼ teaspoon orange zest, ⅛ teaspoon turmeric

Brown smoothie (Note: Don't judge a smoothie by its color—you will chocolove it!): ½ cup (150 ml) water, 1 tablespoon cacao powder, 1 teaspoon mesquite powder, 2 tablespoons Brazil nuts, 1 date, a pinch of cinnamon

White Smoothie

Black Smoothie

Green Smoothie 2

Pink Smoothie

Purple Smoothie

Yellow Smoothie

Pink smoothie: ½ cup (150 ml) apple juice, ½ cup (100 g) strawberries, ½ small red beet, 1 piece of ginger (to taste)

White smoothie: ¾ cup (200 ml) water, 1 small apple (peeled and chopped), 1 small piece of ginger or ground ginger to taste, 1 banana, ¼ teaspoon maca powder, 1 tablespoon cashew butter (see recipe on page 14)

Black smoothie: ¼ cup (50 ml) *Lait de* Coconut (page 2) or BPA-free canned coconut milk, 1 tablespoon black sesame seeds, ¼ cup (50 ml) fresh-squeezed orange juice, 1 date

Green smoothie #2: ¾ cup (150 ml) water, 2 tablespoons Brazil nuts, 1 date, 1 teaspoon spirulina powder, ½ avocado, ¼ to ½ teaspoon maca powder, 1 teaspoon mesquite powder

Yellow smoothie: ½ cup (100 ml) *Lait de* Coconut (page 2) or BPA-free canned coconut milk, 1 banana, ⅛ teaspoon vanilla powder or extract, ⅛ teaspoon cinnamon, ½ cup pineapple chunks

Purple smoothie: ¾ cup (200 ml) *Lait de* Coconut (page 2) or BPA-free canned coconut milk, 1 teaspoon açai powder, 1 date, 2 teaspoons cacao powder, ⅛ teaspoon vanilla powder or extract, 1 tablespoon chopped fresh mint, 1 teaspoon almonds, 1 tablespoon coconut oil or coconut butter

Smoothies and Shakes Extraordinaire

Bunny Hoptail

SERVES 1

- ♥ ¾ CUP (200 ML) CARROT JUICE (SEE PAGE 93)
- ♥ ½ CUP (100 ML) ALMOND MILK, HOMEMADE (SEE PAGE 2) OR STORE-BOUGHT
- ¼ TEASPOON VANILLA POWDER OR EXTRACT
- TEASPOON NUTMEG

Blend all ingredients in a high-speed blender until smooth. This energizing blend will have you hopping all around town!

You can drink your bunny hoptail at room temperature or warm it up on the stove on a cold day. (Just don't make it too hot: what a shame to destroy all of those excellent enzymes in the carrot juice!)

Tropical Twist

SERVES 1

- ♥ ¾ CUP (150 ML) *LAIT DE* COCONUT (PAGE 2) OR BPA-FREE CANNED COCONUT MILK
- ½ CUP (100 G) CHOPPED FRESH PAPAYA*
- ½ CUP (100 G) CHOPPED FRESH MANGO
- ½ CUP (50 G) CHOPPED FRESH PINEAPPLE**
- JUICE OF 1 LIME
- ♥ ½ TEASPOON MINCED FRESH GINGER
- ¼ TEASPOON VANILLA POWDER OR EXTRACT

Blend all ingredients in a high-speed blender until smooth.

*The black seeds of papaya are edible! Don't be scared! They may be slightly spicy and bitter, but they are rich in enzymes and have even been used to rid the body of parasites.

**You may notice that you don't see much pineapple in this book. Confession: I don't like it! However, pineapple has an incredible nutritional profile and shouldn't be forgotten just because it doesn't happen to be in my intimate circle of best friend foods. Pineapple contains bromelain, an enzyme that helps to break down proteins, aids digestion, thins the blood to prevent clotting, and helps to fight inflammation in the body. It's high in potassium and manganese, and since it's low in calories and high in fiber, pineapple is a popular weight-loss tool. Add pineapple to smoothies, dice it and use as a topping for your breakfast cereal or Crème de Chia (page 39), or blend into a tropical sauce for Pancrêpes (page 164).

Blueberry Bliss

SERVES 1

♥ ½ CUP (200 ML) COCONUT WATER

½ CUP (200 ML) *LAIT DE* COCONUT (PAGE 2) OR BPA-FREE CANNED COCONUT MILK

♥ 1 BANANA

½ CUP (100 G) FROZEN BLUEBERRIES, THAWED

1 TEASPOON AÇAI POWDER (OPTIONAL)

JUICE OF 1 LIME

2 TABLESPOONS WALNUTS

2 TABLESPOONS COCONUT FLAKES

¼ TEASPOON VANILLA POWDER OR EXTRACT

♥ ½ TEASPOON MINCED FRESH GINGER OR GROUND GINGER

Blend all ingredients in a high-speed blender until smooth. Enjoy your happiness in a glass.

AÇAI
The antiaging superberry

Açai (pronounced ah-sigh-ee) is a tiny berry filled with antioxidants, amino acids, and essential fatty acids. It tastes like a combination of berries and chocolate and strengthens the digestive and cardiovascular systems and keeps the skin radiant. You'll look and feel ten years younger with just a spoonful! (OK, so it doesn't work *that* quickly, but if you consume it on a regular basis, you will notice a positive change in how you look and feel.) Açai is a great energy booster and a perfect addition to smoothies or desserts or as the star of its own açai bowl mixed with fruit. Plus, like many superfoods, a little bit goes a long way. Açai goes very well with both chocolate and berries since it really brings out those flavors. Oh say can you açai?

Mint Chocolate Miracle Milkshake

SERVES 1

♥ ¾ CUP (200 ML) ALMOND MILK, HOMEMADE (SEE PAGE 2) OR STORE-BOUGHT

½ AVOCADO, PITTED AND PEELED

1 HANDFUL OF SPINACH

1 TABLESPOON CHOPPED FRESH MINT

2 DROPS OF MINT ESSENTIAL OIL (OPTIONAL)

♥ 1 TABLESPOON CACAO POWDER

1 DATE, SOAKED, PEELED, AND PITTED (OPTIONAL)

2 TEASPOONS CACAO NIBS (OPTIONAL)

Blend all ingredients except the cacao nibs in a high-speed blender until smooth. Pour into a glass and top with the nibs. Believe in miracles.

This smoothie is great when you need a mint chocolate fix but it's too cold for ice cream. (If it's not too cold, try the ice cream recipe on page 114.)

Macarena Milkshake

SERVES 1

½ CUP (125 ML) FRESHLY SQUEEZED ORANGE JUICE OR FRESH ORANGE SEGMENTS

♥ 1 BANANA

♥ 1 CARROT, CHOPPED

♥ ½ APPLE, PEELED AND CHOPPED

♥ 1 TABLESPOON LEMON JUICE

½ TEASPOON MACA POWDER

1 TEASPOON ACEROLA POWDER (OPTIONAL, FOR EXTRA VITAMIN C)

½ CUP (100 G) FRESH MANGO, CHOPPED (OPTIONAL, FOR AN EXOTIC TWIST)

Blend all ingredients in a high-speed blender until smooth. Say goodbye to colds and flus, thanks to the vitamin C in this smoothie.

Festival of Green Juices

The Big Green Apple

1 handful of greens of your choice
1 cucumber
1 celery stalk
♥ 1 green apple
♥ 1 slice of ginger

C'est la Green

1 head of romaine
1 cucumber
♥ 3 large carrots
1 fennel bulb
2 celery stalks
1 handful of spinach
♥ Juice of ½ lemon
♥ 1 small slice of ginger (about ½ tablespoon minced)
1 teaspoon chopped fresh parsley

14-Carrot Gold

♥ 14 baby carrots
(or around 3 large carrots)
♥ 1 apple
♥ 1 slice of ginger (to taste)

Rise and Shine

1 orange
1 grapefruit
♥ 1 small slice of ginger
♥ 1 lemon
A pinch of cayenne pepper
♥ 1 small slice of fresh turmeric or a pinch of
turmeric powder

Un-beet-able

1 pear
1 beet
cup (50 g) pineapple
♥ 1 slice of ginger

Dr. Cayenne
Pepper

1 lime
♥ 1 lemon
1 handful of fresh cilantro
1 celery stalk
1 large cucumber
A pinch of salt
A pinch of cayenne pepper

Monsieur
Vegetables

♥ 2 carrots
1 large handful of spinach
2 celery stalks
1 tablespoon chopped fresh parsley

Beauty Juice

For skin glowing with health!
♥ 3 carrots
1 cucumber
♥ ½ apple
1 handful of romaine leaves
1 handful of spinach

Granolove

There are so many granolas on the market today, but making it is so easy, you'll fall in granolove at first bite! Make a big batch and eat for days or share with friends (or anyone you'd like to befriend).

Granolove

MAKES 8 TO 10 SERVINGS

2 CUPS (200 G) GLUTEN-FREE OATS (OR BUCKWHEAT, QUINOA, AND/OR BROWN RICE FLAKES)

½ CUP (50 G) RAW BUCKWHEAT GROATS

♥ ¼ CUP (60 G) COCONUT FLAKES

A PINCH OF SALT

¼ CUP (50 ML) MAPLE SYRUP

¼ CUP (50 ML) LIQUID COCONUT OIL*

♥ ½ CUP APPLESAUCE (HOMEMADE OR ORGANIC AND SUGAR-FREE)

½ TEASPOON CINNAMON

½ TEASPOON VANILLA POWDER OR EXTRACT

♥ ½ TEASPOON GROUND GINGER (OPTIONAL)

Preheat the oven to 350°F (175°C).

Combine the oats, buckwheat, coconut flakes, and salt in a large bowl. Add the remaining ingredients, mix together well, then spread on a rimmed baking sheet.

Bake for around 15 minutes. Mix with a spatula, then cook for another 10 minutes, or until golden brown (but not burned!). Remove from the oven and let cool for at least 10 minutes. (Try to resist eating the entire tray in one sitting. This keeps well for days in a tightly sealed container.)

Depending on the temperature, coconut oil will naturally turn solid or liquid. If it's solid, simply warm it gently over the stove to melt it into liquid form.

To dress up the Granolove, add any of the following before baking: a mashed banana, chopped almonds, crushed walnuts, hulled sunflower seeds, raisins, ginger, ground flaxseed . . . or any of your favorite add-ins!

The photo opposite shows granolove, all dressed up. Warning: Any of these granolove options, when served with coconut yogurt (page 4), may dramatically change your life.

Buckwheat Granolove

AU NATUREL

1 CUP (100 G) RAW BUCKWHEAT GROATS

ALL DRESSED UP (OPTIONAL ADDITIONS)

½ CUP (50 G) NUTS AND/OR SEEDS OF CHOICE (SUNFLOWER SEEDS, PUMPKIN SEEDS, ALMONDS, PECANS, WALNUTS . . .)

½ CUP (50 G) DRIED FRUIT OF CHOICE (RAISINS, FIGS, APRICOTS, DATES, PRUNES . . .)

♥ 2 TABLESPOONS COCONUT FLAKES

½ TEASPOON CINNAMON

♥ 1 APPLE, CORED, PEELED, AND PURÉED

TEASPOON EACH OF THE FOLLOWING SPICES (OR OF AS MANY OF THEM AS YOU HAVE!): CARDAMOM, NUTMEG, GINGER, CLOVES

Soak the buckwheat overnight or for around 8 hours in filtered water. Rinse the buckwheat, add the "all dressed up" ingredients, if desired, and cook it on either:

. . . a tray in a dehydrator. Dehydrate for 8 hours, or until crispy.

. . . a rimmed baking sheet. Bake at 350°F (175°C) for 20 minutes, or until crispy.

TIP
The Dehydrator

The Buckwheat Granolove is much better when prepared in a dehydrator, a machine that looks like a mini spaceship and cooks foods at a veeeeery low temperature. Dehydrators are great for preserving nutrients, but sadly, they don't conserve electricity, so use them sparingly—for example, for this gorgeous granola recipe. Make a lot at one time since it will keep for weeks!

Cereal: Part of This Green Breakfast

I grew up eating breakfast with Tony the Tiger, Cap'n Crunch, Lucky the Leprechaun, and Toucan Sam. Sadly, they probably all have diabetes, arthritis, and obesity issues today, since the cereals they promote are laden with sugar, chemicals, and other atrocities. However, there is nothing like a bowl of sweet, crunchy goodness in a sea of creamy milk to start the day. Enter . . . my grrrrrrrreat versions of some childhood favorites.

Cookie Crisp

SERVES 1

½ CUP (50 G) GRANOLOVE OF CHOICE (PAGE 36)

1 TEASPOON MESQUITE POWDER, CAROB POWDER, AND/OR LUCUMA POWDER

♥ 1 TO 2 TEASPOONS CACAO NIBS

Mix together all of the ingredients in a bowl. Pour *Lait de Nuts* (page 2) or store-bought nut milk of choice on top (I recommend walnut).

Cocoa Puffs

SERVES 1

♥ 1 TEASPOON CACAO POWDER

♥ 1 TEASPOON LIQUID COCONUT OIL

2 TABLESPOONS PUFFED RICE

⅓ CUP (30 G) GRANOLOVE OF CHOICE (PAGE 36)

Mix the cacao with the coconut oil until it forms a liquid sauce. Pour the sauce over the puffed rice, then let it cool for a few minutes and harden. Mix with Granolove. Pour hazelnut milk, homemade (page 2) or store-bought, on top. Go cuckoo.

Luckier Charms

(They're magically delicious.)

SERVES 1

½ CUP (50 G) GRANOLOVE OF CHOICE (PAGE 36)

1 TEASPOON LUCUMA POWDER (OPTIONAL)

YOUR CHOICE OF "MARSHMALLOWS" TO TASTE:

HEARTS—RASPBERRIES OR SLICED STRAWBERRIES

BLUE MOONS—BLUEBERRIES

STARS—PUMPKIN AND/OR SUNFLOWER SEEDS

HORSESHOES—WALNUTS OR CASHEWS

CLOVERS—FRESH SUNFLOWER SPROUTS

POTS OF GOLD—SLICED BANANAS

RAINBOWS—FRESH BEE POLLEN

RED BALLOONS—GOJI BERRIES

Mix together all of the ingredients in a bowl. Pour *Lait de* Plants (page 1) or store-bought plant-based milk of choice over the top, and let the ingredients soak to form a beautiful rainbow!

Crème de Chia

Chia is the most popular seed in school. This South American superfood is the new muse of both the culinary and nutrition worlds, thanks to its unparalleled nutritional profile and unique hydrophilic properties that turn it into a tapioca-like gel when mixed with liquid. Chia is an excellent addition to any meal, but particularly breakfast, since these nutrient-dense seeds will energize and hydrate you all day long!

Crème de Chia

SERVES 1

♥ 2 TABLESPOONS CHIA SEEDS
♥ 1 CUP (250 ML) ALMOND MILK, HOMEMADE (PAGE 2) OR STORE-BOUGHT
¼ TEASPOON VANILLA POWDER OR EXTRACT
¼ TEASPOON CINNAMON
1 DATE, SOAKED, PEELED, AND PITTED (OPTIONAL, IF USING UNSWEETENED ALMOND MILK)

Add the chia seeds to a bowl. Mix all other ingredients in a blender or shaker, then pour over the seeds. Mix well with a spoon. Wait a minute or so, then mix again with a spoon. Leave the bowl on the counter for 15 to 20 minutes, until the seeds absorb the liquid. Mix again with the spoon. Eat as it is, or add more almond milk if you prefer a thinner consistency. Alternatively, place in the fridge and eat later or the next day. This is a perfect meal to make ahead and grab for breakfast in the morning!

CHIA VARIATIONS

The preparation instructions are the same, but with just a few ingredient swaps or added superfoods, you can transform a simple Crème de Chia into an energizing meal or power snack!

Chia Parfait

Add one third of the Crème de Chia to a tall glass or small bowl. Top with granola (like Granolove, page 36) and chopped fresh fruit or dried fruit (think mulberries, goldenberries, or goji berries). Add another layer of chia mixture followed by more granola and fruit, then more crème, then more granola and fruit.

Enerchia

Replace the almond milk with Hippie-Chic Hemp Milk (page 2) or store-bought hemp milk and add ¼ teaspoon maca powder and 1 teaspoon mesquite powder. Top with goldenberries.

Chocochia

Replace the almond milk with Brazil nut milk (homemade—see page 2—or store-bought) and add 1 teaspoon mesquite powder, 1 tablespoon cacao powder, and a pinch of cayenne pepper (optional).

♥ BEST FRIEND FOOD
Chia

Remember chia pets? Awww, weren't they cute? Chia seeds may *seem* adorable and innocent—teeny black or white seeds that look like poppy seeds hanging out at a health food store near you—but they're in fact powerful forces of nature. Chia seeds boast a nearly perfect ratio of omega-3 and omega-6 oils and are a great source of fiber and protein. They help regulate blood sugar levels by ensuring a slow release of carbs and slow conversion of those carbs into glucose so your energy levels won't fluctuate.

Chia has more calcium than milk, more potassium than bananas, more iron than spinach, and more vitamin C than oranges! It's great as a stand-alone meal or snack in the form of Crème de Chia, but is also a terrific vegan alternative to eggs in baking recipes (just mix 1 tablespoon chia seeds with 3 tablespoon water to replace an egg), and you can sprinkle the seeds over any meal to add crunch and protein or blend them into smoothies, soups, or dressings to thicken them.

Dress all in black chia or use the white seeds, which are identical in nutrition and flavor, but a bit more "glam" for presentation purposes.

Le Pain Quotidien (Homemade Bread!)

A toast! To the bread that will change your life! I offer you this recipe in honor of my great-grandfather, a baker who had plenty of dough, even during the Great Depression. This bread is—are you sitting down?—gluten-free, vegan, yeast-free, soy-free, and, I promise, not flavor-free! Though it may not be a boulangerie baguette, it's the new loaf of my life: hearty and dense, yet it doesn't feel like a brick in your stomach. Plus, it's so easy to make—no need to knead!—and it toasts perfectly. Use your dough right away or be frugal and store it in the fridge or freezer for a long time.

This bread is tasty on its own or topped with avocado, Happy Hummus (page 54), or Better Butter (page 6). Toast it for the best flavor and texture and transform into a sandwich.

MAKES 1 SMALL LOAF (AROUND 10 SLICES)

♥ 1 CUP ALMONDS
1½ CUPS (300 G) PUMPKIN SEEDS
1 CUP (120 G) BROWN RICE FLOUR (OR QUINOA FLOUR)
½ CUP (100 G) SUNFLOWER SEEDS
¼ CUP (50 G) SESAME SEEDS
2 TABLESPOONS PSYLLIUM HUSK POWDER
♥ 2 TABLESPOONS CHIA SEEDS
SALT AND BLACK PEPPER TO TASTE
1 TABLESPOON CHOPPED FRESH HERBS OR ¼ TEASPOON SPICES (OPTIONAL)
2 CUPS (500 ML) COLD, FILTERED WATER

Preheat the oven to 350°F (175°C).

Spread the almonds, sunflower seeds, sesame seeds, and pumpkin seeds on parchment paper on a baking sheet and toast until fragrant (5 to 10 minutes), turning partway through for even toasting.

Add the almonds and 1 cup (200 g) of the pumpkin seeds to a food processor and process into a fine powder.

Transfer this "flour" to a big bowl and add all of the other ingredients except the water. Mix together well, then add the water. Let it sit for at least 1 hour, or until all of the water is absorbed. The dough should be very firm and dense.

Grease a loaf pan with some coconut oil and add the dough. Press down with a spoon. Bake for around 1 hour, until the top is browned and a toothpick stuck into the middle comes out clean. You can start checking it at 45 minutes depending on your oven, but it usually takes at least 1 to 1½ hours. Remove and allow the loaf to cool completely in the pan. (Note: This step will be difficult since you will be tempted by a stunning, great-smelling loaf of freshly baked bread, but trust me!) Once it's cool, slice and enjoy! If it doesn't seem cooked enough inside, toast it to firm it up.

VARIATION

For a sweet version, replace ¼ cup (50 g) of the pumpkin seeds or almonds with hazelnuts and/or pecans and add 1 to 2 tablespoons maple syrup, ½ teaspoon cinnamon, and ¼ cup (50 g) dried fruit (e.g., raisins, chopped figs, or apricots). Topped with coconut or almond butter and banana slices, it is, quite simply, heaven.

PSYLLIUM HUSKS
a boost for your bowels!

Psyllium is pronounced like "silly-yum." This is not a coincidence, since this ingredient ups the YUM factor in baked goods. Psyllium is a magical binding ingredient that comes from a plant most commonly found in India and helps gluten-free bread stick together. Psyllium is most often sold as a laxative, thanks to its absorbent fiber that not only sweeps the colon free of toxins but also soothes the digestive tract since it soaks up so much water. Psyllium can help get things moving, but it can also bulk up the stool in cases of diarrhea. Now let's get back to baking!

You can find psyllium husk in powder form in most health food stores or online. It sounds fancy, but it's not too expensive, and a little bit goes a long way.

Le Pain Perdu (French Toast)

"No bread left behind!" What we Americans call "French toast," the French call le pain perdu, which literally means "the lost bread." It's a way of transforming old, stale bread into a sweet treat. Think of it as CPR for your ailing bread. Obviously, our pain quotidien (page 40) is so spectacular that there will rarely be any of it "lost" and in need of a makeover, but if the occasion arises (or you want to use other bread), voilà: a recipe for easy "French toast." This is great for kids (cut the bread pieces into fun shapes using cookie cutters!) and for impressing guests for brunch.

SERVES 2 (OR A FEW CHILDREN)

- ♥ 1 LARGE RIPE BANANA (AROUND ½ CUP MASHED)
- ♥ 1 CUP (250 ML) ALMOND MILK, HOMEMADE (SEE PAGE 2) OR STORE-BOUGHT
- ¼ CUP (30 G) ALMOND FLOUR, HOMEMADE (PAGE 14) OR STORE-BOUGHT
- 1 TABLESPOON ARROWROOT POWDER
- ¼ TEASPOON VANILLA POWDER OR EXTRACT
- ¼ TEASPOON CINNAMON
- 1 TEASPOON GROUND FLAXSEEDS
- ♥ 1 TABLESPOON COCONUT OIL
- 4 SLICES *LE PAIN QUOTIDIEN* (PAGE 40) OR OTHER GLUTEN-FREE BREAD

In a large bowl, mash the banana well with a fork. Add all of the other ingredients, except for the bread. Stir well. The mixture should be liquidy but still nice and thick. Warm up a pan on the stove over medium heat, then grease with more coconut oil.

Dip a bread slice into the batter slowly and let it absorb the batter for a few seconds so it is coated on all sides. (Don't be afraid to get messy!) Add to the pan and cook for 3 to 4 minutes, until golden brown. (Cook 2 slices at once if the pan is big enough.) Flip it over and cook until the other side browns and the inside is cooked through, around 3 more minutes. Transfer to a plate and repeat with the remaining bread. Top each serving with fresh berries, Sweet Butter (page 6), a drizzle of maple syrup, and/or almond butter.

Avocado Tartines

Tartine is a fancy French word for, well, toast topped with a spread, otherwise known as an open-faced sandwich. Tartines are great for a quick breakfast or anytime snack, or served with a side salad for an easy lunch. Tartines can be sweet (think: almond butter, page 14, mashed banana, NOtella, page 76 . . .) or savory. My favorite tartine is très simple: mashed avocado sprinkled with spices or mixed with fresh herbs or veggies du jour.

Avocado Tartine au Naturel

MAKES 1 SERVING

2 SLICES *LE PAIN QUOTIDIEN* (PAGE 40) OR OTHER GLUTEN-FREE BREAD

♥ 1 SMALL AVOCADO, PITTED AND PEELED

A PINCH OF CAYENNE PEPPER

♥ 1 TEASPOON LEMON OR LIME JUICE

SALT AND PEPPER TO TASTE

Toast the bread. In a bowl, mash the avocado and other ingredients together with a fork. Spread onto the toast. *Voilà!*

HURRIED AND CURRIED AVOCADO TARTINE

Add a pinch of curry powder to the top of your Avocado Tartine au Naturel.

HERBED AVOCADO TARTINE

Chop up some fresh basil, chives, cilantro, and parsley and mix into the mashed avocado mixture.

MISO-CARROT TARTINE

Grate 1 small carrot and mix with 1 teaspoon of miso paste and a splash of lemon juice. Top the avocado toast with this mixture.

CHOUCROUTE GARNIE TARTINE

(One of my all-time favorite combinations!) Top your Avocado Tartine au Naturel with 1 to 2 tablespoons sauerkraut.

AVOCADO AND WHITE BEAN TARTINE

Mix together ¼ cup (15 g) white beans, mashed avocado, lemon juice, olive oil, salt/pepper, and fresh or dried herbs. Spread onto toast.

SWEET AVOCADO TARTINE

Mash an avocado in a bowl with ½ banana. Spread onto toast. Top with a pinch of cinnamon and/or a drizzle of maple syrup.

B.L.T.

Add a layer of coconut or eggplant "bacon,"* a layer of lettuce, and a sliced tomato (plus the always optional but always awesome avocado).

*COCONUT OR EGGPLANT "BACON"

Surgeon *green*eral's warning: This does not taste like bacon, look like bacon, or resemble bacon in any way. It should never be compared to actual bacon. I call it bacon because, like bacon, it adds a salty and crispy element to recipes. Think of it as six degrees of Vegan Bacon—it's a stretch, but in the end, it all comes back to bacon.

Add 1 cup (250 g) coconut flakes or eggplant (sliced lengthwise into very thin strips, around ¼ inch/¾ cm thick) to a bowl. If using eggplant, toss with salt and olive oil and marinate for at least 10 minutes. Toss the oiled and salted eggplant or coconut flakes with 1 tablespoon maple syrup, 1 tablespoon coconut aminos or tamari, 1 tablespoon apple cider vinegar, and salt and pepper to taste. Add a pinch of paprika or cayenne pepper for an extra kick. Let marinate for at least 1 hour, preferable for 3 or more.

Bake at 350°F (175°C) for 10 to 15 minutes, or dehydrate for around 8 hours, until crispy.

Spring

My playlist for coming back to life in springtime

I Can See Clearly Now JIMMY CLIFF

Shake It Out FLORENCE & THE MACHINE

Ooh Child THE FIVE STAIRSTEPS

Change Your Mind SISTER HAZEL

Let It Go IDINA MENZEL

Burn the Pages SIA

Tomorrow Is Gonna Be Better JOSHUA RADIN

Brand New Day STING

Break the Shell INDIA ARIE

Breathe Again SARA BAREILLES

Under the Bridge RED HOT CHILI PEPPERS

The World I Know COLLECTIVE SOUL

Anything Could Happen ELLIE GOULDING

Shake It Off TAYLOR SWIFT

In the mood for spring

Spring is a time of regeneration and reconstruction after the cold, darkness, and often illness associated with winter. In the springtime, flowers bloom, seeds sprout, and the sun shines down, enveloping the earth in a blanket of warmth. After months of hibernation, our bodies wake up and kick back into gear. Spring is a transitional period during which both body and mind undergo a transformation. Before it can savor summer's pleasures, the body first needs to rid itself of the toxins accumulated during the winter months. Oh, oui—spring is detox time! It's the moment to get rid of what isn't serving us and nourish our bodies and minds with positive energy on both a psychological and nutritional level. Even Mother Nature rests in the winter, but as soon as the first signs of spring come, she heads back to work. Fruits, vegetables, herbs, and other plants are more varied, more colorful, and more flavorful.

Paris in the springtime is as good as the song says, but I also like springtime everywhere. It's my favorite season, especially at the market. After months of squash, potatoes, and leeks (as much as I do love them), the freshness of those first spring peas, crisp asparagus, or sweet strawberries is truly magical. It's a rainbow of flavors—and health benefits!

I definitely have spring fever; do you?

Breathe

When the first rays of sunshine and the warm rains of spring arrive,
our energy levels rise little by little, we breathe better, we feel stronger,
and all of this works wonders on our mood as well.

Delicious detox: Au revoir, toxins!

When you hear the word "detox," what do you think of? Not drinking a sip of alcohol for three weeks after partying a little bit too hard? Consuming nothing but juices and tasteless broth so that you can fit into your bikini over the summer? OK, let's rewind.

The concept of "detox" is very simple. We need to empty the body of what is hurting it and welcome what will help to nourish it, both physically and emotionally. It means starting to lighten up meals and opting for foods adapted to the change in temperature outside and, consequently, in the body. A "detox" will be more effective in the long term if it's done little by little, every day instead of a radical, extraordinary, superdetox session. Spring lasts for a few months, so that gives you an entire season to purify yourself from the inside out!

In Chinese medicine, spring is the season of the liver and the gallbladder, the two organs primarily responsible for detox in the body. According to this philosophy, the liver makes our "qi" (energy) flow smoothly throughout the body, so to keep it moving we need to make sure this energy isn't blocked by toxicity in these organs. Acupuncture reduces tension and unblocks anything getting in the way of that qi. If you're on pins and needles waiting to find time to get to the nearest Chinese medicine practitioner, don't worry; you can still do so many things at home to detox. Think: yoga, tai chi, waking up early (it gets your liver going!), moving around outside in the fresh air, eating greens and sour foods (like apple cider vinegar or sauerkraut), or drinking cleansing teas.

In Chinese medicine and also in traditional Ayurvedic medicine from India, health is synonymous with balance. When we get sick, this means that there is an imbalance somewhere in body or mind. In the springtime, we need to focus on getting our digestive systems back in balance. Detoxifying ourselves of what we don't need (inflammatory foods, negative thoughts, and so on) gives us space to welcome in a positive energy that can last for the rest of the year. And guess what color is associated with both the liver and springtime in Chinese medicine? You guessed it—green! So get your green on this season—fresh herbs, leafy greens, sprouts, and microgreens all support the liver and just might help the qi to dance through our bodies happily and make us smile and dance around (yes, you're allowed!) at the same time.

Seasonal produce

FRUIT

Apricots

Kiwis

Lemons

Rhubarb

Strawberries

VEGGIES

Artichokes

Asparagus

Beets and beet greens

Carrots

Dandelion greens

Fava beans

Fennel

Garlic

Green onions

Mint

New potatoes

Peas

Radishes

Spinach

Spring onions

Swiss chard

Watercress

Détox yoga

By Mika de Brito

Mika de Brito *is the king of yoga cool in France. Mika is the cofounder of Yogalab, a unique and mesmerizing mélange of movement and music in partnership with French singer-songwriter Marco Prince. From studios across Paris to his vast country home in Les Cevennes in the French countryside, this French yogi has created his own style of Vinyasa Krama, a blend of physical, dynamic practice with a focus on breathing and spirituality. Mika is all about bringing yoga to everyone—no crazy gurus or esoteric metaphysical experiences, just movement and music, asanas and art. Mika is filled with positive energy, and his classes are designed to free the mind and the body of negativity in all forms.*

mika-yoga.fr

Nothing is better than a healthy mind in a healthy body. However, we shouldn't look at all of the toxins in our bodies or minds in a negative way. They are all part of a natural process. For example, whenever we use our muscles, we produce waste, and our bodies need to get rid of this waste. The best way to detox is to get rid of this waste little by little on a daily basis. I recommend a vinyasa sequence, a dynamic succession of postures done in a specific order, with a particular rhythm, and of course relaxation at the end. Learn how to breathe, to relax, to truly sleep! And day after day, think of at least one positive thought—that's also what detoxing is about!

1. NAULI

Here, we focus on a "churning" in the stomach that promotes the "intestinal fire," the digestion of food, but also on the ways that we "digest" the experiences in our lives. Try to do this exercise on an empty stomach! Standing up, with your hands on your knees, bend your knees just a bit. Hold your breath and try to "empty" your belly and bring your belly button in as much as possible for around 1 minute (without forcing yourself, especially if you're new to this!). I recommend doing this exercise regularly, even daily.

2. TATRAKA

Sit in lotus position (with your legs crossed) and light a candle. Stare at the candle until your eyes tear a bit, then stop.

1

2

3

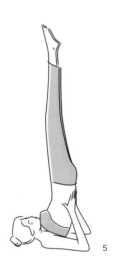

5

3 AND 4. UTTKATASANA WITH A TWIST

In a vinyasa, certain postures like twists or inversions are recommended for detox since they promote lymphatic circulation. Uttkatasana (or chair pose) is a great pose for detox, especially with a twist! In Tadasana (standing, with your hands by your side), bend your knees and stretch your arms in the air—inhale and exhale. Place your hands in prayer position over your heart then "twist" to the left by placing your right elbow on your left knee. Stay there for five breaths then do the same thing on the other side. A tip: When you place your elbow on your knee, the palms of your hands should be pressing against each other, your forearms should be aligned, and your knees are still bent in "chair pose" position. It's important here to protect your back and your pelvic area when you twist. Try not to "wind into the posture" and hurt yourself when you twist, but instead try to continue to stretch your spinal cord and open the space between your shoulders and ears. The pressure of your elbow on your knee will help you to naturally contract your ab muscles!

5. SARVANGASANA

Sarvangasana, or shoulder stand, is known as "the mother of asanas." It's beneficial for all parts of the body. Lie down on your mat or on the floor and raise your legs in the air so that they are vertical and form a right angle with the rest of your body. Place your hands on your lower back, and let the weight of your body rest on your shoulders with your elbows on the ground. Stay in this position for around 30 seconds at first, then try to stay up for longer, little by little, until you can stay there for around 2 or 3 minutes.
Note: This pose is not recommended if you are pregnant, menstruating, or have just had a meal. If this pose is uncomfortable for you for any reason, try Adho Mukha Svanasana (AKA "downward dog," where your heart will still be below your head—see page 83).

6. SAVASANA

This is also known as corpse pose. Lie down on your back with your arms by your sides and the palms of your hands facing the ceiling, your shoulders resting on the ground. Try not to move. Relax your forehead, your jaw, your eyes; relax your tongue as well (your tongue articulates every thought you have, so let it rest!). With each breath, your body should become lighter, free of all of its limitations. With each exhalation, feel the weight of your body on the ground. Try not to pay attention to the air coming in and going out; just breathe naturally. Your spirit should be very calm. Often, our minds can become cluttered simply by trying *not* to think! Try to think about nothing; just lie there still and observe the silence. Shhhhhh!

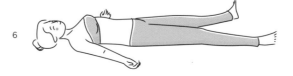

6

Inner Peas: Perfect Pea Purée

One of my favorite spring sports is . . . shelling peas! This may not strike you as a particularly athletic endeavor, but I find it to be both relaxing and rewarding. There is nothing like cracking open those first pea pods of spring and savoring the crunchy, fresh flavors of the tiny pearls inside. When I was a little girl, I used to hum while eating peas and, I confess, I still do! This perfect pea purée may just make you sing, too. Serve this purée as a side dish, as a spread on toast or crackers, atop a salad, or as a creamy pesto for pasta or grains. It's unpealieveable! If you don't share my enthusiasm for shelling peas, feel free to substitute thawed frozen peas here. Finally—whirled peas!

MAKES 2 SERVINGS

1 CUP (200 G) SHELLED PEAS (THAWED, IF FROZEN)

2 TABLESPOONS TAHINI

♥ 1 TABLESPOON LEMON JUICE

1 TEASPOON LEMON ZEST

1 GARLIC CLOVE, PEELED AND SLICED

A PINCH OF CUMIN

2 TABLESPOONS CHOPPED FRESH MINT

SALT AND PEPPER TO TASTE

Steam the peas for 1 minute only! Vegetables that are *al dente* keep their nutrients intact. (Plus, who likes mushy, wrinkled peas?) Immediately place the peas under cold running water to stop the cooking. If desired, reserve some of the cooled peas for mixing in just before serving (this makes for a coarser texture with some crunch). Add the rest of the peas and the tahini, lemon juice and zest, garlic, cumin, and mint to a food processor or blender and blend until smooth and creamy. If you make the purée with frozen peas, you may wish to add a handful of fresh peas at the end. Add salt and pepper to taste.

PEAS
Give Peas a Chance

Peas are called *petits pois* in French. They may be "petite," but they pack a powerful punch! These legumes are a great source of plant-based protein. They are rich in phytonutrients and low in fat and calories. They help to regulate blood sugar, thanks to their fiber and protein content, and contain so many vitamins (A, B, C, and K) and minerals (potassium, phosphorous, magnesium, calcium, iron, zinc, copper, manganese, and selenium). Yes, all of that in those teeny-tiny green balls—oh my pod!

Kale Spa Day

The Queen of Greens took her time gaining power in France (kale and other members of the cabbage family were traditionally "foods of the poor"), but she has finally arrived in all of her royal splendor.

Kale Chips

MAKES 2 SERVINGS OR 1 BIG BOWL TO SNACK ON

1 GARLIC CLOVE

4 HUGE HANDFULS OF KALE (ANY VARIETY, BUT CURLY KALE IS BEST)

2 TABLESPOONS NUTRITIONAL YEAST

1 TABLESPOON OLIVE OIL

A PINCH OF SALT

2 PINCHES OF CAYENNE PEPPER (OPTIONAL, FOR A SPICY KICK)

Oh no, my friends, I'm not joking: Raw kale needs a good massage before it's ready to go out . . . onto your plate. Otherwise, it will be very hard to chew and to digest, and you may feel like you're eating rubber. So caress it, knead it, rub it until it starts to relax and shrink. Don't be shy—get down and dirty!

Peel and mince the garlic. Remove the thick stems and central ribs and slice the kale into thin strips. In a bowl, mix the kale with the nutritional yeast, olive oil, salt, and cayenne (if using). Massage the kale well with your hands. The massage should last for around 20 seconds to 1 minute.

TWO WAYS TO COOK:

The "tanning salon" version: Preheat the oven to 300°F (150°C). Add the kale chips to a baking sheet and cook for around 12 minutes. Turn them over and cook for another 5 minutes. The chips should be crispy, but don't burn them!

The "sauna" version (in a dehydrator): Add the kale to a dehydrator and cook at 115°F (45°C) for 8 to 12 hours, until crispy.

Don't hesitate to double, triple, quadruple, or multiply this recipe by 100—these chips last for a long time at room temperature in a closed bag or glass jar (that is, if you and your friends and family don't devour them before that! Bet ya can't eat just one!).

Kale Spa Salad

MAKES 1 SERVING

♥ ½ AVOCADO

2 GENEROUS HANDFULS OF KALE (ANY VARIETY, BUT I PREFER CURLY KALE HERE)

♥ 1 TABLESPOON LEMON JUICE

½ TABLESPOON OLIVE OIL

♥ ½ TABLESPOON HEMP SEED OIL OR YOUR FAVORITE PLANT-BASED OIL (FLAXSEED OIL, PUMPKIN SEED OIL, AVOCADO OIL . . . OR A BLEND)

SALT AND PEPPER TO TASTE

A PINCH OF CAYENNE PEPPER

1 SMALL TOMATO OR 1 HANDFUL OF CHERRY TOMATOES

2 TABLESPOONS HEMP SEEDS

Pit, peel, and chop the avocado into small cubes. Add the kale leaves to a bowl, then add the lemon juice, olive oil, hemp seed oil, salt, and pepper. Massage the kale for a few minutes until both of you are very relaxed. Chop the tomato if using one small tomato. Add the avocado, tomato, and hemp seeds to the bowl.

KALE
Queen of Greens

The Queen of Greens certainly merits her crown. Kale is very, very rich . . . in nutrients. Kale supports the immune system and gives us energy, thanks to its magnesium and potassium. Rich in fiber, it slows the passage of glucose in the blood and stabilizes blood sugar. It also helps to fight against bad cholesterol invading the body's regal kingdom of health.

Like any queen, kale needs pampering. Try:

A hot stone massage, AKA SAUTÉ it. Add to a pan with some coconut or olive oil, onions, and garlic. Sauté for a couple of minutes, until wilted.

A steam bath, AKA STEAM it in a steamer!

A swim, AKA SOAK it in vegetable/miso broth or warm water until soft.

Happy Hummus

Do you know the fairy tale "The Princess and the (Chick)pea?" If you think your digestive system is too sensitive for legumes like chickpeas, hummus may just be your solution to a happily ever after. This creamy concoction, a staple of Middle Eastern cuisine, is such a great, digestion-friendly way to enjoy the protein-packed chickpea. This recipe makes a basic, classic hummus, but don't be afraid to add your favorite herbs, spices, or even other vegetables for more flavorful and exotic versions.

Très ChicPea Classic Hummus

MAKES 1 BIG BOWL

1 CUP (150 G) COOKED CHICKPEAS (SEE PAGE 18; SOAK THEM OVERNIGHT AND COOK WITH KOMBU TO MAKE THEM MORE DIGESTIBLE) OR DRAINED AND RINSED CANNED CHICKPEAS

2 TABLESPOONS TAHINI

A PINCH OF CUMIN

2 TABLESPOONS OLIVE OIL

SALT AND PEPPER TO TASTE

GARNISHES:

1 TEASPOON PARSLEY

1 TEASPOON SESAME SEEDS

1 TEASPOON OLIVE OIL

1 GARLIC CLOVE, PEELED AND MINCED (*VERY* OPTIONAL)

Go !

Blend the chickpeas, tahini, cumin, and olive oil in a blender or food processor until smooth and creamy. Add salt and pepper to taste. Transfer to a bowl and top with the garnishes.

CHICKPEAS
Garbanzo-là-là!

Chickpeas, otherwise known as garbanzo beans, are a great source of plant-based protein and fiber, vitamins, and minerals. Their low glycemic index, tryptophan, and capacity to reduce cholesterol make them a wonderful ally for health. They star in hummus and falafel but are also great additions to salads. Try roasting chickpeas in some olive or coconut oil for a perfect protein-packed snack!

Red Pepper Hummus

MAKES 1 BIG BOWL

1 GARLIC CLOVE (*VERY* OPTIONAL)

1 RED BELL PEPPER

1 CUP (150 G) COOKED CHICKPEAS (SEE PAGE 18) OR DRAINED AND RINSED CANNED CHICKPEAS

2 SUN-DRIED TOMATOES (PREFERABLY DRY AND SALT-FREE; SALTED OR OIL-PACKED ARE OK, BUT ADJUST THE OLIVE OIL AND SALT IN THE RECIPE ACCORDINGLY)

♥ 1 TABLESPOON LEMON JUICE

1 TEASPOON LEMON ZEST

2 TABLESPOONS TAHINI

¼ TEASPOON CUMIN

2 TABLESPOONS OLIVE OIL

A PINCH OF PAPRIKA

SALT AND PEPPER TO TASTE

Preheat the oven to 400°F (200°C). Peel and chop the garlic (if using), and clean the red pepper and remove its white membranes and seeds.

Place the pepper in the center of a baking dish and roast it for around 30 minutes, until tender with wrinkly, blackened skin. Remove it from the oven, cover it, and let it "sweat" for around 15 minutes. Remove the skin and cut the pepper into slices.

Blend the chickpeas, red pepper slices, garlic, sun-dried tomatoes, lemon juice and zest, tahini, cumin, olive oil, and paprika until smooth and creamy. Add salt and pepper to taste.

Sexy Spring Salad with Mustard-Miso Vinaigrette

OK, so cabbage may not seem like the sexiest vegetable around, but in fact, this cruciferous-fabulous food is rich in fiber and antioxidants to keep your skin glowing. (Note: Red cabbage is particularly rich in antioxidants.) Dulse is a vitamin and mineral powerhouse that cleanses the body of heavy metals, promotes thyroid function, and supports the liver—all key elements of a healthy detox. Not to mention fennel and carrots, beauty foods extraordinaire! I've dressed up these healthy veggies in a tangy sauce to keep things interesting. This salad is light, crunchy, and flavorful, perfect for transitioning to the warmer weather and great for detox season.

MAKES 1 SERVING

FOR THE MUSTARD-MISO VINAIGRETTE:

♥ 1 TABLESPOON LEMON JUICE (SEE NOTE)

1 TEASPOON LEMON ZEST

1 TEASPOON DIJON MUSTARD (PREFERABLY APPLE CIDER VINEGAR–BASED)

♥ 1 TEASPOON MISO PASTE

1 TEASPOON MAPLE SYRUP

1 TABLESPOON OLIVE OIL

1 TABLESPOON NUTRITIONAL YEAST (OPTIONAL)

SALT AND PEPPER TO TASTE

FOR THE SALAD:

½ FENNEL BULB

¼ CUP (50 G) THINLY SLICED RED CABBAGE

♥ 1 MEDIUM CARROT

♥ 1 AVOCADO

2 GENEROUS HANDFULS OF MESCLUN

♥ 1 HANDFUL OF DULSE

1 TABLESPOON CHOPPED FRESH CHIVES

Blend all vinaigrette ingredients, except salt and pepper, in a blender or whisk by hand. Add salt and pepper to taste.

Core and thinly slice the fennel. Drown (yes, go for it!) the raw fennel and cabbage in the dressing. Let them sit for a few minutes to absorb the dressing (or—even better—refrigerate overnight).

Peel or wash then grate the carrot. Pit, peel, and slice the avocado. When you're ready to eat, add the mesclun, dulse, chives, carrot, and avocado and mix together.

Note: I use A LOT of lemon in this book. Lemon is a staple in green cooking—it adds flavor and sweetness and detoxifies and alkalinizes the body at the same time. In order to get your taste buds used to the tartness, if you want to add less lemon than my recipes call for at first and work your way up, feel free!

FENNEL
A light bulb with stomach superpowers

Want to laugh? Try to pronounce the word for "fennel" in French: *le fenouil* (pronounced "luuuuh feeeeen ouiiii"). After years of living in France, I still cannot pronounce the word. Luckily, no pronunciation is necessary to eat it! Fennel is low in calories but rich in fiber and vitamins A, C, E, and B9, great for strengthening the immune system. Fennel is filled with calcium, magnesium, potassium, and iron and fights viruses and inflammation. It aids digestion and helps to fight flatulence, diarrhea, and constipation. These are not very glam topics, *oui*? Fine, we won't speak another word—just add some fennel to your next meal as your top-secret defense against tummy troubles, and don't worry, your veggie secret is safe with me.

Beet Rawvioli with Faux-mage

How do you make ravioli without pasta or cheese? Beets me! Actually, it's very easy. Adaptable to any season, these plant-based ravioli are elegant and impressive, but so simple to make.

SERVES 1

1 MEDIUM BEET (ANY VARIETY, BUT I ESPECIALLY LOVE CHIOGGIA, OR STRIPED, BEETS—THEY ARE GORGEOUS WHEN SLICED!)

1 TABLESPOON OLIVE OIL

3 TO 4 TABLESPOONS HERBED FAUX-MAGE (PAGE 5)

1 HANDFUL OF ARUGULA

1 TEASPOON TRUFFLE OIL (OPTIONAL)

♥ JUICE OF ½ LEMON

SALT AND PEPPER TO TASTE

Peel the beet, then cut it into very thin slices with a mandoline. You can also do this with a knife; just go very slowly and be careful not to cut yourself!

Mix the beets with the olive oil and let sit in a dish at room temperature for at least 10 minutes, preferably for 30 minutes to overnight (in the latter case, leave in the refrigerator).

Add a spoonful of faux-mage to half of the beet slices, then top each with another beet slice to make a mini sandwich.

Add the arugula to a bowl or plate. Top with the rawvioli, then finish with truffle oil, if using (or more olive oil), lemon juice, salt, and pepper.

ADAPT THIS RECIPE TO OTHER SEASONS!

Try butternut squash rawvioli in the fall, zucchini rawvioli in the summer, or turnip rawvioli in winter.

BEETS
A lipstick-colored root

Beets' strong concentration of methionine facilitates the elimination of toxins from the body. They are also rich in betanin, which stimulates the breakdown of fatty acids in the liver. Raw or cooked, beets add a sweet flavor to juices and meals, especially during "detox" periods like springtime!

If you notice that your urine turns red after eating beets, don't panic! This phenomenon comes from the betaines that are absorbed by the intestines, which don't pose any threat to your health! So turn up the beet!

Magnifique Millet with Spring Vegetables

Millet is appropriately pronounced "mi-YAY!" in French. "YAY!" will likely be your reaction after eating this colorful and flavorful dish that is, in sum, spring on a plate. Millet may be the title food here, but it actually serves as supporting actor to special guest stars: fresh, seasonal produce (adaptable year-round using anything you find at the market). Say it with me now (in your best French accent, please): YAY for millet!

MAKES 2 SALADS

½ CUP (50 G) DRY MILLET

6 SMALL RED RADISHES

8 ASPARAGUS SPEARS (WHITE OR GREEN)

♥ 2 CARROTS

2 FRESH SPRING (GREEN) GARLIC CLOVES

♥ 1 TABLESPOON COCONUT OIL

½ CUP (50 G) CHOPPED FRESH GREEN ONIONS

2 HANDFULS OF FRESH SPINACH

½ CUP (50 G) SHELLED PEAS

1 HANDFUL OF ARUGULA AND/OR MUSTARD GREENS

1 HANDFUL OF FRESH HERBS OF CHOICE

♥ JUICE OF 1 LEMON

1 TABLESPOON OLIVE OIL

1 TEASPOON APPLE CIDER VINEGAR

1 TO 2 TABLESPOONS NUTRITIONAL YEAST (OPTIONAL)

SALT AND PEPPER TO TASTE

MILLET
It's not just for birds (really!)

Like quinoa, millet is a grain that is perfect for replacing pasta, couscous, or bulgur. Millet is a beautifying food thanks to silica, which strengthens nails, hair, and skin. It's also easily digested and a great source of carbohydrates, protein, vitamins B1, B2, B5, A, and C, as well as calcium, potassium, magnesium, sodium, fluoride, silica . . . OK, I'll stop. Millet does everything you can imagine, other than perhaps washing your dishes once you're done eating (if you find a grain that does this, please send it my way).

On its own, millet doesn't have much taste, but it's the perfect food to highlight whatever veggies or sauces you mix with it.

For best nutrition, add the millet and a pinch of salt to a bowl of water, cover, and soak overnight or during the day. Rinse and drain before cooking. If you don't remember to soak . . . OMG YOU MIGHT DIE! Just kidding, *pas de problème*, just rinse the millet and follow the rest of the directions.

Add the millet to a small pot over medium heat and lightly toast for 1 to 2 minutes. Then add 1 cup (250 ml) water if you soaked the millet, or 1½ cups (375 ml) water if not. Bring to a boil then reduce the heat to low, cover, and simmer for around 15 minutes if presoaked, or 20 minutes if not, until the millet has absorbed the water (but isn't too mushy!). Let it sit in the covered pot off of the stove for around 5 more minutes until it's fluffable (a word I invented to describe what happens when one places a fork into perfectly cooked millet).

Rinse and cut off the tops of the radishes. Halve or chop into pieces depending on their size.

Snap the asparagus spears at their natural breaking point, then cut the tender parts into small pieces. Peel or wash the carrots, then grate. If you're using fresh garlic, chop into small pieces or slice thinly. If you're using regular garlic, peel and grate.

In a small pot over medium heat, heat the coconut oil and add the green onions. Sauté for around 1 to 2 minutes, until the onions become translucent. Add the radishes, asparagus, carrots, spinach, and peas (and any other seasonal spring veggies you wish), and sauté for just around 1 minute, so they are tender but still quite crisp. Turn off the heat.

Add the millet and mix together so the millet becomes warmed, but not hot or mushy. Top with the arugula and fresh herbs and, just before serving, add the lemon juice, olive oil, vinegar, and nutritional yeast. Add salt and pepper to taste.

Wrap Me Up! (Healthy Wrap Sandwiches)

I'm a wrap star! Yes, I'm Becca Rhymes, in the same crew as Farro Williams, The Roots, and Kale-ye West. Gimme a beet! It's so simple to be a wrap star: Just take a nori sheet, brown rice wrap (using the crêpe recipe on page 64), collard leaf, or large piece of romaine lettuce; add everything you want inside; roll it up; and (hip hop) hooray, it's ready! Collard back, yo!

"The Notorious G.R.E.E.N." Collard Wrap

MAKES 1 WRAP

- 1 LARGE COLLARD LEAF
- ♥ ¼ AVOCADO
- JUICE OF 1 SMALL LIME
- A PINCH OF CUMIN
- A PINCH OF CORIANDER
- A PINCH OF CAYENNE PEPPER
- ♥ 1 TEASPOON SPIRULINA POWDER
- ♥ 1 SMALL CARROT, PEELED AND GRATED
- ♥ 1 TABLESPOON HEMP SEEDS
- SALT AND PEPPER TO TASTE
- 1 TEASPOON PUMPKIN SEED OIL OR OLIVE OIL (OR HEALTHY, PLANT-BASED OIL OF CHOICE)

Destem the collard by cutting out the thick white stem in the center *very carefully* with a paring knife. Scoop out the avocado flesh into a small bowl, then add most of the lime juice and the cumin, coriander, cayenne, and spirulina and mash together with a fork. Place the collard on a cutting board or plate and add the fillings vertically along one long side of the leaf, leaving a margin on each side, starting with the avocado mixture, then the carrots, hemp seeds, salt, and pepper. Drizzle with the oil and the remaining lime juice.

Fold the longer sides of the collard over the filling to cover. Then, from one shorter end, start rolling the leaf up until everything is covered, like a burrito. You can eat it as it is or slice it in half.

Note: Plan to make 1 to 2 wraps per person for an appetizer portion and 3 to 4 each for a light main with a side salad.

♥ BEST FRIEND FOOD
Spirulina: The sexiest superfood

Spirulina is a seaweed that is 70 percent protein and more easily absorbed by the body than soy or beef, making it one of the best plant-based protein sources on the planet. Rich in vitamins, minerals, and chlorophyll, spirulina provides the energy needed for proper functioning of the brain and the immune system. Because it is so nourishing, spirulina is great for weight loss since it can help to curb appetite, but it's also so rich in nutrients that it is often given to children suffering from malnutrition.

"Nori by Nature" Sweet Potato Wrap

MAKES 1 WRAP

- ♥ 1 SWEET POTATO
- 1 HANDFUL OF SPINACH
- ½ TEASPOON CHOPPED FRESH CHIVES
- ♥ 1 TABLESPOON MISO BUTTER (PAGE 6)
- 1 NORI SHEET

Peel, dice, and steam the sweet potato until soft, 7 to 10 minutes. Smush the sweet potato with a fork and mix in the spinach, chives, and miso butter. Place the nori sheet on a plate, fill vertically with a generous amount of the sweet potato filling, then fold the remaining nori over the filling and roll. Wet the final edge of the nori with some water so that it sticks closed. Eat as is, like a nori burrito, or cut in half.

Note: The sweet potato puree with miso butter can also be eaten on its own or as a side dish for any meal—it's a quick, nutritious, and belly-soothing bowl in just minutes!

"Miso Elliott" Creamy Almond Wrap

MAKES 1 WRAP

♥ 1 CARROT

1 SMALL PIECE OF DAIKON RADISH

1 TABLESPOON SPROUTS OR MICROGREENS

½ TEASPOON CHOPPED FRESH CHIVES

♥ 2 TABLESPOONS ALMOND BUTTER, HOMEMADE (SEE PAGE 14) OR STORE-BOUGHT

♥ 1 TEASPOON LIGHT MISO PASTE

♥ 1 TABLESPOON LEMON JUICE

1 MEDJOOL DATE, PITTED AND CHOPPED

1 NORI SHEET

Peel and grate the carrot and radish. Mix in a bowl with all of the other ingredients except the nori. Place the nori sheet onto a plate. Add the filling and roll it up (as on page 62). *Voilà!*

Other wrap ideas

"QUINOA LATIFAH" GUACAMOLE WRAP

1 gluten-free corn or brown rice tortilla (or Savory Crêpes, opposite) stuffed with ½ cup (50 g) cooked quinoa and guacamousse of choice (page 86).

"THE BEETY BOYS" WRAP

Roast or steam a beet until cooked but not mushy, then cut in half and slice thinly. Add to a nori sheet with 1 to 2 tablespoons faux-mage (page 5) and some arugula.

"THE FRESH PEAS OF BEL AIR" WRAP

1 Savory Crêpe (opposite) or romaine leaf stuffed with Perfect Pea Purée (page 50), sun-dried tomatoes (soak in warm water if too chewy), basil, and toasted sunflower seeds.

Savory Crêpes

These perfect Parisian crêpes can also easily be transformed into savory wraps! Cover each one with a dish towel so they stay soft and pliable, then add your favorite ingredients to make wonderful wrap sandwiches.

1 CUP (120 G) BROWN RICE FLOUR OR QUINOA FLOUR (OR A MIXTURE)

¼ CUP (30 G) CHICKPEA FLOUR

1 TABLESPOON ARROWROOT POWDER

SALT AND PEPPER TO TASTE

½ TEASPOON DRIED HERBS/SPICES, SUCH AS THYME, HERBES DE PROVENCE, BASIL, OREGANO, AND TURMERIC (OPTIONAL)

1 TABLESPOON OLIVE OIL

1 TEASPOON APPLE CIDER VINEGAR

¾ CUP (200 ML) WATER

♥ 1 TABLESPOON COCONUT OIL OR OLIVE OIL

Mix the flours, arrowroot powder, salt, pepper, and herbs (if using) together by hand in a large bowl. Pour the olive oil, vinegar, and water over the top and mix again until it becomes a homogenous batter.

Add the oil to a saucepan over medium heat. Pour the batter into the pan and tilt the pan a few times to spread the batter evenly all the way to the edges. Cook until the batter starts to bubble, then flip over and continue to cook until lightly golden brown. Stuff with filling of choice (see suggestions below), then fold in two and enjoy. Or, if using as a wrap, place on a plate and cover with a dish towel until ready to use.

A FEW FILLING OPTIONS

Faux-mage of choice (page 5), pear slices, arugula, and toasted sunflower seeds

Hummus (page 54), a handful of greens, and a drizzle of olive or sesame oil

Avocado, Hempesto (page 10) or Parsley Pistou (page 8), and grated carrots

Coconut bacon (page 42), sautéed onions (in coconut or olive oil), and faux-mage of choice (page 5)

White Asparagus Velouté

In America, we call a tall, lean person a "string bean." The French say asperges *("asparagus")! Personally, I much prefer the name "asparagus"—it's much fancier than a string bean! Voilà: a creamy velouté that honors this supermodel-shaped vegetable. White asparagus is ubiquitous in France in springtime, but if you can't find the white variety where you are, go green (always a great option!).*

SERVES 1

6 ASPARAGUS SPEARS

1 SMALL FENNEL BULB

1 GARLIC CLOVE

¼ CUP (40 G) COOKED WHITE BEANS (SEE PAGE 18) OR DRAINED AND RINSED CANNED WHITE BEANS

¼ TEASPOON HERBES DE PROVENCE BLEND (OR DRIED THYME)

1 TABLESPOON OLIVE OIL

½ CUP (100 ML) VEGETABLE BROTH, MADE FROM A BOUQUET GARNI (SEE PAGE 161) OR STORE-BOUGHT, OR MORE IF NEEDED

SALT AND PEPPER TO TASTE

GARNISHES:

1 TABLESPOON FRESH SPROUTS

1 TABLESPOON CHOPPED FRESH SEASONAL HERBS

Wash the asparagus and break them with your hands—this will happen naturally at the point where the woody bottom meets the edible part. Core and chop the fennel bulb. Steam the fennel for around 2 minutes, then add the asparagus. Continue to steam for 2 minutes, just until the asparagus and fennel are tender, then run them under cold water to stop the cooking. Cut the asparagus into small pieces. Peel and chop the garlic.

Add the beans, asparagus, fennel, garlic, herbes de Provence, and olive oil to a blender and blend until creamy, adding the broth gradually and as needed. Add salt and pepper to taste, then serve topped with the garnish.

ASPARAGUS
The supermodels of the vegetable world

Asparagus is like a luxury brand's capsule collection: expensive and ephemeral. It is born and dies in the springtime—it's around only from April until June. This detox-friendly vegetable is so necessary for this season of transition. Asparagus is a natural diuretic, a fancy word to explain the fact that it'll flush those toxins right out of you. Asparagus also happens to be an aphrodisiac, perfect for the season of love!

Asparagus is rich in vitamins A and C and contains some B vitamins, potassium, phosphorous, and fiber. White asparagus doesn't have the same chlorophyll content as its green cousins, but its nutritional profile is nearly identical nonetheless.

White asparagus doesn't like to be alone. It's best when married with a sauce. Steam it to keep it tender—it's too fragile to be braised or sautéed. Be gentle with your luxury vegetables, please!

Carrot Cake

Carrot cake sounds healthy, but the traditional recipe is decidedly not. This green, clean, and très gourmet version boasts the same flavors as the original version, but without sugar, butter, cream cheese . . . and without cooking, too! (Don't worry, the carrots stay!) This dessert is perfect for springtime—light, yet filling.

SERVES 1

♥ ½ CUP (60 G) GRATED CARROT (AROUND 1 LARGE CARROT, OR USE THE PULP FROM YOUR CARROT JUICE)

2 TABLESPOONS WALNUTS

♥ 2 TABLESPOONS ALMONDS

3 MEDJOOL DATES, SOAKED AND PITTED

2 TABLESPOONS RAISINS

¼ TEASPOON CINNAMON

⅛ TEASPOON NUTMEG

♥ ¼ TEASPOON GROUND GINGER

A PINCH OF VANILLA POWDER OR EXTRACT

A PINCH OF SALT

FOR THE ICING:

2 TABLESPOONS CASHEWS

♥ 1 TABLESPOON LEMON JUICE

♥ 1 TABLESPOON COCONUT BUTTER (OR COCONUT OIL)

1 MEDJOOL DATE, SOAKED, PEELED, AND PITTED

A PINCH OF VANILLA POWDER OR EXTRACT

WATER, COCONUT WATER, OR ALMOND MILK AS NEEDED

Strain the grated carrot in a nut milk bag to release their liquid. If using carrot pulp from juice, no need to do anything!

Combine the carrots, walnuts, almonds, and 3 dates in a food processor to form a thick dough. Add the mixture to a bowl with the raisins, cinnamon, nutmeg, ginger, vanilla, and salt. Mix by hand. Add the dough to a muffin tin and press down to fill the cup halfway or use a round mold to form it into a circle.

TO MAKE THE ICING:

Add the cashews, lemon juice, coconut butter, date, and vanilla to a small blender and mix until smooth and creamy, adding liquid as needed. Using a spatula, spread the icing over the top of the dough, then place in the fridge for at least 1 hour or for several hours/overnight.

♥ BEST FRIEND FOOD
Carrots

"A kiss on the hand may be quite continental, but carrots are a girl's best friend . . ." —Marilyn Monroot

Carrots are rich . . . in carotenoids, beta-carotene, lutein, and zeaxanthin. Beta-carotene is a major investment in your immune and reproductive systems, not to mention a powerful inflammation fighter. Carrots help to prevent certain illnesses, notably cancer and heart problems, and can even slow the aging process. Carrots are a great source of B vitamins and vitamins A and E and are wonderfoods for eye health, protecting against cataracts and other vision problems.

Despite their vast nutritional wealth, these root vegetables remain humble and down to earth. Subtle and sweet, they can add crunch to any recipe when served raw. However, don't be afraid to heat things up! Gently cooking carrots actually helps your body to absorb their famous carotenoids, as does adding a bit of fat, since carotenoids are fat-soluble. Plus, this ravishing root is *très* affordable, so make sure to say yes when proposed one!

Beauty Tips

By Tata Harper

From her big farm in Vermont, Tata Harper creates natural, nontoxic cosmetics based on some of my favorite things to eat, like aloe vera, coconut oil, grapefruit, olive oil, and avocado. All of the products are made right on the farm—it doesn't get more farm-to-facial than that! Glowing goddesses like Gwyneth Paltrow, Christy Turlington, and Julianne Moore are fans of her products, but lucky us, Tata has agreed to share her beauty secrets! Roll out the green carpet and get ready to glow like a superstar!

I'm sure to include in my daily and weekly beauty regimen habits that I know will keep my skin luminous, glowing, hydrated, and healthy long-term. A preventative anti-aging approach is really the best long-term strategy for gorgeous skin, so I've been practicing the below tips for years. The secret to good skin is to take care of it properly, which requires multiple steps daily and special treatments every week or month. Some of the tips and secrets below I learned from my mother and grandmother; others, from holistic health and beauty experts I've met around the world.

1. Hydration

Keep the skin moisturized—properly hydrated skin has a luminosity and glow that dry skin lacks. Use a daily moisturizer and antiaging products that contain natural hyaluronic acid, which is something our skin naturally produces in its deepest layer on its own; it keeps the skin plump and collagen fibers healthy. Moisturizers with humectants (like raw honey, for example) draw in moisture from the environment all day to keep your skin's hydration levels balanced. Using a facial oil on top of your moisturizer, as the last step of your regimen, keeps hydration balanced and protects the skin from environmental damage—but be sure to use an oil with a low molecular weight so it's nongreasy and penetrates quickly.

2. Steam facials

One tip my mother and grandmother taught me is to steam the face with herbal mixes once a week to detoxify the skin. We make an herbal blend now from ingredients grown on my farm, like meadowsweet, calendula, and comfrey—all have amazing benefits for detoxifying, soothing, and cleansing the skin. It's best to do this sort of facial with a facial mask on, like our Resurfacing Mask, to drive the active ingredients of the mask deep into the pores. To do the steam sauna, steep one tea bag of blended herbs in a bowl of hot water and lean your face over it; put a towel over your head to trap all the steam. Let the steam penetrate and work its magic until the water cools, and then rinse off your mask—it feels great!

3. Enzyme exfoliating masks

Another thing I learned growing up was to occasionally treat the skin to an exfoliating mask treatment made from fresh fruits like papaya and pineapple, both of which have special enzymes that are great for detoxifying and deep-cleaning the skin while fighting bacteria and promoting glow. I love making my own masks in the food processor—it leaves the skin softened, brightened, and free of the daily buildup of dead skin and environmental toxins. (See one of Rebecca's recipes opposite.)

Xoxo, Tata

Tata Harper, the queen of green cosmetics, is founder and CEO of Tata Harper Skincare, tataharperskincare.com

Chocolate Mask

Cacao contains antioxidants that have antiaging properties and prevent wrinkles. It stimulates circulation and keeps the skin glowing. More importantly, you'll be smearing chocolate all over your face. Any questions?

♥ ¼ CUP (100 G) CACAO POWDER
¼ CUP (25 G) COOKED OATMEAL (LEFTOVER FROM BREAKFAST, OR 2 TABLESPOONS OATS MIXED WITH ¼ CUP HOT WATER)
1 TEASPOON BAKING POWDER

Blend all of the ingredients with a spoon to form a thick paste. Apply the mask to your face, spreading evenly. Leave on for 10 to 20 minutes. Rinse well with water.

Chocolate Bath

Oh yes, every woman's fantasy come true: a chocolate bath! (Go on, indulge yourself—you can thank me later.)

♥ 2 CUPS (400 ML) ALMOND MILK, HOMEMADE (SEE PAGE 2) OR STORE-BOUGHT
♥ 3 TABLESPOONS CACAO POWDER
2 TABLESPOONS COCONUT SUGAR
2 TABLESPOONS NATURAL, ODORLESS LIQUID SOAP

Blend the almond milk, cacao powder, and coconut sugar in a blender or shaker until mixed. Pour into a bowl and add the soap. Pour the mixture into a warm bath while the water is running. Hop in. Close your eyes. Dreams can come true (just don't fall asleep!).

♥ BEST FRIEND FOOD
Cacao

Want to hear the best news in the history of the world? Chocolate is good for you! *Oui oui*, true story. Chocolate is healthy and beautifying and the most *unguilty* of pleasures that exists! Note: When I say "chocolate," I do *not* mean sugar-laden chocolate bars or buttery chocolate chip cookies. I'm talking *le chocolat* in its purest form, namely cacao.

Cacao is rich in flavonoids, antioxidants that promote heart health: They promote the dilation of blood vessels, helping to lower blood pressure and prevent heart failure. They also help fight bad cholesterol and have positive effects on memory and concentration.

Cacao contains magnesium, a mineral that naturally reduces stress levels. And if chocolate makes you smile, it's thanks to its theobromine, a natural mood booster. To be consumed in extreme bliss . . . OK, OK, and moderation, too!

Mousse au Chocolove

This chocolate mousse is the ultimate comfort food: It's easy to digest and soothing to both body and mind, thanks to a silky texture and feel-good chemicals that boost endorphins and serotonin levels in the brain. Unlike classic mousse au chocolat, this version uses a (not-so) secret ingredient to obtain a creamy consistency: the astounding avocado! No need for cream or eggs; the avocado alone adds sultry smoothness, with the addition of dates, vanilla, cinnamon, and an optional superfood boost from carob and mesquite that accentuates the chocolate flavor without adding sugar.

SERVES 1 CHOCOHOLIC (OR 2 TO 3 OTHER PEOPLE)

♥ 1 LARGE AVOCADO

1 MEDJOOL DATE

♥ 1 *VERY* GENEROUS TABLESPOON RAW CACAO POWDER

⅛ TEASPOON VANILLA POWDER OR VANILLA EXTRACT

⅛ TEASPOON CINNAMON

♥ ¼ CUP (50 ML) NUT MILK (HOMEMADE—SEE PAGE 2— OR STORE-BOUGHT), COCONUT WATER, OR WATER

A PINCH OF HIMALAYAN OR SEA SALT

1 TEASPOON MESQUITE POWDER (OPTIONAL)

1 TEASPOON CAROB POWDER (OPTIONAL)

VANILLA
Eau d'innocence

Vanilla is an antiaging powerhouse, rich in antioxidants, vitamins, and minerals to keep both your skin and *you* innocent. This aphrodisiac fights cancer and depression and even helps calm the mind—it's a sweet sidekick for *la vie en healthy*! Pure vanilla bean is ideal, but vanilla powder is a great way to add vanilla flavor without any effort. Vanilla extract is fine, too; just look for organic varieties with the smallest amounts of fillers or alcohol. This subtle yet ubiquitous flavoring is an excellent addition to sweet treats but also lends itself to savory dishes, like a pumpkin soup or butternut squash risotto. It's the perfect match for chocolate and is great in a vinaigrette atop, for example, roasted beets or sweet potato.

Halve, pit, and scoop out the flesh of the avocado. Soak the date in hot water until soft, then remove the pit and peel. Add all ingredients to a Vitamix (preferable) or food processor and blend until smooth. Add more liquid as needed.

Tips: Top with some cacao nibs and fresh fruit if you're fancy! You can also easily turn this into a chocolate shake; just add more liquid to thin it out and pour into a glass. This is much creamier and more delicious using a nut milk, particularly a homemade cashew milk.

SPREAD THE MOUSSE AU CHOCOLOVE!
MORE VARIATIONS ON THIS CLASSIC:

MINT MOUSSE AU CHOCOLOVE

Add 1 to 2 drops of peppermint essential oil and ½ tablespoon chopped fresh mint into the mousse and blend, then garnish with more mint leaves.

MOUSSE AU CHOCOLÉ!

Add a pinch of cayenne pepper and ¼ teaspoon maca powder.

MOUSSE AU CHOCORANGE

Add 1 to 2 drops of orange essential oil and top with orange zest.

MOUSSE AU CHAI-COLOT

Add 1 to 2 drops of cinnamon bark essential oil and a pinch each of nutmeg, cloves, ginger, black pepper, and cardamom. Optional: Add 1 teaspoon of lucuma powder.

MOUSSE AU CHOCAÇAI

Add 1 teaspoon of açai powder. Top with fresh berries and cacao nibs.

Le "Chic" Cake (No-Bake Cheesecake)

I was born in New York City, world capital of le cheesecake, and my mother's recipe is famous across the world (or at least across my world), but le best cheesecake I've ever had was in Paris. That crème! That crust! However, since the original version isn't so chic for the insides (again, that crème! That crust!), I have taken the liberty to invent my own version: le chic cake. Sorry, Maman, but there's a new cheesecake in town!

MAKES 2 SMALL CHIC CAKES

FOR THE CRUST:

½ CUP (50 G) PECANS (YOU CAN SUB ALMONDS, PISTACHIOS, OR WALNUTS HERE)

3 MEDJOOL DATES, SOAKED AND PITTED

♥ 2 TABLESPOONS COCONUT FLAKES

½ TEASPOON CINNAMON

FOR THE CREAM CHEESE (THAT IS OBVIOUSLY NEITHER CREAM NOR CHEESE FILLED!):

♥ 1 TABLESPOON COCONUT OIL

½ CUP (50 G) CASHEWS, SOAKED UNTIL SOFT (AT LEAST 1 HOUR, PREFERABLY SEVERAL)

1 MEDJOOL DATE, SOAKED, PEELED, AND PITTED

♥ 1 TABLESPOON LEMON JUICE

¼ TEASPOON LEMON ZEST

¼ TEASPOON VANILLA POWDER OR EXTRACT

TOPPING:

2 TABLESPOONS STRAWBERRY COULIS WITH GOJI BERRIES (PAGE 11)

♥ ¼ TEASPOON LEMON ZEST (OPTIONAL)

PIECE OF ADVICE TO ACCOMPANY YOUR PIECE OF CHIC CAKE
Fat is phat

You may have noticed by now that all that is green isn't necessarily "light." This chic cake, for example, is rich in flavor, but also in calories and fat content—these are the "good" fats and the calories are far from "empty," but they are still calories and fat. So please enjoy a small (French-sized!) portion of this chic cake instead of a slice the size of your head, AKA New York style!

TO MAKE THE CRUST:

Combine all ingredients in a food processor until it forms a dough. Divide the dough between two round molds on a plate and press down firmly. Let the crusts sit while you prepare the cream cheese layer.

TO MAKE THE CREAM CHEESE:

Warm the coconut oil in a small saucepan on low heat until it liquefies. Transfer the oil and all other ingredients to a blender and blend until creamy. Add water if necessary.

Pour the cream cheese over the crusts in their molds, then refrigerate for at least 1 hour, preferably several, until they harden.

Before serving, pour the coulis over the top.

CHIC CAKE VARIATIONS

Make your chic cakes even more chic with a quick change of accessories using each season's most fashionable fruits!

IN THE SUMMER: CHERRY CHIC CAKE

Add ¼ cup (50 g) pitted cherries to the cream cheese ingredients before blending. Chop a few more cherries into small pieces and mix into the cream cheese by hand before spreading over the crust. Top with a few more cherries for decoration.

IN THE FALL: CARAMEL APPLE CHIC CAKE

Add ¼ cup (50 g) peeled and diced apples to the cream cheese ingredients before blending. Top with Caramel Sauce (page 11) instead of the berry coulis.

IN THE WINTER: CHOCOLATE-ORANGE CHIC CAKE

Add 1 tablespoon cacao powder and replace the lemon juice and zest with orange juice and zest before blending the cream cheese layer. Top with cacao nibs and more orange zest.

NOtella Spread

Like any American child, I grew up on peanut butter and jelly and—quelle horreur— fluffernutter sandwiches, AKA peanut butter and Marshmallow Fluff between two pieces of (white! processed!) bread. In France, Nutella is the staple "kid" food. The real Nutella has added sugars, milk powder, and other emulsifiers, but who needs them? Chocolate and hazelnuts are a winning combination on their own, from both a nutritional and flavor perspective. Spread this creamy cacao on tartines (page 42), rice cakes, or crackers; use it as a dip for fruits like strawberries, bananas, or apples; add it to Pancrêpes (page 164); or tap into your inner child and eat it out of the jar with a spoon while no one is looking!

Go !

MAKES 1 SMALL JAR

½ CUP (100 G) HAZELNUT BUTTER, HOMEMADE (SEE PAGE 14) OR STORE-BOUGHT (NO SUGAR ADDED)

♥ 2 TABLESPOONS CACAO POWDER

½ TEASPOON VANILLA POWDER OR EXTRACT

♥ 1 TEASPOON COCONUT SUGAR (OPTIONAL)

Mix all ingredients in a bowl with a spoon until homogenous.

Store in a closed glass jar for several days . . . or weeks, if you don't finish it before!

COCONUT SUGAR

What? I thought we were going sugar-free?

Don't worry: Even though coconut sugar looks like sugar, tastes like sugar, and—oh—it's *called* sugar, it's not sugar. At least, it's not the refined white table sugar you're accustomed to. Confused? Coconut palm sugar is made from the sap of the coconut palm tree—it is extracted, then boiled and dehydrated. Coconut sugar is less processed than "real" sugar, so it keeps most of its nutrients intact. It contains small amounts of magnesium, zinc, iron, phosphorous, potassium, and vitamins B1, B2, B3, and B6. It has a rich, caramel flavor and can easily be substituted for sugar or brown sugar in recipes. Coconut sugar has a slightly lower glycemic index than granulated sugar does, but its calorie content is pretty much the same, so as with other sweeteners (honey, maple syrup . . .), don't overdo it please.

NOtella
Spread

Summer

Positive playlist for a sunny day

Brighter Than the Sun COLBIE CAILLAT
Walking on Sunshine KATRINA & THE WAVES
Firework KATY PERRY
Sunshine Song JASON MRAZ
Happy PHARRELL WILLIAMS
Good Day GREG STREET FEATURING NAPPY ROOTS
Get Lucky DAFT PUNK
Start Me Up THE ROLLING STONES
Up All Night ONE DIRECTION
Long Time Sun SNATAM KAUR
Believer AMERICAN AUTHORS
La Vie en Rose EDITH PIAF
Beautiful Day JOSHUA RADIN

In the mood for summer

Finally, summer is here! According to Ayurveda, summer is pitta season. According to traditional Chinese medicine, it's yang season. Whatever school of thought you belong to—whether it be ancient Indian wisdom, Chinese medicine, or common sense—I think we all can agree that, in summertime, (1) it's hot, and (2) we need to cool off, in all senses of the term. OK, so maybe you don't need to be a Zen master to figure that out, but aren't you more comfortable knowing that the ancient experts approve? So let's all cool off and enjoy ourselves, shall we? It's essential to our survival!

In summer, farmers markets transform into a gallery of plant art. Fruits and vegetables are abundant. Quel choix! What a wealth of colors, scents, and flavors!

Even if we may feel like eating lighter and less this time of year, this doesn't mean that we need to be satisfied with just a tiny tomato salad at lunchtime or piece of watermelon to snack on. Check out the end of this chapter—some of my friends, who happen to be culinary artistes, have kindly shared their secrets to creating green, clean, and chic meals at home that look and taste like a fancy chef prepared them! So join our party. As the French say, plus on est de fous, plus on rit! *This literally means "the more birdbrains we are, the more we laugh," otherwise known as "the more the merrier!" I say, the more the greenier! So come on, you birdbrains, let's get fired up—it's summertime!*

Be radiant
Say bon voyage to boring food!

Summer is all about heading off on vacation (or, at the very least, dreaming about it) and embarking on new adventures. Perfect timing! Thanks to a plethora of seasonal fruits and vegetables, summer is the ideal season to innovate and get inspired by dishes from all over the world. Even if you're camping out at home, send your taste buds on a trip with twists on traditions from across the globe!

Water you waiting for? Get your H₂O on!

Before you head out into the sun, remember that the best summer survival tip of all is . . . hydration! We all know we're supposed to drink more water, especially in the warm weather. Drink filtered, not bottled, water and you'll save money by not buying plastic and help the earth at the same time—win, win! Pour filtered water into a stainless steel or glass water bottle and carry it with you by day. The best option is a home filtration system—they're expensive, but a great investment in your health. Otherwise, opt for a small, countertop version, especially one with a *très* chic design like my favorite, Soma. You can also *eat* your water via produce bursting with water—which happens to be in season just when we need it most.

Watermelon

When I was younger, I was the watermelon-eating champion every year during my summer camp's relay race. My prize? Glowing skin, energy, immune defenses . . . and a ribbon. Watermelon is the ultimate summer superfood. High in water content and low in calories, watermelon is a great source of vitamin C and lycopene, a carotenoid known for preventing many diseases. I don't recommend gorging on watermelon eating-contest-style, but a nice slice on a hot day is sweet summery perfection. (Note: Watermelon is best when eaten on its own, since it has such a quick digestion time that it can upset your stomach if you combine it with other foods.)

Blueberries

Blueberries are powerhouses of antioxidants, anthocyanins, flavonoids, and so many other crazy substances whose health benefits are unparalleled. Blueberries help the brain function and may prevent diseases like Alzheimer's and Parkinson's, thanks to their selenium, potassium, copper, zinc, manganese, B vitamins, and vitamins A, C, and E. They are low in calories, reduce belly fat, and boost metabolism, making them a great weight-loss food. Blueberries also help firm the skin and fight against blemishes. It's the antiaging fruit *par excellence*.

Seasonal foods

FRUIT

Apricots

Blueberries

Cherries

Figs

Honeydew melon

Peaches

Plums

Raspberries

Tomatoes

Watermelon

VEGGIES

Bell peppers

Corn

Cucumbers

Eggplant

Fennel

Green beans

Summer squash

Zucchini

Yoga for Self Confidence

by Elena Brower

Elena Brower *is one of the most esteemed yoga teachers in the world. Gwyneth Paltrow, Christy Turlington, and Eva Mendes are among her* très chic *international clientele. Elena proves that, with just a few easy yoga postures, we can all feel like superstars—it's all about self-confidence. Elena is an expert in female issues ranging from pre- and post-natal yoga to hormone balancing to,* bien sûr, *self-esteem. Her classes always incorporate off-the-mat emotions into the on-the-mat physical practice. Elena is the author of* The Art of Attention.

elenabrower.com

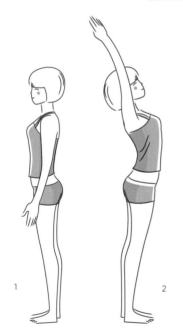

1   2

Elena Brower is a yoga goddess who shares a little bit of her light to keep us glowing all summer long.

Yoga practice lends us time with our physical strength, capacities, and sensitivities. Even a few minutes of focused practice gives me a fresh start, a new vista, and a revitalized sense of myself and my purpose. Why? With the five poses below, we oxygenate the blood, bring the muscles to the bones, open space in those muscles, and rewire our brains. The rewiring is what I experience most profoundly; each time I'm in a doubtful or fearful place, a short practice brings me back, cools me off, and reminds me of who I am and how I move in this world. May this practice bring you deep peace within yourself.

1. STAND TALL IN TADASANA, MOUNTAIN POSE

For three to five breaths, feel your feet on the floor, lengthen your legs, and grow your spine taller. Let your face soften and turn your palms to face forward. Listen to these three to five breaths and feel your own presence.

2. URDHVA HASTASANA

Stretch your arms HIGH. Reach as far above you as you can, every finger, and breathe as deeply and as slowly as you can for three to five breaths. Then reach your arms out to the sides as far as you can, every finger, for three to five long, thoughtful breaths. Then interlace your hands behind you and reach as far back and high as you can, stretch your elbows open, and breathe, as deeply and as slowly as you can, three to five breaths. Inhabit your entire body; breathe to the borders of your skin and feel the comfort and confidence of arriving with awareness into your own body.

3. BOW FORWARD INTO UTTANASANA, STANDING FORWARD BEND

Cooling, contemplative, and centering, this pose feels like a quiet cocoon. Make your legs stronger by lifting the muscles up toward your hips; spread out and lengthen your toes. Touch the floor if you can, or your shins if that's easier, and lengthen the top of your head down toward the floor as you make your legs longer and taller for three to five breaths, or as long as 1 minute.

4. STEP BACK INTO ADHO MUKHA SVANASANA, DOWNWARD FACING DOG

Stretch from your heart through your hands. Ground and lengthen your fingers. Breathe deeply and deliberately to reach your seat high. Keeping that, bend your knees slightly, make your legs stronger, then reach your heels toward the floor, but not to touch. Take three to five breaths and slowly build your stamina in this pose: 30 seconds, 1 minute.

5. STEP YOUR RIGHT FOOT FORWARD AND TURN YOUR BACK HEEL DOWN TO THE FLOOR AT A 45-DEGREE ANGLE FOR PARSVAKONASANA, SIDE ANGLE POSE.

Stand well on your back foot, with the whole sole of that foot down, and make that leg strong. Bring your right forearm onto your front thigh, and send your left arm long over your left ear. Breathe slowly into both lungs evenly, then lengthen your back leg longer and bend your front knee more deeply. Breathe three to five breaths here; soften your eyes. Come up to stand and switch your feet for the second side.

3

4

5

Eggplant and Olive Tapenade

As soon as the warm weather arrives, the French flock to outdoor terraces and anxiously await apéro *time. Just before dinner, friends or family meet to drink rosé wine or other aperitifs and nosh on small hors d'oeuvres to whet their appetites for the meal ahead. Tapenade is a classic Provençale dish that usually contains olives, capers, anchovies, and olive oil. It's a naturally healthy food, but I've lightened it up even more with another summer favorite, eggplant! The eggplant,* AKA aubergine *in French, makes this dish lighter, more hydrating, and even creamier—olive it, and I think you will, too! It's aubergenius!*

MAKES 1 SMALL BOWL

OLIVE OIL

1 LARGE EGGPLANT

SALT TO TASTE

12 SMALL PITTED OLIVES (LOOK FOR VINEGAR-FREE VARIETIES)

½ TEASPOON HERBES DE PROVENCE BLEND (OR A MIX OF ANY OF THE FOLLOWING DRIED HERBS: THYME, OREGANO, ROSEMARY, BASIL, MARJORAM, FENNEL, SAVORY)

♥ JUICE OF 1 LEMON

PEPPER TO TASTE

Preheat the oven to 350°F (175°C). Coat a baking sheet with just a bit of olive oil. Cut the eggplant in half lengthwise.

Lightly salt the open halves of the eggplant (just a pinch!) then leave them on the counter for 15 to 30 minutes to "sweat" (feel free to do the same outside while you wait—it's summer!).

Place the eggplant halves face down on the prepared baking sheet. Bake for around 30 minutes, until the eggplant is tender. Remove from the oven and let cool for 15 minutes.

With a spoon, remove the flesh of the eggplant and place it into a blender or food processor with the olives, herbs, lemon juice, and 1 tablespoon olive oil. Blend until creamy. Add salt and pepper to taste.

Tapenade isn't just for toast! It's great on salad, on pizza (with my socca crust on page 106), or simply eaten by the spoonful!

OLIVE OIL
Mediterranean-chic!

In the vegetable oil family, olive is definitely the most popular—it's the cheerleader of oils, used in so many different culinary preparations. It's a staple of the famous Mediterranean diet. Olive oil is filled with fats, but these fats are the source of its heart-health benefits. Olive oil is also rich in polyphenols, antioxidants that fight bad cholesterol and aging. Olive oil is best used as a dressing in order to keep all of its nutrients intact, but it's also a healthy cooking oil for low or medium heat.

Guacamousse

Guacamole should be its own food group. It definitely tops my own personal food pyramid. While commonly used for dipping chips or stuffing into a burrito, it shines all by itself. Guacamole was invented by the Aztecs and perfected in Mexico, but it is, after all, a mousse, and therefore fits in as a delectable green accompaniment to any French meal. Mash with a fork, a traditional mortar and pestle, or a food processor or blender for a more mousse-y consistency. Anything goes! This summer staple is always a crowd-pleaser (shhh, don't tell your guests it's a health food, too!).

Simple Guacamousse

Once upon a lime . . .

SERVES 1 AVOCADO-LOVER (OR 3 TO 4 AS A SNACK OR APPETIZER)

♥ 1 AVOCADO
♥ 1 TEASPOON LEMON JUICE
  1 TEASPOON LIME JUICE
  A PINCH OF CUMIN AND CAYENNE PEPPER
  1 TABLESPOON CHOPPED FRESH CILANTRO
  1 TEASPOON CHOPPED FRESH CHIVES
  1 TEASPOON OLIVE OIL
♥ 1 TEASPOON SPIRULINA POWDER (OPTIONAL, FOR AN EVEN GREENER GUACAMOUSSE)

Cut the avocado in half, remove the pit, and scoop out the flesh with a spoon. Add to a bowl with the other ingredients and mash with a fork until mixed well but still chunky.

Crazy Guacamousse

Hemp! This guacamousse is out of control!

SERVES 1 AVOCADO-LOVER (OR 3 TO 4 AS A SNACK OR APPETIZER)

♥ 1 AVOCADO
  ½ CUCUMBER
  ½ FRESH MANGO
  1 SMALL TOMATO
  1 GARLIC CLOVE (OPTIONAL)
  ½ SMALL RED ONION (OPTIONAL)
♥ 2 TEASPOONS LEMON JUICE
  1 TEASPOON LIME JUICE
  1 TABLESPOON CHOPPED FRESH CILANTRO
♥ 1 TEASPOON HEMP, OLIVE, FLAXSEED, OR PUMPKIN SEED OIL
  A PINCH EACH OF CUMIN AND CORIANDER
  A PINCH (OR MORE—GO CRAZY!) OF CAYENNE PEPPER
  SALT AND PEPPER TO TASTE
  1 TABLESPOON PUMPKIN SEEDS, SOAKED OR TOASTED
  1 TEASPOON CHOPPED FRESH CHIVES

Cut the avocado in half, remove the pit, and scoop out the flesh with a spoon. Peel the cucumber and mango and dice into tiny cubes. Cut the tomato into small pieces. Peel and chop the garlic and onion (if using). Add all ingredients except the pumpkin seeds and chives to a bowl and mash with a fork until mixed well but still chunky. Top with the pumpkin seeds and chives.

Avocado

It's no secret—I've been madly in love with avocado for a long time now. I'm avocadobsessed. It's not just a crush—avocado totally loves me back.

Avocados are packed with monounsaturated fats, which are *good* fats responsible for so many health benefits, like reducing cholesterol and heart-disease risk and even protecting against colon and breast cancers. These fats are essential for a functioning brain, glowing skin, and balance in the body. Of course, like anything, they should be enjoyed in moderation, but repeat after me, my friends: "I'm not afraid of fats!" Whew! Doesn't that feel good?

Avocado is rich in vitamin E, an essential nutrient to protect against illness and keep the skin radiating beauty. It also contains beta-sitosterol, which helps fight bad cholesterol, and folate, which is essential for all women, especially pregnant women. Avocado is filled with fiber and is healing for the digestive tract. Avocados also contain vitamin K, calcium, and vitamin C, not to mention those elusive omega-3 fatty acids (yes, more fatty friends!) that our body cannot produce so we must get them from foods.

Avocado is nature's own butter. Its unique consistency allows it to replace butter, mayonnaise, or cream in recipes from sauces, dressings, salads, smoothies, soups, or sandwiches to desserts. It makes any meal creamy and smooth. Avocado marries well with both savory and sweet concoctions.

Like any serious relationship, make sure to choose your avocado carefully. Don't judge by outward appearances—until you open up the avocado, you have no idea what it has to offer. Avocados should be soft to the touch, but don't wait too long or they will no longer be available . . . to be eaten.

Tip: If you bought an avocado that isn't quite ripe but you are dying to make one of the avocado-based recipes in this book, just place it in a paper bag and surround it with ripe fruits to accelerate the maturation process.

BEAUTY RECIPE
Green Chic Avocado Face Mask

INGREDIENTS
♥ 1 AVOCADO
♥ 1 TABLESPOON ALMOND OIL
♥ 1 TABLESPOON SPIRULINA POWDER∗

∗Spirulina can also serve as a green—and chic—eye shadow!

Avocado helps to reduce wrinkles, heal scars, and soften and hydrate the skin. The Aztecs used avocado as a beauty product, so why can't we? Add spirulina to infuse your skin with antioxidants.

Halve, pit, and scoop out the flesh of the avocado and add to a bowl with the oil and spirulina. Mash with a fork until creamy. Apply the mixture all over your face (making sure not to cover your eyes!). Leave for around 15 minutes, then rinse well. (Don't hesitate to lick your lips—this is the most delectable face mask ever!)

Sophisticated Summer Rolls

These summer rolls look fancy and sophisticated, but they're so easy to make. Just stop, drop, and roll!

FOR 3 ROLLS/1 SERVING

FOR THE DIPPING SAUCE:
- ♥ 1 TEASPOON COCONUT AMINOS OR TAMARI
- 2 TEASPOONS TOASTED SESAME OIL
- ♥ 2 TEASPOONS LEMON JUICE
- ½ TEASPOON MINCED GARLIC (OPTIONAL)

FOR THE FILLINGS:
- ♥ 1 AVOCADO, HALVED AND PITTED
- ♥ 1 CARROT
- ½ SMALL CUCUMBER
- ¼ RED BELL PEPPER
- 3 SHEETS OF BROWN RICE PAPER (IF YOU CAN'T FIND IT, WHITE RICE PAPER IS FINE)
- 2 TABLESPOONS TAHINI
- A HANDFUL OF SPROUTS
- 1 TABLESPOON SESAME SEEDS, TOASTED FOR MORE FLAVOR, OR JUST SOAKED (IF YOU WANT TO KEEP THINGS RAW!)

Mix all of the ingredients for the dipping sauce in a small bowl.

Peel and slice the avocado, carrot, and cucumber into thin slivers. Remove the white membrane and the seeds from the pepper and slice that thinly, too.

Dip a rice paper into a bowl of room-temperature water for a few seconds. Place the rice paper onto a plate. Spread some of the tahini in the center, then add a third of the veggies and some sesame seeds. Drizzle some more tahini on top. Starting with the side closest to you, fold the rice paper over the filling, then fold in the corners and roll until it forms a tight burrito-like roll, and stick together. Cut in half. Repeat the process with the other two rice papers.

Place the rolls on a plate. Serve with the dipping sauce and garnish with the remaining sesame seeds.

SPROUTS
They're alive!

Sprouts are "living" foods that are bursting with nutrients: vitamins, minerals, enzymes, fiber, antioxidants, chlorophyll, and plant protein. Sprouting makes these grains and seeds more digestible and the nutrients more easily absorbed by the liver and the pancreas. Sprouts are truly wonderfoods, and I highly recommend adding just a handful to anything and everything you eat—not only are they pretty, crunchy, and tasty, but their enzymes will help digest any meal. *Vive la* sprout! (Literally!)

Colorful Black Bean Salad with Mango Sauce

This salad is a fiesta on a plate! Black beans turn this into a rich, "meaty" dish that is lightened up by a refreshing mango sauce, crunchy bell peppers, and hydrating cucumber. It's a rainbow of color, flavor, and fun that is also easy to make ahead (just add the avocado at the end!). Leftovers just get tastier!

SERVES 2

¼ RED BELL PEPPER

¼ ORANGE BELL PEPPER

¼ YELLOW BELL PEPPER

♥ 1 CARROT

½ SMALL FENNEL BULB

½ SMALL CUCUMBER

1 LARGE HANDFUL OF BABY SPINACH OR SALAD GREENS

1 CUP (100 G) COOKED BLACK BEANS (SEE PAGE 18) OR DRAINED AND RINSED CANNED BLACK BEANS

1 TABLESPOON CHOPPED CHIVES

1 HEAPING TABLESPOON CHOPPED FRESH CILANTRO, PLUS A HANDFUL FOR GARNISH

2 TABLESPOONS PUMPKIN SEEDS

♥ 1 AVOCADO, PITTED, PEELED, AND THINLY SLICED

LIME SLICES

FOR THE MANGO SAUCE:

½ RIPE MANGO

1 TEASPOON CHOPPED GREEN ONIONS

JUICE OF 1 LIME

1 TABLESPOON OLIVE OIL

⅛ TEASPOON CORIANDER

SALT AND PEPPER TO TASTE

CAYENNE PEPPER TO TASTE

Clean the bell peppers, remove the white membranes and seeds, and slice thinly. Wash or peel then grate the carrot. Core and thinly slice the fennel. Chop the cucumber into small cubes. In a bowl, combine the prepared veggies, spinach, beans, chives, and a heaping tablespoon of the cilantro.

Toast the pumpkin seeds in the oven (5 minutes at 400°F/200°C) or over the stove (3 minutes over medium heat) making sure not to burn them. They'll start to pop when they're done!

TO MAKE THE SAUCE:

Peel and cut the mango into pieces. Add all sauce ingredients to a blender and blend until creamy.

Pour the sauce over the beans and veggies. (Yes, *all* of the sauce. Don't think, just do it.) Mix together well. Transfer to a plate and add salt, pepper, and cayenne to taste. Top with the pumpkin seeds, additional handful of cilantro, avocado slices, and lime wedges.

Serve over a bowl of brown rice or quinoa for a hearty summer meal, stuff into a collard wrap, or spread on a tartine for a savory breakfast.

MANGO
Beauty fruit!

Nicknamed the "queen of fruits," mango is definitely noble nourishment. Mangoes are a great source of beta-carotene (which gives them their bright orange hue), vitamin A, B vitamins, and antioxidants. This fruit is ideal for soft skin and a healthy body, not to mention that it's bursting with water and is so refreshing and hydrating, making it a perfect food for summer.

Mango has also been scientifically proven (by . . . me!) to make you smile. (It's so good that it will naturally turn up the corners of your mouth upon tasting. Try it.)

Look for ripe mangoes; they are not only tenderer and tastier, but also richer in fiber. 1, 2, 3, manGO!

Green Beans with Orange and Hazelnuts

Oranges are vitamin C powerhouses that boost immunity, support the kidneys, and energize the body. Orange juice and zest are uplifting and invigorating, and just a splash adds so much flavor to any meal. The tanginess of the orange contrasts so well with the aromatic and rich toasted hazelnuts, for a unique mélange of flavor and texture, especially when combined with crunchy green beans.

SERVES 1

1 TABLESPOON HAZELNUTS

1 CUP (200 G) GREEN BEANS

1 TABLESPOON RAISINS

FOR THE ORANGE VINAIGRETTE:

½ TEASPOON ORANGE ZEST

2 TEASPOONS HAZELNUT OIL (OR UNTOASTED SESAME OIL)

1 TEASPOON OLIVE OIL

1 TABLESPOON FRESHLY SQUEEZED ORANGE JUICE

♥ ½ TEASPOON MINCED FRESH GINGER (OPTIONAL)

SALT AND PEPPER TO TASTE

Toast the hazelnuts in the oven (5 to 10 minutes at 400°F/200°C) or on the stove (2 to 3 minutes over medium heat), making sure not to burn them!

Lightly steam the green beans for 2 to 3 minutes, then rinse them in cold water to keep them crunchy. Mix together the green beans, toasted hazelnuts, and raisins.

TO MAKE THE VINAIGRETTE:

Set some of the orange zest aside for the garnish. Mix the rest of the ingredients together by hand or in a blender. Season to taste.

Add the vinaigrette to the green bean mixture, then add the rest of the orange zest.

This is a great side dish, or you can serve it as the pièce de résistance over a bowl of greens and grains (try wild or black rice for a change!).

Summerthyme Green Soup

Easy to make, refreshing, and flavorful, this soup will help you chill out on a hot summer day. It offers a perfect balance of taste and texture and is easy to make ahead of time, then grab to enjoy during an outdoor picnic. It's one of my favorite recipes of all time (particularly summertime)! It takes advantage of the plethora of herbs in full green bloom this season. Out of (fresh) thyme? You can also add any dried herbs you like.

SERVES 2

♥ 1 LARGE AVOCADO, HALVED AND PITTED
1 CUCUMBER
♥ 1 CARROT
1 SMALL FENNEL BULB
♥ 1 TABLESPOON LEMON JUICE
1 TEASPOON APPLE CIDER VINEGAR
1 LARGE HANDFUL OF ARUGULA
1 HANDFUL EACH OF MINT, BASIL, CILANTRO, CHIVES, AND PARSLEY
1 TABLESPOON CHOPPED FRESH THYME (OR ¼ TEASPOON DRIED)
1 TABLESPOON OLIVE OIL OR PUMPKIN SEED OIL OR HEMP SEED OIL
1 SMALL TOMATO OR 2 SUN-DRIED TOMATOES (OPTIONAL)
A PINCH OF CAYENNE PEPPER
SALT AND PEPPER TO TASTE
UP TO ¼ CUP (75 ML) WATER (IF NEEDED)

GARNISHES:

♥ 1 TO 2 TABLESPOONS HEMP SEEDS
1 HANDFUL OF FRESH SPROUTS OR MICROGREENS

Peel and dice the avocado, cucumber, and carrot. Core and chop the fennel into small pieces. Add all of the ingredients (except garnishes) to a blender and blend until smooth and creamy.

If you are using a standard blender and not a Vitamix, you may need to add water gradually until you reach your desired consistency.

Pour into bowls, top with hemp seeds and sprouts, and serve, or pour into a jar or glass container and take on the road!

For skinsational spirulina soup, simply replace the thyme and the mint with even more cilantro, and add a pinch each of cumin and coriander and 2 teaspoons spirulina powder.

THYME
A thyme to remember

Are you already exhausted by all of the fun you're having this summer? Take a thyme out! This healing herb has antiseptic and antibiotic properties, so it helps treat colds or infections and clear up your skin. It's a great detox food to support the liver, and it can help relieve asthma and bronchitis. It can also aid digestion and reduce bloating—good news for bikini season!

CILANTRO
A magical herb!

Cilantro is one of the most popular herbs out there, and also the most *un*popular! Ask anyone how they feel about cilantro and they'll either scream "I LOVE it!" or wrinkle their noses and declare their hatred for it. Whichever camp you're in, there's no denying its extraordinary detox properties. Cilantro helps to rid the body of heavy metals and soothe chronic inflammation. It literally removes, or "chelates," toxic metals from the nervous system and bodily tissues, the causes of so many problems ranging from hormonal imbalances to cancer to depression, thyroid problems, food allergies, parasites, and other unpleasant symptoms of toxicity.

Cilantro is a great remedy for arthritis, menstrual problems, anemia, and eczema and keeps the skin glowing thanks to vitamins A and C.

Chilled Carrot Velouté with Cashew Crème

The French are known for their creamy soup called velouté, which literally means "velvet" en Français. Chilled soups are perfect for the summertime—they are easy to prepare in advance and stay fresh for a couple of days. Just add the ingredients, blend, and let chill in the fridge while you chill outside under the sun. The soup is creamy even without the Cashew Crème de la Crème, but it's a great complement.

MAKES 1 SERVING

FOR THE SOUP:

♥ ½ AVOCADO, PITTED

½ GARLIC CLOVE (OPTIONAL)

♥ 1 CUP (250 ML) CARROT JUICE (FROM FRESH CARROTS IN A JUICER OR CARROTS BLENDED WITH WATER THEN STRAINED)

2 TABLESPOONS MACADAMIA NUTS OR CASHEWS

♥ 1 TABLESPOON LEMON JUICE

1 TEASPOON COCONUT AMINOS OR TAMARI

♥ 1 TEASPOON MISO PASTE

♥ 1 TEASPOON MINCED FRESH GINGER

1 TEASPOON CHOPPED FRESH CHIVES

1 TO 2 TABLESPOONS CASHEW CRÈME DE LA CRÈME (PAGE 6)

BLACK PEPPER

OPTIONAL TOPPINGS:

♥ 1 TABLESPOON GRATED CARROT (PURPLE CARROTS ARE *TRÈS* PRETTY IF YOU CAN FIND SOME!)

1 TABLESPOON GRATED RAW BEET

1 TABLESPOON FINELY DICED CUCUMBER

1 TEASPOON CHOPPED FRESH CHIVES

1 TEASPOON SESAME SEEDS (TRY BLACK SESAME SEEDS!)

1 TEASPOON GOMASI-OH-LÀ-LÀ! (PAGE 7)

Go!

Peel and slice the avocado and garlic. Blend all of the soup ingredients except for the cashew crème in a blender with a pinch of pepper. Refrigerate the soup for at least 30 minutes, longer if possible. Pour the chilled soup into a bowl, top with the cashew crème, and garnish with toppings of choice.

Note: The "finishing touches" turn this soup into an artful masterpiece and a meal in its own right. Feel free to add whatever toppings you'd like to transform this into your dream bowl!

♥ BEST FRIEND FOOD
Ginger

Ginger is ugly. But it's always there for us and helps us when things aren't going our way. It's a true best friend. Perhaps not the prettiest, but certainly the most loyal and one of the most interesting and multitalented. It's no coincidence that ginger is a root since this food is very balancing, stabilizing, and helps to keep us quite literally down to earth.

Ginger, AKA Zingiber officinale, is antibacterial, antiviral, and anti-inflammatory. It warms the body, boosts the immune system, lowers fever, improves energy, acts as an aphrodisiac, stimulates the appetite, eases nausea, soothes the intestines, reduces bloating, lowers the toxicity levels of certain foods, fights against muscle pain and arthritis, protects the liver, protects the body against certain cancers, and can make you fly. OK, so perhaps not the last feature (I just wanted to see if you were paying attention), but it's true that ginger helps pretty much all of the body's systems in one way or another. What a miracle root!

Fresh ginger is perfect for herbal tea, but ginger powder is also great, particularly when blending into drinks, soups, or warm winter wonderbowls (page 000). Ginger is a welcome addition to both sweet and savory dishes, although it is naturally spicy, so adapt to it little by little.

Salade Niçoise

This salad is so Nice! But also so American, thanks to Julia Child, who brought this French Riviera favorite to US shores. This salad is the epitome of French "simple, but elegant" cooking and is filling and flavorful, yet cool and refreshing.

Even without the traditional eggs, tuna, or anchovies, it's a hearty meal disguised as a salad. The seaweed pâté adds a salty, "fishy" flavor, and the rest of the ingredients are standard Niçoise inclusions. Feel free to sub another protein of choice: tempeh, tofu, nuts, seeds, or another veggie pâté.

Julia and I strongly urge you to separate each ingredient and arrange them next to each other on the plate. "A bountiful arrangement in bowl or platter is so handsome to behold that I think it a cruel shame to toss everything together into a big mess," Julia wrote.

SERVES 2

FOR THE TUNO PÂTÉ:
¼ CUP (50 G) SUNFLOWER SEEDS
♥ ¼ CUP (25 G) ALMONDS
♥ 2 TABLESPOONS DRIED DULSE
♥ 1 TEASPOON MISO PASTE
♥ ½ TEASPOON COCONUT AMINOS OR TAMARI
♥ 2 TEASPOONS LEMON JUICE

FOR THE VINAIGRETTE:
1 SMALL SHALLOT, CHOPPED
2 TABLESPOONS MUSTARD VINAIGRETTE (PAGE 10)

FOR THE SALAD:
1 CUP (200 G) SMALL RED POTATOES
1 CUP (200 G) GREEN BEANS
1 LARGE TOMATO
4 CUPS (800 G) LETTUCE OR MIXED SALAD GREENS OF CHOICE
½ CUP (100 G) COOKED WHITE BEANS (SEE PAGE 18) OR DRAINED AND RINSED CANNED BEANS
2 TABLESPOONS CHOPPED FRESH PARSLEY
2 TABLESPOONS CHOPPED FRESH BASIL
2 TABLESPOONS CHOPPED FRESH CHIVES
2 TABLESPOONS BLACK OLIVES (PREFERABLY NIÇOISE!), PITTED AND HALVED
2 TEASPOONS CAPERS (OPTIONAL)

To make the pâté, soak the sunflower seeds and almonds overnight or for at least 1 hour. Rinse the dulse very well with water. Pat dry with a paper towel or dishcloth or let dry in a sieve while you prepare the rest of the ingredients. Rinse the sunflower seeds and almonds and add to a food processor with the other pâté ingredients, including the dulse. Pulse into a coarse consistency. Place in a small glass container and pat down well, then store in the refrigerator until ready to use.

In a small bowl, whisk together the vinaigrette ingredients.

Steam the potatoes (or roast at 350°F/175°C with a splash of olive oil, salt, and pepper). Steam the green beans for just a few minutes, then rinse with cold water so they maintain their crunch. Wash and slice the tomato into wedges.

Add salad greens to a bowl and mix with half of the vinaigrette. Divide between two serving bowls. Add 1 serving of the pâté to each bowl. Divide the green beans, potatoes, white beans, and tomatoes between the bowls, arranged in separate rows next to each other.

Top the salads with the parsley, basil, chives, olives, and capers (if using). Drizzle the remaining vinaigrette over the top.

Le Burger

As soon as the warm weather rolls around, Parisians flock to café terraces to soak in the sun. Dining inside when the sun is shining is a cardinal sin in France. In recent years, le hamburger (that's French for . . . hamburger!) has become a national bistro favorite. This lighter version of the classic burger and fries is great for the hot summer months, when our bodies need energy to do so many things—run, swim, hike, or exercise our social skills—instead of digesting a gut-unfriendly meal. Cook these burgers on the grill, on the stove, or in the oven, but be sure to eat them outside, no excuses!

MAKES 2 BURGERS

FOR THE BURGERS:

¼ CUP (50 G) DRY MILLET

1 SMALL RED ONION

♥ 1 CARROT

1 BEET (OPTIONAL)

2 GARLIC CLOVES

2 CELERY STALKS

1 GENEROUS HANDFUL OF FRESH SPINACH

♥ 1 TABLESPOON COCONUT OIL

1 TEASPOON COCONUT AMINOS OR TAMARI

♥ 2 TABLESPOONS QUINOA, OAT, OR BROWN RICE FLOUR

A PINCH OF CUMIN AND/OR CORIANDER

A PINCH OF BLACK PEPPER

A PINCH OF CAYENNE PEPPER

A PINCH OF SALT

2 VEGAN, GLUTEN-FREE HAMBURGER BUNS, SLICES OF TOAST (SEE RECIPE ON PAGE 40), OR ENGLISH MUFFINS

LETTUCE

1 TOMATO, SLICED

SPROUTS

TO MAKE THE BURGER:

Soak the millet overnight, then drain, rinse, and add to a saucepan. Lightly toast for around 1 minute. Add ½ cup (125 ml) water and cook until all of the water is absorbed, 15 to 20 minutes. (Note: This should be cooked until a bit "mushy," less firm than for a salad or other dish.)

Peel and chop the onion; peel and grate the carrot (and the beet, if using); and peel and crush the garlic. Slice the celery thinly and chop the spinach.

Add ½ tablespoon of the coconut oil to a saucepan over medium-low heat, then add the onions and garlic and sauté for 1 to 2 minutes. Add the carrots, beets (if using), celery, spinach, and coconut aminos and sauté for another 1 to 2 minutes. Pour the vegetable mixture into a bowl with the cooked millet, flour, and spices.

Divide the millet mixture in two, form into balls with your hands, and press down to form round patties (use a round metal biscuit cutter to make a perfect shape, if desired).

COOK ACCORDING TO ONE OF THE FOLLOWING METHODS:

Add the remaining ½ tablespoon of coconut oil to the pan, still on the stovetop over medium-low heat. Cook for around 5 minutes, or until lightly browned, then flip and continue cooking until the other side is browned (but not burned!), around 5 more minutes.

Preheat an outdoor grill to high and lightly coconut-oil the grill. Grill the patties for 3 to 5 minutes on each side, or until browned with grill marks but not blackened.

Preheat the oven to 400°F (200°C). Line a baking sheet with parchment paper or coat with olive or coconut oil. Add the patties and bake for around 15 minutes, then flip over and continue to bake until cooked through, 10 to 15 minutes more.

Place the patties on the burger buns. Top with the lettuce, tomato, and sprouts. Serve with a handful of fries and ketchup (recipes opposite).

Tip: For an even lighter version, replace the burger buns with a few crackers, or romaine or collard leaves.

Root Veggie Frites

SERVES 2
- ♥ 1 SWEET POTATO
- 1 PARSNIP
- ♥ 1 CARROT
- ♥ 1 TABLESPOON COCONUT OIL
- SALT AND PEPPER TO TASTE

Preheat the oven to 375°F (180°C).

Peel or scrub the sweet potato, parsnip, and carrot and cut into long, thin slices and place in a bowl. Melt the coconut oil. Pour it over the vegetables, add salt and pepper, and mix thoroughly. Place on a baking sheet and bake for around 20 minutes, then rotate and continue to cook until soft when pierced with a fork but still crunchy on the outside, 5 to 10 more minutes.

Ketchup:

MAKES 2 SERVINGS
1 DATE, SOAKED AND PITTED
2 SUN-DRIED TOMATOES
1 MEDIUM FRESH TOMATO
2 TABLESPOONS OLIVE OIL
1 TEASPOON APPLE CIDER VINEGAR
SALT AND PEPPER TO TASTE

Soak, pit, and peel the date. Soak the sun-dried tomatoes in warm water for 5 to 10 minutes, until soft. Add all ingredients to a blender or food processor and process until smooth.

Cauliflower Steak Frites

Le hamburger *may be in the spotlight now, but* steak frites *is of course the most traditional French bistro food. Why not have your steak and eat it, too? You can, and feel good about it, if you replace the steak with cauliflower (chou-fleur)—the other other other other white meat!—and use baked root veggie "fries." If you're really hungry, serve the steaks right alongside your veggie burgers—it's a great combo!*

SERVES 2
½ HEAD OF CAULIFLOWER
2 TEASPOONS OLIVE OIL
SALT AND PEPPER TO TASTE
1 BATCH ROOT VEGGIE FRIES (ABOVE)

Using a sharp knife, cut the cauliflower lengthwise into slices around 1 inch (2.5 cm) thick. If you have trouble digesting raw cauliflower or prefer it extra tender, steam the cauliflower briefly. Add the olive oil to a sauté pan on medium heat. Place the cauliflower into the pan and cook for around 5 minutes, or until lightly browned, then flip over and continue to cook. The cauliflower should be fork-tender but still crunchy. Alternatively, bake in a 400°F (200°C) oven for around 5 minutes on each side. Season with salt and pepper, and serve with veggie fries.

Pretty-in-Pad Thai

My pad Thai is a very liberal interpretation of the original street food, but it still has a touch of the exotic. Nothing is fried, and it's filled with healthy ingredients. Kelp noodles absorb all of the deliciousness of this creamy sauce, but protein-packed mung bean noodles, soba, or any veggie- or grain-based noodle will do.

SERVES 1

♥ 1 CARROT

½ SMALL CUCUMBER

½ SMALL RED BELL PEPPER

♥ 1 CUP (100 G) KELP NOODLES, COOKED, MUNG BEAN NOODLES, COOKED. 100% BUCKWHEAT SOBA NOODLES, OR VEGGIE NOODLES MADE FROM CARROTS, DAIKON, OR PARSNIPS (SEE TIPS BELOW)

FOR THE SAUCE:

♥ 1 SMALL PIECE OF GINGER (TO TASTE)

1 SMALL GARLIC CLOVE

♥ 1 TABLESPOON COCONUT OIL

¼ CUP (50 ML) *LAIT DE* COCONUT (PAGE 2) OR BPA-FREE CANNED COCONUT MILK

♥ 1 TABLESPOON ALMOND BUTTER, HOMEMADE (PAGE 14) OR STORE-BOUGHT

2 TEASPOONS LIME JUICE

1 TEASPOON COCONUT AMINOS OR TAMARI

♥ 1 TEASPOON MISO PASTE

½ MEDJOOL DATE, SOAKED, PEELED, AND PITTED (OR 1 TEASPOON MAPLE SYRUP)

A PINCH OF CAYENNE PEPPER, OR TO TASTE

2 TO 3 TABLESPOONS WATER

GARNISHES:

A HANDFUL OF SPROUTS

A HANDFUL OF CILANTRO

1 TEASPOON FRESH CHIVES, CHOPPED

1 TABLESPOON GOMASI-OH-LÀ-LÀ! (PAGE 7) OR SESAME SEEDS

½ LIME, HALVED (OPTIONAL, TO GARNISH)

Wash or peel, then grate the carrot. Wash and chop the cucumber and bell pepper. To make the sauce, peel the ginger and garlic and chop or mince. Blend all sauce ingredients in a blender until smooth and creamy.

Pour the sauce over the cooked noodles and mix well. (If you're using kelp noodles, this dish is much better if you let them soak in the sauce for 30 minutes or, even better, several hours in the refrigerator. And don't be afraid to drown them in sauce—they need a good swim!)

Add the carrot, cucumber, and bell pepper to the noodles and mix well. Garnish with the sprouts, cilantro, chives, and gomasio before serving. Serve with lime wedges and squirt on top as a gourmet finishing touch.

Tips: If you're using kelp noodles, first, prepare yourself—they look and feel like plastic and are absolutely tasteless without anything added to them. DO NOT abort your mission now; I promise you'll be rewarded later. Soak the noodles for around 30 minutes in water, then rinse them very well.

If you're making veggie noodles, peel and cut the tops off some carrots, daikon, or parsnips. Place in a spiralizer to make noodles!

Alternatively, cook the soba noodles according to package directions then rinse with cold water.

RED BELL PEPPER
The bell of the ball

Like our friend the tomato, the bell pepper is, in fact, a fruit. It's rich in vitamin C and antioxidants, but low in calories. It's a very anti-inflammatory food, and its lycopene can fight cancer and other illnesses—making this the *real* Dr. Pepper. Plus, vitamin C builds collagen, so it keeps the skin looking beautiful, and it helps the body absorb iron, so try adding bell peppers to any iron-rich meal (think quinoa, spirulina, beans, lentils . . .). Slap on your sexy nightshades and head into the sun!

Cabinet Curry

*Looking to whip up some curry in a hurry? Look no further than your exotic . . . pantry!
This simple but fabulous version skips some traditional Thai ingredients (like galangal, chiles,
lemongrass, and Kaffir lime leaves), although if you can get your hands on them at an Asian
market or a good supermarket, they will make this even tastier. Thai cuisine is flavorful
and spicy, but also quite light, making it perfect for summer.*

SERVES 1

1 SMALL ZUCCHINI

♥ 1 CARROT

1 SMALL SHALLOT

1 SMALL GARLIC CLOVE

½ BELL PEPPER (RED, ORANGE, YELLOW, OR A COLORFUL MIX!)

1 SMALL TOMATO

♥ 1 TABLESPOON COCONUT OIL

2 TABLESPOONS WATER

1 HANDFUL OF BABY SPINACH

½ CUP (100 ML) *LAIT DE* COCONUT (PAGE 2) OR BPA-FREE CANNED COCONUT MILK

⅛ TEASPOON CUMIN

⅛ TEASPOON CORIANDER

♥ ⅛ TEASPOON TURMERIC (OR GRATED FRESH TURMERIC IF YOU'RE FANCY!)

♥ ½ TEASPOON MINCED FRESH GINGER OR GROUND GINGER

A PINCH OF CAYENNE PEPPER

JUICE OF 1 LIME

1 LEMONGRASS STALK (OPTIONAL)

1 HANDFUL OF FRESH BASIL, PLUS MORE FOR GARNISH

1 HANDFUL OF FRESH CILANTRO, PLUS MORE FOR GARNISH

1 CUP (100 G) COOKED BROWN OR RED RICE (SEE PAGE 18)

1 TABLESPOON CHOPPED FRESH MINT

1 TEASPOON COCONUT AMINOS OR TAMARI

1 TABLESPOON COCONUT FLAKES (OPTIONAL)

Wash and dice the zucchini and carrot into tiny pieces. Peel and chop the shallot, then peel and mince the garlic. Wash the pepper, remove the membranes and seeds, then cut into thin slices. Wash and dice the tomato.

Warm the coconut oil in a sauté pan over medium heat. Add the shallot and garlic and sauté for 1 to 2 minutes, then add the carrots. Pour 2 tablespoons water onto the pan and continue to simmer for another 2 to 3 minutes.

Add the zucchini, bell pepper, tomato, spinach, coconut milk, cumin, coriander, turmeric, ginger, cayenne, and a splash of the lime juice. If using lemongrass, rinse it, then cut off a 1-inch (2.5 cm) piece. Peel off the outer layer and discard. Add the whole inside piece to the curry mixture. Cover and simmer for another 5 minutes, or until the veggies are tender (but not mushy!). Remove the lemongrass.

Turn off the heat, add a handful of the basil and cilantro, and mix well. Add the rice to a bowl, then add the curry. Top with the additional basil and cilantro and the mint, coconut aminos, and coconut flakes (if using). Add another splash of lime juice.

CUMIN
Smelly, but sexy

Don't be scared—cumin has a very strong smell, but it's also an intense health-boosting spice. It fights insomnia, indigestion, nausea, colds, and respiratory problems, as well as strengthens the immune system. It's also rich in iron and antioxidants. So don't turn up your nose at this special spice—cumin get it!

Summer Lovesagne Napoleon

Whether you're feeding an army or just yourself, this Napoleon is revolutionary. It is abounding with flavor and nutrition. This is a perfect summer dish, since it is rich and protein-packed, yet still cooling and light. You can make this ahead of time and let it marinate in the refrigerator while you marinate outside in the sun. This is one of my favorite recipes for this sunny season. Careful: It may just conquer your world.

SERVES 1

1 SMALL ZUCCHINI

2 TABLESPOONS OLIVE OIL

1 LARGE HANDFUL OF BABY SPINACH

♥ 1 TABLESPOON LEMON JUICE

1 TEASPOON APPLE CIDER VINEGAR

SALT AND PEPPER TO TASTE

PISTACHIO PESTO:

1 HANDFUL OF FRESH BASIL, PLUS EXTRA FOR GARNISH

¼ CUP (100 G) RAW PISTACHIOS, PLUS EXTRA FOR GARNISH

1 HANDFUL OF ARUGULA

♥ 1 TABLESPOON LEMON JUICE

1 GARLIC CLOVE, PEELED (OPTIONAL)

2 TABLESPOONS OLIVE OIL

SALT AND PEPPER TO TASTE

1 TABLESPOON NUTRITIONAL YEAST (OPTIONAL)

1 SERVING OF FAUX-MAGE AU NATUREL (PAGE 5)

1 SERVING OF *SAUCE TOMATE* (PAGE 9) OR STORE-BOUGHT TOMATO SAUCE

Think about making most—or all!—of this in advance. For example, in the morning before heading to the beach!

Wash the zucchini, then cut it in half vertically. Using a mandoline or a very sharp knife, cut the halves into very thin slices. Salt the zucchini slices and mix with 1 tablespoon of the olive oil, then lay them on a plate to absorb the salt, "sweat," and marinate. You can do this the night before or leave for a few hours, but even an hour or so will be fine.

Combine the spinach, lemon juice, vinegar, and remaining 1 tablespoon of olive oil in a bowl with a pinch of salt and pepper and mix together with your hands. Set aside while you prepare the rest of the ingredients.

TO MAKE THE PESTO:

Blend all pesto ingredients in a food processor into a coarse consistency.

TO ASSEMBLE:

Place one third of the zucchini slices on a plate or in a lasagna pan. Top with a layer of half of the faux-mage, then continue to create layers with some of the pesto, half of the tomato sauce, and half of the spinach mixture. Top each slice with faux-mage, then pesto, then tomato sauce, then the spinach mixture. Top with another layer of zucchini slices, then repeat. Finish with a layer of zucchini slices, then top with a few pistachios and basil leaves. (You should only use about half of the pesto; save the rest for another day.)

Serve with a simple arugula salad with some lemon juice and olive oil (or, for an even more glam version, truffle oil . . . *oh là là!*).

Taco Belle

These raw tacos are perfect for a fiesta with friends. You can make everything ahead of time and don't even need to warm anything up once your guests arrive. You can simply enjoy your company without spending the evening slaving over the stove! These tacos are "meaty" yet refreshing. It's a party on a platter! Olé!

MAKES 4 TACOS

FOR THE WALNUT "MEAT":

1 CUP (100 G) WALNUTS

♥ 2 TEASPOONS COCONUT AMINOS OR TAMARI

CAYENNE PEPPER (TO TASTE—DON'T BE AFRAID TO SPICE THINGS UP!)

¼ TEASPOON CUMIN

1 TABLESPOON OLIVE OIL

FOR THE SOCIAL SALSA:

2 LARGE TOMATOES OR 1 CUP (100 G) CHERRY TOMATOES

½ CUCUMBER

½ RED, ORANGE, OR YELLOW BELL PEPPER

¼ CUP (50 G) CHOPPED RED ONION (OPTIONAL)

1 GARLIC CLOVE (OPTIONAL)

♥ 1 TEASPOON LEMON JUICE

1 TABLESPOON OLIVE OIL

2 TEASPOONS CHOPPED FRESH CHIVES

♥ ½ TEASPOON COCONUT NECTAR OR COCONUT SUGAR

A PINCH OF CAYENNE PEPPER

SALT AND PEPPER TO TASTE

♥ 2 AVOCADOS OR 1 CUP CRAZY GUACAMOUSSE (PAGE 86)

2 LIMES

4 LARGE ROMAINE LETTUCES (OR CORN TORTILLAS OR SAVORY CRÊPES—SEE PAGE 64)

¼ CUP TO ½ CUP (60 TO 125 ML) CASHEW CRÈME DE LA CRÈME (PAGE 6)

♥ 4 CARROTS, GRATED

¼ CUP CHOPPED FRESH CILANTRO

TO MAKE THE WALNUT "MEAT":

Pulse all ingredients in a food processor so that the mixture is chunky.

TO MAKE THE SOCIAL SALSA:

Dice the tomatoes. Peel and dice the cucumber. Wash the bell pepper, remove the membrane and seeds, then dice. Peel and mince the garlic (if using). Stir together the tomatoes, cucumber, bell pepper, garlic, onion, lemon juice, olive oil, chives, coconut nectar, and cayenne with a spoon. Add salt and pepper to taste.

TO ASSEMBLE THE TACOS:

Pit, peel, and cut the avocados into thin slices. Cut the limes into quarters.

Place a lettuce leaf on each plate. Add a spoonful of the walnut meat, then a few avocado slices, a spoonful of salsa, and a spoonful or two of cashew crème, and a quarter of the grated carrot, then top with cilantro. Squirt with lime juice. Fold the lettuce leaf and take a bite (go ahead, get messy!). *Olé!*

Tip: Social Salsa is of course great for a taco party, but it can also be eaten on its own, as a dip for Kale Chips (page 52), in a wrap (page 62), or for a refreshing addition to salad or pasta.

Socca Pizza

La vie without pizza is such a sad thought. (And probably one that crossed your mind the moment you parted ways with our old friend gluten, n'est-ce pas?) But never fear—socca is here. This flatbread from the south of France is made of chickpea flour (and is naturally vegan and gluten-free). The French traditionally eat it as an apéritif, but the protein, fiber, vitamins, and minerals in chickpea flour also make this a great base for a light summer meal, especially when topped with seasonal veggies or sauces.

MAKES 1 PIZZA

1 CUP (130 G) CHICKPEA FLOUR
SALT AND PEPPER TO TASTE
½ TEASPOON CHOPPED FRESH THYME
3 TABLESPOONS OLIVE OIL
1 CUP (150 ML) WATER
♥ 1 TABLESPOON COCONUT OIL

In a big bowl, mix the chickpea flour with the salt, pepper, and thyme. Add olive oil, then the water, and mix until the dough is thick but still liquid, like pancake mix. Let it sit on the counter, covered, either overnight, all day long, or for a few hours.

Preheat the oven to 400°F (200°C). Place a cast-iron skillet in the oven to heat up. When the oven is preheated, take out the skillet, coat with the coconut oil, and pour the chickpea mixture over it so that the entire pan is coated. Bake for 8 to 10 minutes, until the dough is firm and the sides are golden brown, but the center is still quite yellow. Flip over the socca pancake and bake for another 8 to 10 minutes. Remove from the oven and place on a plate. You can slice and eat it plain or add your favorite pizza toppings.

I recommend the following:

GREEN PIZZA

Add ¼ cup (80 ml) Green Chic Sauce (page 10), a few sun-dried tomatoes, and a few fresh basil leaves.

MARGHERITA PIZZA

Add ¼ cup (80 ml) *Sauce Tomate* (page 9) or store-bought tomato sauce, a few tablespoons faux-mage of choice (page 5), and a few fresh basil leaves. Just before serving, add Almond Crumble (page 7).

_BEET_PERONI PIZZA

Peel and thinly slice a red beet using a mandoline or paring knife. Toss the beet slices in olive oil, salt, and pepper and roast at 400°F (200°C) for around 5 minutes on each side. Add ¼ cup (80 ml) *Sauce Tomate* (page 9) or store-bought tomato sauce to the socca, some fresh basil leaves, and the roasted beet slices.

WORLD CUP OF SOCCA

Spice it up with your favorite fare from everywhere! A few ideas:

1. Add cumin, coriander, and cayenne pepper to the batter, then top with avocado, cilantro, and jicama.

2. Add curry powder to the batter then top with leftover Baby Dahl (page 160).

3. Top with Eggplant and Olive Tapenade (page 84).

Tip: You could take your traveling socca team on the road, but it's best when eaten hot, straight out of the oven.

Matchia Breakfast Bowl

This "matchia" bowl is the love child of two of my favorite superfoods: matcha and chia. It's an easy preparation that is not only green but also perfect for summertime since it is hydrating and energizing. I like fresh berries on mine, but you can add any fruits, nuts, and seeds you like.

SERVES 1

♥ 2 TABLESPOONS CHIA SEEDS

1 TABLESPOON GOJI BERRIES, SOAKED (OPTIONAL)

1 TABLESPOON DRIED MULBERRIES (OPTIONAL)

OTHER DRIED FRUIT TO TASTE

♥ ¾ CUP (150 ML) ALMOND MILK, HOMEMADE (SEE PAGE 2) OR STORE-BOUGHT

½ TEASPOON MATCHA POWDER, OR TO TASTE (START SLOWLY AND WORK YOUR WAY UP)

¼ TEASPOON VANILLA POWDER OR EXTRACT

A PINCH OF CINNAMON

♥ A PINCH OF GROUND GINGER

1 DATE, SOAKED, PEELED, AND PITTED, OR 1 TEASPOON MAPLE SYRUP

½ CUP (50 G) RASPBERRIES

½ CUP (50 G) BLUEBERRIES

Add the chia seeds and goji berries, mulberries, and other dried fruit (if using) to a small bowl. Combine the almond milk, matcha, vanilla, cinnamon, ginger, and date in a blender. Pour over the chia seed mixture. Mix with a spoon. Let sit for around 1 minute, then mix again. Let the bowl sit on the counter at room temperature for around 1 hour, stirring occasionally if you can. When the chia absorbs the liquid and it starts to look like a gelatinous rice pudding, top with the raspberries, blueberries, and even some granolove (page 36) if you like, and eat straight away, or refrigerate for several hours or overnight.

Peach Crumble, Two Ways

There's nothing like biting into a fresh, juicy peach on a hot summer's day. It is truly nature's candy! The French expression avoir la pêche *(literally, "to have the peach") means to be filled with energy. Peaches' natural sugars and water content definitely do provide a burst of energy! The French are obsessed with "le crumble"—it's a staple dessert on most restaurant menus across the country. I too adore a warm peach crumble,* bien sûr, *but when peaches are perfectly ripe and juicy, I find it a shame to cook them, so I've also added a peachy keen raw version that will help you "have the peach" on those hot summer nights.*

Baked Peach Crumble

SERVES 1

2 SMALL, RIPE PEACHES (PREFERABLY ORGANIC!)

¼ CUP (50 G) BLUEBERRIES

♥ 1 TABLESPOON LEMON JUICE

¼ TEASPOON CINNAMON

¼ TEASPOON VANILLA POWDER OR EXTRACT

1 TEASPOON MAPLE SYRUP

1 TEASPOON ARROWROOT POWDER

♥ 1 TABLESPOON ALMOND FLOUR, HOMEMADE (PAGE 14) OR STORE-BOUGHT

FOR THE CRUMBLE:

1 TABLESPOON PECANS

¼ CUP (40 G) GLUTEN-FREE OATS OR QUINOA FLAKES

♥ ½ TABLESPOON COCONUT OIL

1 TEASPOON MAPLE SYRUP

¼ TEASPOON CINNAMON

¼ TEASPOON VANILLA POWDER OR EXTRACT

A PINCH OF SALT

Preheat the oven to 350°F (175°C).

Wash and dice the peaches and mix with the blueberries, lemon juice, cinnamon, vanilla, maple syrup, arrowroot, and almond flour. Add the mixture to a small oven-safe bowl or pan. Leave it aside while you prepare the crumble.

TO MAKE THE CRUMBLE:

Pulse the pecans in a grinder or food processor to form smaller bits, but not a fine flour. Mix the pecan pieces with the oats, coconut oil, maple syrup, cinnamon, vanilla, and salt. Spread the oat mixture over the fruit and bake for around 25 minutes, until the oats are lightly browned and the fruit is warm.

Serve topped with a spoonful of vanilla ice cream (page 114) or coconut yogurt (page 4).

Raw Peach Crumble

SERVES 1

2 SMALL, RIPE PEACHES

1 MEDJOOL DATE, SOAKED, PITTED, AND PEELED

♥ 1 TABLESPOON LEMON JUICE

¼ TEASPOON VANILLA POWDER OR EXTRACT

¼ TEASPOON CINNAMON

♥ 1 TABLESPOON ALMOND SLIVERS

FOR THE CRUMBLE:

2 MEDJOOL DATES, SOAKED AND PITTED

1 TABLESPOON PECANS

1 TABLESPOON WALNUTS

¼ TEASPOON CINNAMON

A PINCH OF SALT

Cut the peaches into small pieces. Place half the peach pieces and the date, lemon juice, vanilla, and cinnamon in a blender and blend until smooth. Mix the rest of the peach chunks in by hand. Add the fruit mixture to a bowl or spread out over a plate.

TO MAKE THE CRUMBLE:

Combine the dates, pecans, walnuts, cinnamon, and salt in a food processor into a crumbly dough.

With your hands, sprinkle the crumble over the fruit mixture. Top with the almond slivers.

5-Ingredient Fruitwiches

These fruitwiches are easy to make and très kid-friendly.
They're a perfect energizing snack or grab-and-go quick breakfast.

SERVES 1 (OR A FEW KIDS)

♥ 2 TABLESPOONS ALMOND BUTTER, HOMEMADE (PAGE 14) OR STORE-BOUGHT*

¼ TEASPOON CINNAMON

¼ TEASPOON VANILLA POWDER OR EXTRACT

SWEETENER OF CHOICE (1 MEDJOOL DATE, ½ TEASPOON COCONUT SUGAR OR NECTAR . . .)

¼ TO 1 TEASPOON MACA POWDER (OPTIONAL, FOR A GROWN-UP FRUITWICH)

♥ 1 LARGE BANANA OR 1 APPLE

Add the almond butter, cinnamon, vanilla, sweetener, and maca (if using) to a bowl and mix together by hand.

If using a banana, you can (1) slice the banana in half lengthwise then spread the almond butter mixture on one side and top with the other slice or (2) slice it into thin bites horizontally to make several mini fruitwiches. You can also coat the banana with almond butter then roll it around in your favorite toppings (hemp seeds, coconut flakes, cacao nibs . . .) and slice thinly to make . . . banana sushi! If using an apple, core and slice it thinly horizontally. Stuff a small teaspoonful of almond butter mix in between two slices. You can serve with toothpicks to make them less messy to eat, but hey, who's watching? Have fun!

*Many schools today prohibit nut butters due to allergies. You can easily replace the almond butter with sunflower seed butter for an allergen-free option to pack in a school lunch.

CINNAMON
The spice that makes everything nice!

Cinnamon is an aromatic spice that goes with everything. It soothes the stomach and supports brain function. It has an antibacterial and antifungal effect. It's rich in antiaging antioxidants to make the skin glow, and it protects the body against illness. It makes foods taste sweeter, plus lowers blood sugar and prevents sugar from transforming into fat in the body. It would be a cinnamon not to eat this spice as much as possible!

♥ BEST FRIEND FOOD
Apples

"An apple a day keeps the doctor away." True story. Apples are a gold mine of health benefits! They're very energizing, and since they are composed of 85 percent water, they are also hydrating and detoxifying. Apples are rich in fiber, especially pectin, a soluble fiber that aids digestion, prevents diarrhea, and regulates cholesterol levels in the body.

"Split"-Second Banana Ice Cream

"I scream, you scream, we all scream for . . ." STOP right there. Ice? And cream?
No wonder everyone is screaming. This combination is a digestion nightmare. It's cold.
It's dairy. And it's likely filled with copious amounts of sugar. Le scandale! But what is a childhood
(or an adulthood, for that matter?) without licking off a melty cone or bowl of ice cream on a hot
summer's day? Not much of one, I say. You'll go bananas once you
try this life-changing treat. Feel free to scream.

MAKES 1 SERVING

♥ 2 OR 3 RIPE BANANAS

A MEDJOOL DATE (SOAKED, PITTED, AND PEELED),
MAPLE SYRUP, STEVIA, OR COCONUT SUGAR
(OPTIONAL, IF YOU HAVE A SWEET TOOTH)

You'll need a good blender or food processor for this recipe.

Peel the bananas and chop into 1-inch (2.5 cm) pieces. Place in the freezer, preferably in a glass container, until frozen and hard. Add to your blender or food processor and blend until smooth and creamy. *Voilà!* Magic! Eat it right away before it melts!

Here are some flavoring ideas:

MINT CHOCOLATE CHIP

Add 1 tablespoon cacao powder, a pinch of vanilla powder or extract, 1 to 2 drops of mint essential oil and/or a handful of fresh mint leaves, and blend. Mix in 1 tablespoon cacao nibs by hand.

VANILLA

Add ¼ teaspoon vanilla powder or extract and blend.

CHOCOLATE

Add 1 tablespoon cacao powder, 1 teaspoon mesquite powder, and a pinch of vanilla powder or extract and blend.

CARAMEL

Add 1 date, ½ tablespoon carob powder, and ½ tablespoon mesquite powder and blend.

COCONUT ALMOND FUDGE

Mix 1 tablespoon of almond butter with 2 teaspoons cacao powder in a small bowl. Add to prepared ice cream, along with 2 teaspoons coconut flakes and 1 tablespoon toasted almonds, and mix together by hand.

STRAWBERRY

Add ¼ cup strawberries to the ice cream and blend, then add another ¼ cup of chopped strawberries and mix by hand.

ESSENTIAL OILS
Oil là là!

Essential oils are natural compounds from the seeds, stems, roots, flowers, and bark of plants. They have been used for centuries for their healing properties for both mind and body—in Egypt, Greece, Rome, Persia, China, and India. It was a French chemist, René-Maurice Gattefossé, who rediscovered essential oils and began more in-depth analysis of the wonders of aromatherapy in the early twentieth century. You've likely spotted essential oils in your favorite perfumes or body products, but they do much more than smell great. They are natural first aid kits and flavorful cooking ingredients, helpful for cleansing the body, treating physical ailments, boosting your mood, and even cleaning your house.

Peppermint is my favorite essential oil—it freshens breath, cures a sore throat, eases digestion, and can soothe aches and pains all over the body. It's also especially delicious when mixed with chocolate. Lavender is calming to the mind and body; rose balances hormones; clove is great for the mouth and teeth and can treat headache and stomach aches; and lemon balm acts as a natural antidepressant. These are just some of the myriad health benefits of essential oils. Add to natural beauty remedies, or try a few drops in your recipes. Just make sure you buy a top-quality oil (I like Young Living) and go slowly. Remember: This may be natural medicine, but it's still quite powerful, so do your research and talk to a health professional before you go crazy.

BeautiFuel Banana

Avoir la banane, or "to have the banana" in French, means to be feeling great—an appropriate expression, since this fruit always seems to make me feel fabulous. This simple mix of some of our dearest Best Friend Foods hydrates the skin, repairs damaged or dry hair, and softens the skin on our feet (often a casualty of those summer days running around barefoot on the beach!).

♥ 4 RIPE BANANAS
♥ 2 RIPE AVOCADOS
♥ 2 TABLESPOONS COCONUT OIL
♥ JUICE OF 1 LEMON (OPTIONAL, FOR OILY SKIN)

♥ BEST FRIEND FOOD
Banana

I'm convinced I'm part monkey. Bananas have always been my ultimate comfort food. Bananas may have developed a bad reputation since they are quite high in (natural!) sugars, but we can't forget all of their other health benefits. Bananas are rich in fiber and vitamins A, B complex, C, E, and K, and they contain folate (an essential nutrient for pregnant women). They're also very high in potassium, minerals, and electrolytes (that hydrate the entire body), important for digestion and muscle function. Bananas are easy to digest, and mashed banana is a great remedy for diarrhea, as well as a fantastic hangover helper after a night out.

Bananas make smoothies and desserts naturally smooth and sweet without any added cream or sugar. They should be eaten when ripe—and this often means a brown and spotted peel. It's just a sign of maturity—no need to fear!

Peel the bananas and pit and peel the avocados and add the flesh to a bowl with the coconut oil and lemon juice (if using). Mash with a fork until creamy.

Spread a quarter of the mixture all over your face, but avoid your eyes!

Spread another quarter of the mixture over your scalp and hair (try putting on a shower cap afterward; it will keep things less messy!). Spread another quarter of the mixture on the bottoms of your feet.

Sit and allow the nutrients to absorb into your skin for 15 to 20 minutes. Meanwhile, take the last quarter of the mixture, grab a spoon, and . . . eat it! (Optional: Add your favorite sweetener or some cinnamon.)

Rinse your hair and face with warm water, and wash your feet.

Banana helps to soothe burns, so if you've gotten too much sun, apply some of the mixture and it will help reduce redness and pain.

Banana skins are also very rich in potassium and make a great natural remedy for under-eye circles or puffiness since they fight against water retention. Even if the idea of putting banana skins under your eyes doesn't sound so apeeling, it will make you très chic! (And no one has to know you are standing in your bathroom with banana peels on your face! Your secret is safe with me!)

Is your skin oilier than usual in summer? Adding lemon juice to the mixture provides vitamin C and enzymes that help to exfoliate the skin, clear out toxins, and make it shine (in a good way!).

Summer Fête!

You are cordially invited . . .

Summer—'tis the season to invite friends and family over for a big barbecue, a picnic, or a magical summer night (to be spent dancing around in your tightest spandex and varsity jacket, Grease-style). To celebrate this festive season, I've invited some of my favorite foodie friends over for a green party (singing and dancing optional). These chefs from France, the United States, and across the globe have inspired my own cooking and made going green so much fun! They've all RSVPed "Oui!," so voilà: Come join us for a delightful summer soirée with les amis!

ALAIN PASSARD

Every vegetable across the world dreams of one day making it to Alain Passard's kitchen. There, he or she will be transformed into a work of art. (Yes, I said "he or she"—even vegetables are given a gender identity in France and labeled "le" or "la.") Making it to L'Arpège, Chef Passard's Michelin-starred restaurant in Paris, is the equivalent of winning a Veggie Oscar. Chez Passard, the plants steal the show. Before he rolls out the veg carpet to wow his guests with his plant-powered prowess, this world-renowned chef holds a strict casting call on farms in Sarthe and Normandy, handpicks the standouts, then provides first-class transportation for them to Paris every morning, where he coddles them, pampers them, dresses them in designer sauces, and sends them out into the spotlight. This is an A-list establishment for vegetables and celebrities alike, so be sure to visit the next time you're in Paris. In the meantime, Chef Passard has kindly shared a MicheLeffler-starred recipe for the summer. Make this for friends and family and you'll soon be taking reservations at Chez YOU!
alain-passard.com

WILLIAM LEDEUIL

Ze Kitchen Galerie is one of ze best restaurants in Paris, and ze chef consistently turns out zelicious food! Ledeuil's cuisine is modern French with an Asian twist. He was the first to tickle my taste buds with "creamy" sauces made with a coconut milk base, instead of cream, and exotic Asian herbs and spices. For him, "cooking is understanding the nature and appropriate use of each ingredient in order to respectfully let it shine." Every mouthful of Ledeuil's cuisine has its own distinct flavor and texture. It's no surprise that his two restaurants in Paris' 6th arrondissement, just along the Seine, are always packed. The walls may be covered with modern paintings, but the real artful masterpieces are on the plates.
zekitchengalerie.com | kitchengaleriebis.com

CHRISTIAN SINICROPI

I often dream about living in Christian Sinicropi's kitchen at La Palme d'Or restaurant at the Hotel Martinez in Cannes, France. Everything that comes out of his kitchen is absolutely life-changing. Chef Sinicropi thinks about every detail, he artfully constructs every millimeter of every vegetable, and every mouthful of food he serves is the result of several hours of preparation. The scents that emit from the kitchen are indescribable, and I often want to bottle them up into an "Eau de Sinicropi." Chef Sinicropi taught me that the quality of each and every ingredient is so important and that a zest for life is the best addition to any meal. So until your next Riviera rendez-vous, here's a taste of Cannes in your kitchen!
cannesmartinez.grand.hyatt.fr

SARMA MELNGAILIS

I lost my raw food virginity on a cold winter night in NYC . . . and my life has never been the same since. It all happened at the Manhattan raw food mecca Pure Food and Wine. The restaurant attracts the crème de la (cashew) crème of supermodels and superstars, from Gisèle to Bill Clinton to Alec Baldwin, Jake Gyllenhaal, and Gwyneth Paltrow. Pure introduced me to a new world of flavors and showed me that a meal made only of nuts, seeds, and vegetables could be just as gourmet and flavorful as another—if not more. In ancient BC (before chia) times, Sarma Melngailis was already living la vie en green and was the first to prove that raw food could also be quite glamorous. Sarma's cuisine is a constant reminder that one of the key ingredients to a healthy lifestyle is pleasure.
oneluckyduck.com

WHITNEY TINGLE AND DANIELLE DUBOISE/SAKARA LIFE

Whitney Tingle and Danielle DuBoise are the dynamic duo behind Sakara Life, which began as a healthy meal delivery service in NYC and has now expanded across state lines and become a végolution unto itself. I love their philosopheat, which is based on the idea that food is medicine and focuses on balance (there's our favorite word again!) and enjoyment in all areas of life. They say au revoir to juice fasts, agonizing cleanses, and starvation, and bonjour to beautiful meals that can easily be eaten on the road, in the office, or en route to the next jet-setting destination. Sakara Life offers busy urbanites farm-to-fabulous fare for busy days (and mornings and nights!). It feeds celebrities (think Lily Aldridge, Erin Heatherton, Karolina Kurkova, and Lena Dunham) and features celebrity ingredients (think tatsoi, goji berries, and edible flowers). Summer is picnic season, so who better to give us a fashionable al fresco recipe than the reigning queens of green fare "to go"?
sakaralife.com

ELENORE BENDEL ZAHN

This young Swede expresses her love for Mother Earth every day as a nutrition coach, organic farmer, green chef, and blogger extraordinaire. Her passion for cooking and life is contagious; both her writing and her food are filled with so much love. Elenore's food is just like her: healthy, yet adventurous! This young mother gives birth daily to gorgeous dishes filled with colors and flavors, sprinkled with a dash of optimism and a glowing smile.
earthsprout.com

DAPHNE CHENG

Chef Daphne Cheng is the epitome of green and glam. This young, creative chef is always experimenting in the kitchen and whipping up tasty, artful masterpieces of la haute gastronomie. Oh, and by the way . . . it all just happens to be vegan. Her exclusive supper club has played host to artful masterpieces of incredibly gourmet cuisine and VIPlant-lovers. The moment I tasted her food, it was love at first bite. Daphne's cuisine is original, beautiful, and often mind-blowing. She is the queen of "veganizing" the classics, so I asked her to revamp one of my favorite French dishes: la quiche!
daphnecheng.com

ALISON JOHNSON/ ROSE BAKERY

I see La Vie en Rose . . . bakery! Ever since the day I discovered this cozy Franco-British café in Paris years ago, I have been hooked on their farm-to-table fare. No longer just a tiny spot on the rue des Martyrs, Rose Bakery has now expanded to several addresses in Paris, London, New York, and Tokyo, but it hasn't lost its home-cooked flare. When I was told I needed to avoid gluten and dairy, my first reaction was, "But doctor, how can I live without Rose Bakery's muffins?" Thankfully, Alison—the pastry chef at Rose Bakery's très chic tea room at Le Bon Marché department store—had the solution!

BÉATRICE PELTRE

Béatrice Peltre, AKA Béa, is a French food writer, stylist, and blogger based in Boston. Her French-infused cooking with an American twist captured my heart when I discovered her lovely blog La Tartine Gourmande years ago when I was first dipping my feet in la vie en green. Her recipes are all gorgeous and tasty—oh, and did I mention gluten-free? She speaks fluent Franglais as well as fluent vegetable, so we have a lot to talk about. But let's cut the chatter—it's time to eat!
latartinegourmande.com

THIERRY MARX

This vivacious chef extraordinaire boasts several Michelin stars and is a star in his own right. His unique Asian-fusion French fare has made him a culinary legend in France. He sees food as a pleasure and as a shared experience that should be both beautiful to look at and tantalizing to the taste buds. He may serve fancy food, but Chef Marx is très down-to-earth and practices a very healthy lifestyle when he's not behind the stove. To him, cooking is both a physical and mental sport. A loyal devotee of tai chi, this meditating globetrotter also plays the Japanese taiko drums and never leaves home without a pair of chopsticks—"They are like an extension of my hands," he says. He uses moving meditation as a way of dealing with even the toughest culinary French critics and approaches every dish, and everyone he meets, with a youthful exuberance.
mandarinoriental.fr/paris

Rainbow Tomato Carpaccio with Raspberries and Purple Basil

"Voilà: a beautiful and colorful recipe that is perfect for summer." —Alain Passard

SERVES 4

4 TO 5 TOMATOES IN A MIXTURE OF COLORS AND VARIETIES (GREEN ZEBRA, BLACK RUSSIAN . . .)

2 YOUNG RED ONIONS, PEELED

1 HANDFUL OF RASPBERRIES

12 FAVA BEANS (PEELED)

2 ROSEMARY SPRIGS

1 SMALL BUNCH OF PURPLE BASIL

A GOOD OLIVE OIL

FLEUR DE SEL

FRESHLY GROUND BLACK PEPPER

Cut the tomatoes and onions into thin slices. Place them onto the plate. Add the raspberries, fava beans, rosemary, and purple basil leaves. Pour olive oil over the top and season with fleur de sel and pepper. That's all! *Bonne table!*

TOMATO
A red-hot beauty food extraordinaire

You say tomato, I say *la tomate* . . . However you pronounce the name of this popular fruit (*oui oui,* tomato is a fruit despite the fact that it is typically consumed in savory dishes), there's no denying its plethora of health benefits. Low in calories and bursting with water, tomatoes hydrate the body, especially when consumed raw. However, when you cook them, they become even richer in lycopene, the antioxidant that gives tomatoes their red color. However (and whether or not) you cook them, tomatoes are a great source of vitamin C, B vitamins (including folate—yeah!), vitamin A, iron, and calcium.

Stuffed Zucchini Flowers with Tomato-Galangal Confit

Zucchini flowers are so glamorous. However, they're often served battered, fried, and stuffed with cheese. Luckily, Chef Ledeuil has swooped in to save some zucchini flowers from this fate.

SERVES 4

8 ZUCCHINI FLOWERS (2 PER PERSON)

FOR THE STUFFING:

5 YOUNG GREEN ONIONS
1 CUP (250 ML) OLIVE OIL
2 GARLIC CLOVES
1 STALK OF LEMONGRASS, CUT IN HALF
2 CUPS (300 G) PEELED, DICED YELLOW SUMMER SQUASH (PEELS RESERVED)
CELERY SALT TO TASTE
3 CILANTRO SPRIGS, CHOPPED

FOR THE CHANTERELLE GARNISH:

4 CUPS (400 G) CHANTERELLE MUSHROOMS
1 LEMONGRASS STALK
2 TABLESPOONS OLIVE OIL
SALT AND PEPPER TO TASTE
2 GARLIC CLOVES, MINCED
2 LONG CHINESE CHIVES, CHOPPED
A HANDFUL OF THAI BASIL, CHOPPED

FOR THE TOMATO-GALANGAL CONFIT:

6 RIPE TOMATOES (AROUND 2¼ POUNDS/1 KG TOTAL)
5 TABLESPOONS OLIVE OIL
1 SWEET ONION, MINCED
3 GARLIC CLOVES, MINCED
♥ ONE 3½-OUNCE (100 G) PIECE OF GINGER, MINCED
2 LEMONGRASS STALKS
2 GALANGAL BULBS
6 TABLESPOONS PLUS 2 TEASPOONS RICE VINEGAR
SALT AND PEPPER TO TASTE

TO MAKE THE STUFFING:

Wash and chop the green onions. Heat one third of the olive oil in a nonstick pan over low heat and add the green onions, 1 garlic clove, and half of the lemongrass. Cook until translucent. Transfer to a bowl.

Heat one third of the olive oil in the pan and add the yellow squash, remaining garlic, and remaining lemongrass. Sauté until the squash is very soft. Remove the lemongrass. Mash with a fork, mix with the onions, and season with celery salt.

Sauté the squash skins in the remaining olive oil for around 1 minute, then add them and the cilantro to the squash mixture. Set aside.

TO MAKE THE CHANTERELLE GARNISH:

Wash the chanterelles well twice. Cut the stalk of lemongrass in half. Warm 2 tablespoons of olive oil over the stove with the lemongrass. Season with salt and pepper and sauté the chanterelles for around 2 minutes. Turn off the heat, remove the lemongrass, and add the garlic, chives, and basil.

TO MAKE THE TOMATO-GALANGAL CONFIT:

Destem the tomatoes and cut into pieces. Stir well, then use a sieve or cheesecloth to strain their juices into a bowl.

Heat the olive oil in a sauté pan over medium-low heat, add the onion, garlic, ginger, lemongrass, and galangal, and cook for a few minutes, stirring frequently, until the onions are translucent. Add the tomato juice and vinegar. Season with salt and pepper.

Bring the mixture to a boil, then reduce the heat to low and simmer for 30 to 40 minutes. It will become very creamy and tasty. Remove the lemongrass and galangal before serving.

FINAL TOUCHES:

Cook the zucchini flowers for 5 minutes in a bamboo (or other) steamer. Divide the zucchini flowers and mushrooms among four plates and top with the tomato-galangal confit.

Zucchini Art

Turn your home into a Michelin-starred French Riviera restaurant with this simple but elegant recipe from my favorite chef in Cannes!

SERVES 10

6 YELLOW SQUASH

10 MINI GREEN ZUCCHINI

4 TRUMPET ZUCCHINI (LONG, SKINNY ZUCCHINI)

1 BUNCH OF ROUND RADISHES

1 FRESH GREEN ONION

1 CUCUMBER

2 PINK GARLIC CLOVES

PM OLIVE OIL*

PM AGED RED WINE VINEGAR

PM FLEUR DE SEL**

PM GROUND BLACK PEPPER

6 VEGAN EGG EQUIVALENTS (AGAR-AGAR, VEGETABLE GELATIN, ETC.; SEE PAGE xiii)

♥ PM LEMON JUICE

*Secrets of a French chef revealed: Here, PM means *pour mémoire*, or "according to taste." For all of these condiments, it's up to you to decide how much you want to add.

**Literally "flower of salt," you can find fleur de sel in most gourmet markets, or you can substitute sea salt or Himalayan pink salt.

Peel 5 of the yellow squash (reserving the peel), halve, and remove the seeds. Purée the flesh. Do the same for 9 of the mini green zucchini and 4 of the trumpet zucchini, keeping them separate from the yellow squash. (Discard the zucchini peel.)

Slice the radishes, green onion, and cucumber into slices around ½ inch (1 cm) thick. Peel the garlic and crush or puree it. Mix these together and add the garlic. Add the olive oil, vinegar, and fleur de sel. Stir the mixture together then marinate in the refrigerator for 2 to 3 hours.

Combine three quarters of the yellow squash purée, fleur de sel, and pepper in a small pot or Dutch oven. Heat on the stovetop until warm, but not quite boiling. Add the egg replacement, stir well, then pour the mixture into a round baking mold or cake pan and let it sit in the refrigerator for around 3 hours, until firm. Once firm, make 10 "royales" by cutting out circles using a 1½-inch (4 cm) round cookie cutter. Return them to the fridge.

Cut the remaining mini zucchini *en brunoise*—that is, in tiny cubes around ⅒ inch thick. Stir together one quarter of the zucchini puree with the *brunoise*, then season with olive oil, fleur de sel, and lemon juice. Top each of the yellow royales with some of the mixture.

With the skin of one of the remaining yellow squash, form ¼-inch (.5 cm) rings, each with a ⅒-inch hole, so they resemble little flowers (see photo). Add olive oil and lemon juice to taste. Set them aside.

Make two "gazpachos," one yellow, one green. To do this, divide the refrigerated onion-cucumber-radish between two bowls. Add the remaining three quarters of the zucchini purée to one bowl and the remaining one quarter of the yellow squash purée to the other. Blend each gazpacho separately and place them in the refrigerator.

When ready to eat, remove the royales from the refrigerator and top with the squash-skin "flowers." Remove both of the gazpachos from the refrigerator and pour some of each slowly over each royale.

Zucchini Fettuccine with Creamy Pine Nut Alfredo Sauce

"Voilà: a creamy, rich, and satisfying pasta dish without the flour and gluten of traditional noodles and without the cheese and butter of a traditional Alfredo sauce. Nutritional yeast adds a 'cheesy' flavor, and it's also a great source of B vitamins.

"In the summertime, you can find 'goldbar' yellow squash—it's a variety of squash with a dark yellow skin. It's long and straight like a zucchini, making it easier to julienne. If you can't find it, you can use any zucchini or summer squash for the noodles or a mix of green and yellow.

"In the summer, you can usually find lemon basil at the farmers market, but regular basil is fine, too."
—Sarma Melngailis

SERVES 2

FOR THE ALFREDO SAUCE:

1 CUP (200 G) RAW PINE NUTS

3 TABLESPOONS OLIVE OIL

♥ ¼ CUP (60 ML) LEMON JUICE

1 TABLESPOON NUTRITIONAL YEAST*

½ TEASPOON SEA SALT

FOR THE PASTA:

2 OR 3 GOLDBAR SQUASH (OR OTHER SUMMER SQUASH)

SEA SALT

½ CUP (70 G) RAW PINE NUTS

½ TEASPOON WALNUT OIL OR OLIVE OIL

½ CUP (50 G) CAPERS

1 HANDFUL OF LEMON BASIL LEAVES (OR REGULAR BASIL)

FRESHLY CRACKED BLACK PEPPER

*You can buy nutritional yeast at oneluckyduck.com, fresh from Sarma's kitchen!

TO MAKE THE SAUCE:

Place the pine nuts in a bowl and add enough water to cover them. Soak for 1 hour.

Drain off the water from the pine nuts and add them to a blender with the olive oil, lemon juice, nutritional yeast, and salt. Blend until creamy. If the sauce is too thick, add a bit of water to thin it out.

TO MAKE THE PASTA:

Using a vegetable peeler or Japanese mandoline, cut the squash into wide, thin, noodlelike ribbons, working around each squash until you get to the center seeds. Discard the center or save for another use. Place the squash ribbons in a colander, toss with about ½ teaspoon sea salt, and let sit for at least 30 minutes to allow a bit of the liquid to drain out.

In a small bowl, blend the pine nuts with the oil and a pinch of salt.

Place enough "noodles" for two servings into a medium bowl. Add enough Alfredo sauce to generously coat. Add the capers, half of the lemon basil, and a pinch of pepper and mix together.

Divide the "noodles" between two deep bowls, piled high. Add more sauce on top. Garnish with the pine nut mixture and the remaining basil.

Summer Picnic à la Sakara Life

"When you are jet-setting and go-getting, your body does its best to keep up, but the increased amount of internal stress can cause harm if it's not prepared. Fueling it with fresh, plant-based, hydrating whole foods and nutrient-dense superfoods is the best way to support your body and keep your energy up and ready for whatever beautiful things come your way! Both of our recipes come packed with healing phytonutrients and antioxidants that will keep not only your immune system revving, but that radiant skin of yours hydrated and glowing. They also come boasting heart-healthy fats which will aid in plumping jet-lagged skin, promoting restful sleep, and supporting digestion (especially important when eating unfamiliar foods). The fatty acids will also help keep your mind sharp and alert, and have been linked to memory boosting, so that you can remember all of your beautiful experiences of your travels! Bon voyage, loves!" —Danielle DuBoise and Whitney Tingle

On-the-Glow Cucumber-Carrot Salad with Creamy Mint Drizzle

SERVES 4

½ POUND FRESH GREENS OF CHOICE (E.G., ARUGULA)

½ CUCUMBER, DICED

♥ 2 CARROTS, DICED

½ CUP CHOPPED FRESH DILL

2 GREEN ONIONS, DICED

1 CUP (30 G) COOKED WHITE BEANS

♥ 1 TABLESPOON HEMP SEEDS

½ CUP (100 G) PUMPKIN SEEDS

DRESSING:

♥ 1 CUP (250 ML) *LAIT DE* COCONUT (PAGE 2) OR BPA-FREE CANNED FULL-FAT COCONUT MILK

1 CUP PACKED FRESH MINT LEAVES

2 TABLESPOONS OLIVE OIL

2 TABLESPOONS LIME JUICE

2 TABLESPOONS AGAVE NECTAR

½ TEASPOON HIMALAYAN PINK SALT

½ TEASPOON ARROWROOT POWDER

Rinse and dry the greens. In a large bowl, combine the greens, cucumber, carrots, dill, and green onions. Mix in the beans, hemp seeds, and pumpkin seeds.

TO MAKE THE DRESSING:

In a blender, combine the coconut milk, mint, olive oil, lime juice, agave nectar, salt, and arrowroot. Process until mostly smooth (tiny mint speckles will remain). Divide among 4-ounce cups.

Superfood Beauty Bites

MAKES 10 TO 12 BALLS

8 LARGE DATES, PITTED

¾ CUP (75 G) RAW WALNUTS

♥ ½ CUP (50 G) RAW HEMP SEEDS

⅛ TEASPOON HIMALAYAN PINK SALT

♥ 1 TABLESPOON RAW CACAO POWDER

♥ ¼ TEASPOON TURMERIC POWDER

1 TEASPOON BEE POLLEN (OPTIONAL, FOR BEE-GANS ONLY)

1 TEASPOON MACA POWDER

1 TEASPOON LUCUMA POWDER

1 TEASPOON RAW HONEY (OPTIONAL, FOR BEE-GANS ONLY)

OPTIONAL COATINGS:

CINNAMON, SHREDDED COCONUT, RAW CACAO NIBS, OR GOJI POWDER

Combine all ingredients except coatings in a food processor and process until the mixture is crumbly but sticks together. Form into balls and roll in your choice of coatings. Enjoy as is or store in the fridge for the week ahead!

Caramelized Onion Quiche

"This enlightened version of a classic French favorite has all the right qualities: crisp crust, creamy filling, savory flavor, and feel-good vibes. Kala namak (or black salt) is a mineral salt from the Himalayas used in Indian cuisine. The sulfuric compounds it contains lend an eggy flavor to the quiche. If you can't find it, feel free to omit."—Daphne Cheng

FOR THE CRUST:

1¼ CUPS (100 G) GLUTEN-FREE ALL-PURPOSE FLOUR, OR A 50/50 BLEND OF RICE AND POTATO FLOURS

¼ TEASPOON SALT

1 TABLESPOON COCONUT SUGAR

♥ 7 TABLESPOONS COCONUT OR PALM OIL, CHILLED AND CUT INTO PIECES

2 TABLESPOONS ICE WATER, OR MORE AS NEEDED

FOR THE FILLING:

♥ 4 CUPS (800 ML) ALMOND MILK, HOMEMADE (SEE PAGE 2) OR STORE-BOUGHT

10 GRAMS (ABOUT ⅓ OUNCE) AGAR-AGAR POWDER OR FLAKES*

¼ TEASPOON SALT

¼ TEASPOON KALA NAMAK (BLACK SALT; OPTIONAL)

¼ TEASPOON GROUND WHITE PEPPER

♥ ¼ TEASPOON TURMERIC

A PINCH OF FRESHLY GRATED NUTMEG

1 TABLESPOON VINEGAR

2 TABLESPOONS OLIVE OIL

1 ONION, PEELED AND THINLY SLICED

1 TABLESPOON COCONUT SUGAR

OPTIONAL TOPPINGS:

1 SPOONFUL OF RED AND GREEN BELL PEPPERS, DICED

1 SPOONFUL OF HEMPESTO (PAGE 10) OR PARSLEY PISTOU (PAGE 8)

A HANDFUL OF SPROUTS

*This is one of those cases when you really need a kitchen scale! Be precise and love the results.

TO MAKE THE CRUST:

Combine the flour, salt, coconut sugar, and oil in a food processor and process until the mixture resembles coarse crumbs, about 10 seconds. Add the ice water and pulse again 5 or 6 times, until the dough comes together and starts to pull away from the sides of the container. Add a little more water if needed.

Gather the dough into a ball, flatten it into a disk, and wrap in plastic wrap. Refrigerate for at least 1 hour.

On a lightly floured surface, roll out the dough into an 11-inch circle. Fit into a 9-inch fluted tart pan, ideally with a removable bottom, and trim the edges. Refrigerate for at least 30 minutes.

Preheat the oven to 375°F (190°C).

Line the pastry with parchment paper and fill with pie weights or dried beans. Bake until the crust is set, about 12 to 14 minutes. Remove the paper and weights and bake until golden brown, 8 to 10 minutes. Remove from the oven and cool on a wire rack.

TO MAKE THE FILLING:

Combine the almond milk, agar-agar, salt, kala namak, white pepper, turmeric, nutmeg, vinegar, and 1 tablespoon of the olive oil in a small saucepan. Heat over medium heat for 10 to 15 minutes to allow the agar to bloom, whisking occasionally. Bring to a boil and cook, whisking often, for 15 minutes, until the agar has fully dissolved.

In a medium skillet over medium heat, heat the remaining 1 tablespoon of olive oil and cook the onion with the coconut sugar for 20 to 25 minutes, until caramelized and evenly brown. Stir into the almond milk mixture.

Pour into the prepared crust and chill until set, at least 1 hour.

Serve chilled or reheat in a 200°F (95°C) oven before serving, checking with a thermometer to be careful not to let the quiche itself go over 185°F (85°C); otherwise the agar will melt and lose its form. Sprinkle with toppings, if using.

"Mandarisotto": Bean Sprout Risotto with White Foam and Truffles

Thierry Marx can turn even a simple bean sprout into a Michelin star–worthy wondermeal . . . and he did! Just for us. Don't miss this exclusive risotto.

SERVES 6

FOR THE FOAM:
1 CUP (100 G) WHITE BUTTON MUSHROOMS
½ CUP (50 G) TRUFFLES
1 CUP (125 G) CHOPPED SHALLOTS
2 CUPS (500 ML) DRY WHITE WINE
½ CUP (125 ML) ALMOND MILK, HOMEMADE (PAGE 2) OR STORE-BOUGHT
SALT AND PEPPER

FOR THE RISOTTO:
6 CUPS (600 G) BEAN SPROUTS
1 TABLESPOON OLIVE OIL

TO MAKE THE FOAM:

Remove the mushrooms' stems and wipe off the caps. Clean the truffles with a brush and cut out 6 thin strips with a mandoline; set aside. Also set aside 1½ tablespoons (10 g) of whole truffles and a small amount for the garnish. Chop the rest of the truffles; set aside.

Heat a frying pan. Sweat the shallots with the white wine until reduced, then pass through a conical strainer. Return the strained wine to the pan and set aside. Discard the shallots or reserve for a later use.

Cut the button mushrooms into very thin strips and put in a pan with no added fat. Cover up the mushrooms with water and cover the pan with plastic wrap. Cook on low heat for 25 minutes to remove the mushrooms' juice.

Strain the reduction into the white wine reduction. Add the almond milk; strain all into a pot and add salt and pepper to taste.

Cook for 20 minutes on low heat and add the set-aside 1½ tablespoons of whole truffles at the very end. Finally, emulsify in a food processor to form the foam.

TO MAKE THE RISOTTO:

During the cooking of the foam, remove the bean sprouts' heads, keeping their white stems only. With a knife, cut the stems into tiny pieces, around the length of long rice grains.

Heat the oil in a pan and add the sliced bean sprouts. Mix the oil and sprouts over the heat for 15 seconds to 1 minute. Remove from the heat, add salt and pepper to taste, and add the chopped truffles.

Divide the bean sprout "risotto" among six bowls with 1 small strip of truffle. Cover with the foam and finely grate a little bit of truffle on top to garnish.

Sexy Summer Salad with Rolled Butter

"All my greenylicious wishes to you and your summer day and all of your adventures!"
—xoxo, Elenore

**SERVES 4 AS AN APPETIZER;
2 AS AN ENTRÉE**

FOR THE ROLLED BUTTER:

1 CUP (120 G) UNHULLED SESAME SEEDS,
PLUS MORE FOR ROLLING

♥ 1 TABLESPOON VIRGIN COCONUT OIL

1 TABLESPOON NUTRITIONAL YEAST, PLUS
MORE FOR ROLLING

1½ TEASPOONS FLAKY SEA SALT

1½ TEASPOONS APPLE CIDER VINEGAR

FOR THE SALAD:

1 CUP (200 G) BROCCOLI FLORETS

HIMALAYAN PINK SALT, CELTIC SEA SALT,
OR OTHER HIGH-QUALITY SALT

5 KALE LEAVES, SHREDDED

½ HEAD OF ROMAINE

1 HEAD OF YOUR FAVORITE LETTUCE

5 RAINBOW CHARD LEAVES

1 TABLESPOON OLIVE OIL

1 CUP (200 G) SUGAR SNAP PEAS

1 CUP (200 G) STRAWBERRIES, SLICED

FRESHLY CRACKED BLACK PEPPER

TO MAKE THE ROLLED BUTTER:

Blend 1 cup sesame seeds in either
a high-speed blender or a coffee
grinder until flour-like.

In a blender or food processor,
combine the sesame seed flour,
coconut oil, 1 tablespoon nutritional
yeast, sea salt, and vinegar. Process
until a buttery dough is formed.

Sprinkle some more sesame seeds
and nutritional yeast on a piece of
plastic wrap, add the butter, and roll
to form it into any shape you like
(roll, ball, square . . .).

For optimal flavor, let it rest in the
fridge for at least 24 hours.

TO MAKE THE SALAD:

Massage the broccoli florets with a
pinch of salt.

Rinse and prepare all the leafy
greens, add them to a big bowl, and
toss with the olive oil.

Add the sugar snap peas,
strawberries, and crumbles of the
rolled butter. Add salt and pepper to
taste.

Strawberry-Hazelnut Muffins

"This recipe is true to the kind of muffins we make at Rose Bakery every day. They are always naturally sweet, have a tender crumb, and are full of fruit and nuts or whatever surprises us in the pantry. It's a colorful and nutritious option to start the day."—Alison

MAKES 16 MUFFINS

- ♥ ¾ CUP PLUS 1½ TABLESPOONS (100 G) QUINOA FLOUR
- ½ CUP (100 G) ARROWROOT POWDER
- ♥ ½ CUP (60 G) ALMOND FLOUR, HOMEMADE (PAGE 14) OR STORE-BOUGHT
- ⅓ CUP PLUS 1½ TABLESPOONS (65 G) SORGHUM FLOUR
- ⅓ CUP (50 G) BROWN RICE FLOUR
- 2 TEASPOONS BAKING POWDER
- ½ TEASPOON SALT
- ½ TEASPOON CINNAMON
- ♥ ½ CUP (120 G) MASHED RIPE BANANA
- ♥ 2-INCH (5 CM) PIECE OF GINGER, PEELED AND GRATED
- ♥ 1½ TEASPOONS LEMON JUICE
- ⅓ CUP (120 G) MAPLE SYRUP
- ½ CUP PLUS 1½ TABLESPOONS (150 ML) NEUTRAL OLIVE OIL OR VEGETABLE OIL
- 2 TABLESPOONS GROUND FLAXSEEDS, SOAKED IN 6 TABLESPOONS WATER FOR 3 MINUTES
- ½ TEASPOON VANILLA EXTRACT
- ♥ ½ CUP (120 G) ALMOND MILK, HOMEMADE (SEE PAGE 2) OR STORE-BOUGHT
- ABOUT 1 CUP (100 G) HALVED SMALL STRAWBERRIES, PLUS MORE FOR GARNISH
- ½ CUP (60 G) TOASTED HAZELNUTS, CRUSHED

Preheat the oven to 350°F (180°C) and grease 16 muffin cups (or plan to make two batches).

In a large bowl, mix together the quinoa flour, arrowroot, almond flour, sorghum flour, brown rice flour, baking powder, salt, and cinnamon.

In a smaller bowl, mix the banana with the ginger, lemon juice, maple syrup, olive oil, flaxseed mixture, and vanilla extract. Add to the flour mixture, then mix in the milk. Fold in the strawberries and crushed hazelnuts (reserving some nuts for the garnish).

Fill each muffin cup three-quarters full, place 2 or 3 strawberry halves on top, and sprinkle on some hazelnuts.

Bake for 15 to 17 minutes (depending on the pan size and your oven), until a knife inserted into a muffin comes out clean.

Let cool a bit, then invert the pan to release the muffins.

Other variations: plums and poppy seeds, apricots and almonds, chocolate and cherries, dried figs and dates, blueberries and buckwheat, pumpkin and pecans, apple and spices. Add lemon or orange zest for a little brightness, a handful of polenta for crunch, or seeds for a little bite.

Vegetable Tian

"For me, a vegetable tian *is the quintessence of summer: colorful vegetables sliced thinly and layered in a dish. I like to vary the herbs I use to flavor it, depending on what I have handy in the garden. This dish is on the menu once a week during the hot days of summer." —Béa*

SERVES 4 AS A SIDE

OLIVE OIL

1 TO 2 MEDIUM EGGPLANTS, THINLY SLICED*

SEA SALT

1 MEDIUM ZUCCHINI, THINLY SLICED

BLACK PEPPER

1 MEDIUM RED ONION, PEELED AND THINLY SLICED

4 GARLIC CLOVES, PEELED AND FINELY CHOPPED

¼ CUP FINELY CHOPPED COMBINED FRESH THYME, TARRAGON, PARSLEY, AND BASIL

4 LARGE SUN-RIPENED TOMATOES, THINLY SLICED

*I prefer Italian eggplants as they are smaller than other varieties.

Preheat the oven to 300°F (150°C) and grease an 11 x 7-inch (28 x 18 cm) rectangular baking dish with the oil; set aside.

Place the slices of eggplant on a flat surface and sprinkle them with salt. Let rest for 30 minutes, and then pat them dry.

Arrange a layer of zucchini slices along one side of the baking dish, sprinkle with salt and pepper. Add a layer of onion slices next to and slightly overlapping the zucchini. Mix the garlic and herbs together, then spread a quarter of the mixture on top of the onions. Continue with a layer of tomatoes, add onion, season with salt and pepper, and add a quarter of the garlic mixture. Continue with a layer of eggplant, onion, salt and pepper, and a quarter of the garlic mixture. Add zucchini, onion, salt and pepper, and spread with the remaining garlic mixture. Finish with slices of tomatoes.

Drizzle the vegetables generously with olive oil and bake for about 2 hours, or until the vegetables are soft, checking regularly to make sure they don't burn or cook too quickly.

Serve warm as a side.

Fall

My playlist to breathe again in the fall

Just Breathe PEARL JAM
Think Good Thoughts COLBIE CAILLAT
Take It Easy JACK JOHNSON
Three Little Birds BOB MARLEY
Babylon DAVID GRAY
Living in the Moment JASON MRAZ
Let It Be PAUL MCCARTNEY
Crush DAVE MATTHEWS BAND
One INDIA ARIE
This'll Be My Year TRAIN
Defying Gravity IDINA MENZEL
Possibility Days COUNTING CROWS
Don't Worry Be Happy BOBBY MCFERRIN

Fall in France is known as la rentrée—it's the end of vacation (as you know, the French take their vacations very seriously) and the end of those hot summer nights, the big return to reality after a brief yet magical pause on life. It's a motivational time, filled with hope for a new year beginning.

Yes, a new year! I know that technically the new year begins in January, but for me, it has always started in the fall. I was born in early September, so this time of year has always symbolized new beginnings for me. Regardless of your birthday, it's a time to prepare yourself and your body for the winter months. The days get shorter, the air gets cooler, and it's time to get back to school, back to work, or simply back to reality. Like spring, the fall is a period of transition. It's so important to take care of the body to give it the fuel it needs to take on the cold, lack of light, and fatigue that often define winter.

According to Chinese medicine, we're heading from yang season to yin season and, in Ayurvedic terms, from pitta season to vata season. We need to deal with this changeover smoothly and attentively so that we don't tire out our livers or kidneys. Going straight from light salads and cold drinks to hot, thick soups and comfort foods will be a shock to the system. Instead, we need to nourish ourselves with healthy and detoxifying foods, and gradually replace raw and light foods with more cooked and heavier fare as the weather gets colder. A tip: Take advantage of end-of-summer fruits and vegetables as much as possible before your adventures with winter squash, apples, and mushrooms begin.

Reinvent yourself

In the fall, we need to reflect on what we want or need to get rid of in our lives. This means foods, of course, but also toxic situations that are polluting us. It may be the time to start doing yoga or working out if we've stopped, or simply take the time to breathe and think. Fall is really a time of reflection, the time to start from scratch and reinvent ourselves all over again.

Oh My Gourde!
How not to kill yourself while cutting winter squash

Fall is a dangerous time of year. Cutting winter squash is a perilous task. I know this because I have admittedly spent several autumns and winters with my hands covered in Band-Aids. Here's your official squash-slicing survival guide.

How to cut a butternut

Grab a good cutting board and cut off both ends of the squash with a good knife. Cut the squash in half vertically. Warning: this is not easy, so muster all the strength you have (or the strength of a kind neighbor, friend, or significant other), and good luck! You can do it! I believe in you!

Remove the seeds with a spoon. Cut the squash into horizontal slices around 1 inch (2.5 cm) thick. Use a small knife to cut off the skin, leaving only the "meat." Cut the slices again into small 1-inch (2.5 cm) cubes.

Cooking squash

First, wash your squash well! This may mean scrubbing with a brush—they can get down and dirty. To roast, preheat the oven to 350°F (180°C) place the entire squash in the oven, and bake for 5 to 10 minutes. Then, do either of the following:

Cut the squash in half and remove the seeds. Add coconut oil, salt, and pepper and place the squash halves cut side down onto a baking sheet. Continue to cook for 20 to 30 minutes, until soft.

Cut the squash in half and remove the seeds, then cut it into 1-inch (2.5 cm) slices. Spread with coconut oil, salt, and pepper and bake until tender, 15 to 20 minutes, then flip over and bake for another 5 to 10 minutes.

Seasonal produce

FRUIT

Apples

Blackberries

Figs

Grapes

Oranges

Pears

VEGGIES

Beets

Broccoli

Cabbage

Cauliflower

Celery root

Chard

Endive

Jerusalem artichokes

Leeks

Mâche / Lamb's lettuce

Parsnips

Potatoes

Spinach

Sweet potatoes

Turnips

Winter squash

Yoga for Digestion

by Marc Holzman

Marc Holzman and I grew up in neighboring towns in New Jersey, but I found him in Paris, France (isn't life funny?). I quickly became addicted to his unique style of yoga that is gentle and challenging at the same time. Marc's yoga classes are like drugs—I always leave in a euphoric state and feel good from my head to my toes (sometimes both are in the same place at the same time!). Marc is an expert in Ayurveda, AKA "the science of life." Physical yoga postures are important, but Ayurveda blends the physical with the spiritual, the mental, and the emotional. In the fall, many people experience digestive discomfort due to the change of seasons, the change in temperature outside, and the stress associated with returning to work or school. So I asked Marc to give us his tips for conquering la rentrée in Ayurvedic style!

Autumn season is vata season! As the hot summer months of pitta begin to yield to the colder autumn months of vata, the attributes of this season mirror those of the vata individual: dry, rough, mobile, cold, and light.

Ayurveda places a high emphasis on digestion as the key to good health. Stoking your *agni* (digestive fire) is critical for individuals of ALL *doshas* (constitutions), especially for vata individuals who are already prone to digestive disorders like constipation. As temperatures outside begin to drop during autumn (in the outer ecosystem), we want to make sure our inner ecosystem is in tip-top shape in the digestion department.—Marc

1. CHILD'S POSE—BALASANA

Kneel on the floor, big toes together, and widen your knees slightly. Bow forward between the knees for ten breaths. This pose compresses the abdomen and massages the internal organs. For more intensity, fold a blanket under your belly.

2. WIND REMOVING POSE—PAVANAMUKTASANA

Lie on your back, draw your right knee toward your chest, and take five full breaths. Release and repeat with your left knee. Repeat several times, occasionally bringing both knees in simultaneously. This pose massages the ascending and descending colon, so it's aptly named.

1

2

3

3. RECLINED TWIST— JATHARA PARIVARTANASANA

Lying on your back, bend both knees and drop them to each side, looking over your opposite shoulder. Repeat several times, holding each side for five long breaths. This aids in flushing fluids through the system and stimulates digestion.

4. CAT COW

On all fours with straight arms, inhale and arch your back (stick your butt out; lift your chest and gaze). This is the cow position ④. Exhale, look at your belly, and round your upper and lower back completely, like a scared cat ⑤. Repeat slowly for ten repetitions in synch with the breath. Slow movement between these two poses helps gently massage and bring circulation to your abdominal organs. It also gently stretches the spine and helps relieve tension there that can disrupt good digestion.

4

5

5. HERO POSE—VIRASANA

Kneel on the mat with toes pointing straight behind you and sit between your heels (knees close together) ⑥. If this is too intense on your knees, you can also sit on a lift (block or blanket) under the sit bones. Not only does this pose relieve heaviness in the belly from bloating, it also stimulates the points along the stomach meridian (acupuncture points), which runs directly up the center of the leg between the second toe and the top of the thigh.

marcholzman.com

6

Fabulous Fall Tart

The French have mastered the art of the tart. They fill crispy shells with seasonal ingredients and somehow find the perfect balance between consistency and flavor. This tart is gluten-free but still crisp, thanks to a beautiful marriage between chickpea flour and almond flour. This tart is "buttery" (merci beaucoup, coconut oil!) and rich enough in both protein (thanks, chickpeas and almonds!) and taste to be a meal on its own. Bon appé-tart!

MAKES 1 TART, SERVES 4 TO 8 PEOPLE

FOR THE CRUST:

¾ CUP (60 G) CHICKPEA FLOUR

♥ ⅓ CUP (45 G) ALMOND FLOUR, HOMEMADE (PAGE 14) OR STORE-BOUGHT

2 TABLESPOONS (20 G) ARROWROOT POWDER

1 TEASPOON CHOPPED FRESH THYME

1 TEASPOON CHOPPED FRESH ROSEMARY

SALT AND PEPPER TO TASTE

3 TABLESPOONS COLD WATER

♥ 2 TABLESPOONS LIQUID COCONUT OIL

FOR THE VEGETABLE FILLING:

♥ 1 TABLESPOON COCONUT OIL

1 SMALL RED ONION

½ CUP (50 G) JERUSALEM ARTICHOKES

♥ 2 CARROTS

½ HEAD OF CAULIFLOWER

1 PARSNIP

ONE 2-INCH (5 CM) SLICE OF CELERY ROOT

½ CUP (50 G) DICED BUTTERNUT SQUASH (SEE PAGE 141)

SALT TO TASTE

2 HANDFULS OF FRESH SPINACH

TO MAKE THE CRUST:

Mix the dry ingredients in a large bowl. Add the water and liquid coconut oil and blend with a spoon until it forms a thick dough. Form the dough into a ball with your hands, then cover and refrigerate for 30 minutes while the vegetables cook. If you're impatient, 5 to 10 minutes in the freezer will also do the trick!

TO PREPARE THE VEGETABLE FILLING:

Preheat the oven to 375°F (190°C). Warm the coconut oil in a pan for a few seconds over medium heat to make it liquid. Peel and cut the onion, Jerusalem artichokes, carrots, cauliflower, and parsnip into 1-inch (2.5 cm) cubes, then mix them with the squash, coconut oil, and salt. Add the spinach, saving a few spinach leaves for the final touches. Place into an oven-safe dish and bake for 30 to 40 minutes.

TO ASSEMBLE THE TART:

Remove the crust dough from the fridge and spread it out with your hands into a pie pan. Pierce in several different spots with a fork so that the crust can "breathe." Bake for around 15 minutes. Once the crust and vegetables have cooked, place the vegetable mixture into the crust and return to the oven for around 5 more minutes. When you remove the tart from the oven, place a few spinach leaves on top so they melt over the warm tart. Slice and serve with a side salad drizzled with walnut oil, apple cider vinegar, and fresh parsley.

Note: This tart is best with a mix of several vegetables, but if you don't want to buy all of them (or spend time peeling and chopping all of them) you can pick just three or four from the list—that works, too!

Poivrons Farcis (Stuffed Bell Peppers with Quinoa)

These stuffed peppers are a great way to impress guests (or yourself!). Feel free to fill with other grains or veggies or pour your favorite sauce over the top. If you need inspiration, check out my sauce recipes (page 8) and list of healthy grains (page xii). You've got the right stuffing, baby!

SERVES 2

FOR THE STUFFING:

- ♥ ½ CUP (60 G) DRY RED, WHITE, OR A MIX OF RED, WHITE, AND BLACK QUINOA (AROUND 1½ CUPS COOKED)
- ♥ 2 CARROTS
- 1 CELERY STALK
- 1 RED ONION
- 2 GARLIC CLOVES
- ♥ 1 TABLESPOON COCONUT OIL
- ½ CUP (100 G) CHOPPED BROCCOLI
- 2 HANDFULS OF BABY SPINACH
- ½ CUP (80 G) COOKED CHICKPEAS (SEE PAGE 18) OR DRAINED AND RINSED CANNED CHICKPEAS
- 3 SUN-DRIED TOMATOES, CHOPPED
- 2 TABLESPOONS CHOPPED FRESH HERBS: PARSLEY, BASIL, MINT, CILANTRO . . . PICK YOUR FAVORITES!
- A PINCH OF CAYENNE PEPPER (OR, IF YOU'RE BRAVE, SEVERAL PINCHES)
- 1 TEASPOON COCONUT AMINOS OR TAMARI
- 2 RED BELL PEPPERS

DON'T cook the quinoa according to package directions. Cook according to MY directions (see page 18).

TO MAKE THE STUFFING:

Peel or wash, then grate or dice the carrots. Chop the celery. Peel and chop the onion and garlic.

Add the coconut oil to a sauté pan with the garlic and onion and sauté for 1 to 2 minutes over medium heat. Add the carrots, celery, and broccoli and cook for a few more minutes. (Note: If the veggies start to burn, lower the heat and add a splash of water to the pan.)

Add the spinach, mix together once with a spoon or spatula, then turn off the heat.

Transfer the mixture to a bowl with the quinoa, chickpeas, sun-dried tomatoes, herbs, cayenne, and coconut aminos and mix well.

TO MAKE THE PEPPERS:

Preheat the oven to 350°F. "Guillotine" the peppers (i.e., chop off the tops with a knife). Remove the membranes and seeds, but keep the bell pepper "pocket" intact.

Bake the peppers on a baking sheet for 10 to 15 minutes, until they begin to soften. Remove the peppers from the oven and stuff them to the top with the quinoa-vegetable mixture. Bake for another 20 to 30 minutes, until the peppers are cooked through and the quinoa has begun to brown at the top. Serve with a green salad.

CAYENNE PEPPER
Hot stuff!

Cayenne pepper lends a spicy flavor to any dish. It fights pain from conditions like arthritis and combats colds, flu, and bad bacteria. It's a great detox food that boosts metabolism, it aids digestion by increasing the secretion of enzymes, and it can even boost a poor appetite. I recommend adding cayenne to everything!

Pasta au Gratin

I'll be honest with you—we're friends by now, oui?—this is just a swankier French way of making good old mac 'n' cheese. Like macaroni and cheese, French gratins are the ultimate comfort food when the cold weather arrives. Both dishes feature similar ingredients—butter, milk, cheese, and flour—mixed with pasta (or potatoes). My pasta au gratin is true comfort food—you'll feel comfort even after you digest it! This is a great dish to make for kids, then add a few more "adult" ingredients. (I meant truffle oil, greens, or almond crumble—what were you thinking?)

SERVES 2 ADULTS OR 3 TO 4 CHILDREN

1 MEDIUM BUTTERNUT SQUASH (OR AROUND 1 CUP OF SQUASH, CUT INTO 1-INCH/2.5 CM CUBES)

1 GARLIC CLOVE

1 TABLESPOON OLIVE OIL

♥ 2 TEASPOONS MISO PASTE

1 TABLESPOON NUTRITIONAL YEAST

SALT AND PEPPER TO TASTE

2 BOWLS OF COOKED PASTA (PREFERABLY QUINOA, BROWN RICE, OR BUCKWHEAT BASED; THIS IS ALSO SPECTACULAR WITH MUNG BEAN NOODLES)

FOR AN ADULT MAKEOVER:

♥ ¼ CUP ALMOND CRUMBLE (PAGE 7)

2 HANDFULS OF BABY SPINACH

A DRIZZLE OF TRUFFLE OIL

TO MAKE THE BUTTERNUT SAUCE:

Peel and cut the squash into cubes (see my advice on page 141 for how to complete this step injury-free), then steam for 7 to 10 minutes, until fork tender. Peel the garlic. Blend the squash, garlic, olive oil, miso paste, nutritional yeast (if using), salt, and pepper in a blender until creamy. (Alternatively, add the coconut oil, garlic salt, and pepper and roast in the oven, then add the rest of the ingredients.)

TO ASSEMBLE THE GRATIN:

Add the pasta to a deep baking dish. Drown the pasta in the sauce (this is not only allowed, but obligatory!). You can serve it to the kids as it is, or top with almond crumble and place into the oven at 400°F (200°C) to bake for 5 to 10 minutes, until the crumble is golden brown and the dish is warm. Serve on a bed of spinach and drizzle with truffle oil.

Don't hesitate to go nuts with the butternut sauce, but save leftovers to eat within 3 days. Pour over pasta or other grains for a quick meal; thin out with some veggie broth (store-bought or made from a bouquet garni—see page 161) and warm on the stove for instant soup; or let it thicken in the fridge and serve as a dip or spread.

Sobeautiful Soba Salad

Soba is a Japanese noodle made of buckwheat (and sometimes wheat, so check the label to be sure they're gluten-free). Rich in protein, soba can be eaten cold or hot, but I personally prefer it cold in salad form. This salad is nourishing enough for a main course, but still refreshing and light. It keeps well and loves to travel! Take it with you on a picnic or to the office bento-style! Think: a much greener and cleaner version of cup o' noodles (my former favorite "exotic" dish—true story).

MAKES 1 SERVING

2 OUNCES (50 G; AROUND ¼ OF THE AVERAGE PACKAGE) DRY GLUTEN-FREE SOBA NOODLES

♥ 1 LARGE CARROT

½ RED BELL PEPPER

2 TEASPOONS TOASTED SESAME OIL

♥ 1 TABLESPOON LEMON OR LIME JUICE

♥ 1 TEASPOON COCONUT AMINOS OR TAMARI

♥ 2 TEASPOON MISO PASTE

1 TABLESPOON CHOPPED FRESH CHIVES

GARNISHES:

1 TABLESPOON TOASTED SESAME SEEDS OR GOMASI-OH-LÀ-LÀ! (PAGE 7)

♥ ½ AVOCADO, PITTED, PEELED, AND SLICED (OPTIONAL)

Cook the noodles according to package directions, being careful not to overcook (they'll get mushy!). Drain in a sieve and rinse with cold water.

Peel and grate the carrot. Wash the red bell pepper, remove the membrane and seeds, and cut it into thin slices. In a small bowl, whisk together the sesame oil, lemon juice, coconut aminos, and miso. In a large bowl, mix together the noodles, veggies, and chives. Add the sesame oil mixture and toss. Top with the sesame seeds and serve with avocado slices (if using).

BUCKWHEAT
Go buck wild!

Despite its name, buckwheat isn't part of the wheat family. In fact, it's not even a grain, but a fruit seed! And what a sneaky seed it is—it looks like a grain, cooks like a grain, tastes like a grain, but it's the seed of a fruit in the same family as rhubarb. It's naturally gluten-free, ranks low on the glycemic scale, and is high in protein, particularly in the essential amino acids lysine and arginine. What a great bang for your buckwheat! Try buckwheat groats (whole buckwheat kernels) in your morning porridge, cook kasha (groats' roasted cousin) for dinner, or use buckwheat flour in baked goods for a rich flavor. What the buckwheat are you waiting for? Go eat some!

Sweet Potato Boulettes

Boulettes is a cute French word that means "little balls." These little balls of love are an interesting twist on traditional falafel or a great way to top pasta as a veggie version of hearty "meatballs." These are great drizzled with Tahini Hollandaise (page 8) and served with a side salad or grain dish. Or add to a pita, drizzle with tahini, add some roasted eggplant and hummus, and voilà! A healthy falafel sandwich!

MAKES 2 SERVINGS

- ♥ 1 LARGE SWEET POTATO OR 2 SMALLER SWEET POTATOES (TO YIELD AROUND 1 CUP OF 1-INCH/2.5 CM CUBES)
- 1 GARLIC CLOVE
- ½ CUP (60 G) CHICKPEA FLOUR
- ♥ 1 TABLESPOON LEMON JUICE
- 1 TABLESPOON CHOPPED FRESH PARSLEY
- 1 TABLESPOON CHOPPED FRESH CILANTRO
- ¼ TEASPOON CUMIN
- ¼ TEASPOON CORIANDER
- SALT AND PEPPER TO TASTE
- WATER IF NEEDED
- ♥ 1 TABLESPOON COCONUT OIL
- 1 TABLESPOON SESAME SEEDS (OR PINE NUTS IF YOU WANT TO SPLURGE!)

Preheat the oven to 400°F (200°C). Roast the whole sweet potato for 30 minutes to 1 hour, until tender. Let cool for a few minutes, then peel. Add to a bowl and mash with a fork. Peel and thinly slice the garlic. In a separate bowl, mix the garlic, chickpea flour, lemon juice, parsley, cilantro, cumin, coriander, salt, and pepper. Mix in the sweet potato mash to form a soft and sticky dough. If necessary, add some water. Form small balls with your hands. Tip (from my grandmother!): Dip your hands into a bowl of ice and water before forming the dough balls—they will be less sticky!

Grease a baking sheet with the coconut oil. Roll the balls in the sesame seeds to cover them lightly, then place on the sheet. Bake for around 20 minutes, then turn so that they are cooked evenly throughout.

♥ BEST FRIEND FOOD
Sweet potato

Sweet potatoes are my ultimate comfort food. They're sweet and hearty, yet nutritious at the same time. As with all carbs, don't abuse them, but sweet potatoes are much lower on the glycemic index than regular potatoes, so they keep blood sugar and weight balanced. These potatoes are also so sweet . . . for the intestines (*très* anti-inflammatory), on the skin (rich in beta-carotene!), and for the entire body (rich in antioxidants, vitamins, minerals, and fiber!). Choose sweet potatoes with very orange flesh—the more orange it is, the more packed with beta-carotene—but white and purple sweet potatoes are also flavorful and wholesome.

Spaghetti Squash Puttanesca

I think Mother Nature must have some Italian roots—she wants us all to be able to enjoy pasta, so she created a squash . . . in the form of spaghetti! Cut the squash in half, put it in the oven, cook it, and . . . pesto! I mean, presto! (Though feel free to top this with pesto instead of or in addition to the puttanesca sauce; it's delicioso!*) This recipe is perfect for this transition from summer to winter! Serve with a green salad to boost enzymes that will help with digestion.*

SERVES 2

1 SPAGHETTI SQUASH
WATER OR OIL

FOR THE PUTTANESCA SAUCE:

1 MEDJOOL DATE
4 SUN-DRIED TOMATOES
1 LEEK
2 LARGE TOMATOES OR 1 CUP (200 G) CHERRY TOMATOES
½ RED ONION
2 GARLIC CLOVES
2 TABLESPOONS OLIVE OIL
5 OLIVES, PITTED THEN HALVED OR CHOPPED
¼ CUP CHOPPED FRESH BASIL
2 TABLESPOONS CHOPPED FRESH PARSLEY
½ TEASPOON OREGANO (CHOPPED FRESH OR DRIED)
SALT AND PEPPER TO TASTE

GARNISHES:

♥ 1 TO 2 TABLESPOON ALMOND CRUMBLE (PAGE 7)
A FEW OLIVES, PITTED THEN HALVED

Preheat the oven to 350°F (180°C). Cut the squash in half and remove the seeds. Place both halves, open side down, on a baking sheet. Add water or oil so that it doesn't stick. Bake for around 45 minutes, until the squash is fork tender. Remove from the oven.

TO MAKE THE SAUCE:

Soak the date and the sun-dried tomatoes for around 5 minutes in warm water to soften them. Peel and pit the date, then chop both into small pieces.

Clean the leek and cut off the white part toward the bottom. Slice it in half, then slice thinly. Cut the tomatoes into small pieces. Peel and chop the onion and garlic.

Add the olive oil to a small saucepan over low heat and add the leek, onion, and garlic. Cook over low heat for 3 to 4 minutes. Add the date, sun-dried tomatoes, tomatoes, olives, basil, parsley, oregano, and a pinch of salt and pepper. Cook for just a few minutes, until the tomatoes become mushy, but the sauce is still fresh and chunky.

You can top the roasted squash halves with the sauce or remove the "noodles" with a fork, add to a bowl, and then top with the sauce for a more pasta-like look and feel. Before serving, top with the almond crumble and a few more olives.

SQUASH
The face of fall

Squash is anti-inflammatory and helps balance blood sugar. It's rich in alpha and beta-carotene, vitamins A, C, B6, and K, manganese, potassium, copper, and magnesium.

Its phytonutrients and antioxidants will keep your skin glowing, and its folate is great for women, particularly before and during pregnancy (oh baby, it's cold outside, AKA baby-making season!).

Store your squash in a cool, dry place and it will last for months, or peel and chop up a bunch at one time then store in the fridge for a few days.

Champignons of Champions: Buckwheat Bowl with Mushrooms and Pistou

This dish is hearty and rich thanks to the protein-packed buckwheat and flavorful seasonal mushrooms. I recommend a mix of different types—think chanterelles, portobellos, oyster mushrooms, shiitake, cremini . . . Pick your favorites and have funghi!

SERVES 1

¼ CUP (45 G) RAW BUCKWHEAT GROATS OR KASHA

½ CUP WATER

1 CUP (50 G) MUSHROOMS

½ RED ONION

1 GARLIC CLOVE

♥ 1 TABLESPOON COCONUT OIL

1 TABLESPOON CHOPPED FRESH PARSLEY

1 HANDFUL OF SPINACH

2 TO 3 TABLESPOONS PARSLEY PISTOU (PAGE 8)

SALT AND PEPPER TO TASTE

FRESH PARSLEY

Bring the buckwheat to a boil with the water, then cover and simmer gently until the water is absorbed, around 15 minutes.

Wash the mushrooms very well and cut them into small pieces (unless you're using chanterelles—keep them whole!). Peel and chop the onion and garlic. In a saucepan or Dutch oven over medium heat, heat the coconut oil, add the onion and garlic, and sauté until the onions are translucent. Add the mushrooms and sauté for around 5 minutes. Add the cooked buckwheat and sauté for another 3 to 5 minutes. Turn off the heat, then mix in the spinach and the parsley pistou. Add salt and pepper to taste. Garnish with parsley. Serve hot, or eat it cold the next day.

MUSHROOMS
Let's get wild!

Mushrooms are medicine! These sometimes poisonous, sometimes ugly, but usually enjoyable veggies are loaded with nutritional benefits. Mushrooms are very low in calories, but they are also extremely tasty and among the "meatiest" foods in the plant kingdom. Mushrooms are a great source of vitamin D and support the immune system.

That said, it's hard to simply talk about "mushrooms," since there are so many different kinds of mushrooms—more than 500 in France alone!—I'd have to write an encyclopedia to explain them all in detail. In the meantime, *voilà*: my short list of favorite fungi for both flavor and health benefits: *champignons de Paris* (white button mushrooms), portobellos, shiitakes, oyster mushrooms, chanterelles, black trumpet mushrooms, and *reishi* (the new star of the nutrition world for its antioxidant, anti-inflammatory, and even anti-cancer properties—found in teas and nutritional supplements rather than stir-fries).

So Chic Sushi

Why should sushi be reserved for takeout and trendy restaurants? Make it chez vous! These nori rolls are all veggie-filled, but still savory and satisfying. Nori rolls make for an easy lunch at home or on the go, eaten in "burrito" form or cut into slices like "real" sushi. This raw "rice" is made from daikon radish (but feel free to substitute parsnips or turnips, or use brown rice instead).

MAKES 1 NORI ROLL (PREPARE 2 TO 3 ROLLS PER PERSON FOR A MAIN COURSE)

FOR THE "RICE":

1 DAIKON RADISH, OR 1 SMALL PARSNIP OR TURNIP

1 TABLESPOON TAHINI OR ALMOND BUTTER

♥ 1 TEASPOON MISO PASTE

♥ 1 TEASPOON COCONUT AMINOS OR TAMARI

♥ 1 TEASPOON GRATED FRESH GINGER

♥ 1 TABLESPOON LEMON JUICE

1 DATE, SOAKED AND PITTED (OPTIONAL, FOR A SWEET TOUCH!)

FOR THE SUSHI:

1 CUCUMBER

♥ ¼ AVOCADO

♥ 1 CARROT

1 RED BELL PEPPER

1 SHEET OF NORI (PREFERABLY RAW, UNTOASTED)

1 HANDFUL OF SALAD GREENS

2 TEASPOONS CHOPPED FRESH CHIVES

WASABI PASTE (OPTIONAL, FOR A SPICY KICK!)

FOR THE DIPPING SAUCE:

1 TEASPOON COCONUT AMINOS OR TAMARI

2 TEASPOONS TOASTED SESAME OIL

♥ ½ TEASPOON MINCED FRESH GINGER

♥ 1 TABLESPOON LEMON JUICE

To make the "rice," peel and chop the radish into small pieces, then add them to a food processor. Add the rest of the "rice" ingredients and pulse until mixed through, but not liquid or blended. It should look like rice!

Stir together the dipping sauce ingredients in a small bowl.

Peel and cut the cucumber and avocado into thin slices. Wash or peel then grate the carrot. Clean the red bell pepper and slice it thinly. See the remaining instructions on the opposite page.

DAIKON
Totally radish!

Daikon, AKA "white radish" in Japanese, has been used as medicine for centuries in Asia. Daikon is low in calories and high in water content, B vitamins, vitamin C, calcium, potassium, and fiber. It's great for fragile stomachs since it is packed with enzymes that aid digestion.

♥ BEST FRIEND FOOD
Seaweed

Now I understand why the Little Mermaid had such beautiful skin: seaweed! It may look odd and smell fishy, but seaweed is one of the most beautifying foods on the planet. It makes the skin glow and infuses the entire body with vitamins, protein, fiber, omega-3s, and essential minerals (iodine, potassium, iron, calcium . . .). Ariel can also attribute her flawless figure to seaweed, which helps rid the body of heavy metals, reduce water retention (and thus, cellulite!), and accelerate weight loss. Rich in chlorophyll, your new friend from under the sea helps circulation, oxygenates the entire body, gets rid of toxins, and allows you to easily meet Prince Charming after a terrible storm. OK, I can't confirm that last part, but the rest is true—seaweed is a buried ocean treasure!

Step 1 Place the nori sheet onto a plate. Add a generous amount of "rice" (around ¼ cup/60 g) and pat down so that it covers most of the sheet, leaving around 1 inch (2.5 cm) empty on each side.

Step 2 In the center of the roll, add the avocado, veggies, salad greens, and chives.

Step 3 Wet your fingers, then roll the nori sheet, pushing down firmly as you roll so that it comes together tightly. Add some water to the top and bottom edges when you're done rolling so it sticks together.

Step 4 Cut the nori roll in half or in slices around 1 to 2 inches (2 to 3 cm) thick. Serve with the dipping sauce and wasabi, if using.

Baby Dahl

This is my spiced-up version of kitchari, a traditional Ayurvedic meal. It's a wonderful way to detoxify the body any time, but particularly in between seasons. It's a nourishing and warming meal. Red lentils are easy to digest, and they cook in just minutes! Save leftovers to eat the next day warmed over the stove or to eat cold scooped on top of a salad or in a wrap. Enjoy it, dahl face!

MAKES 1 SERVING

- ♥ 1 CARROT
- ♥ 1 SMALL SWEET POTATO
- ½ RED ONION
- 1 GARLIC CLOVE
- ♥ 1 TABLESPOON COCONUT OIL
- ¼ CUP (50G) DRY RED LENTILS
- ♥ ¼ TEASPOON TURMERIC
- ⅛ TEASPOON CURRY POWDER
- ♥ ⅛ TEASPOON MINCED FRESH OR GROUND GINGER
- SALT AND PEPPER TO TASTE
- A PINCH OF CAYENNE PEPPER (OPTIONAL)
- ♥ ¼ CUP (50 ML) *LAIT DE* COCONUT (PAGE 2) OR BPA-FREE CANNED COCONUT MILK
- A HANDFUL OF CHOPPED FRESH PARSLEY AND CILANTRO, FOR GARNISH

Peel and cut the carrot and sweet potato into small pieces. Peel and chop the onion and garlic.

Warm the coconut oil over medium heat in a small pot over the stove. Add the garlic and onion and sauté for around 1 minute, until the onions are translucent. Add the carrot, sweet potato, and red lentils, and mix together. Add the turmeric, curry, ginger, and a pinch each of salt, pepper, and cayenne (if using) and mix again.

Pour enough water over the mixture to cover the vegetables, lower the heat, and simmer for around 15 minutes, until the veggies and the lentils are soft. Add the coconut milk and simmer for another minute or so. Serve warm over a bowl of brown rice or quinoa, or eat on its own. Garnish with parsley and cilantro.

Tips: Feel free to add other vegetables (broccoli, cauliflower, kale . . .) toward the end of the cooking process to make a hearty stew.

To turn this into a soup, add more liquid (coconut milk or water) and blend with an immersion blender or Vitamix. Store in the refrigerator for 2 to 3 days.

SOUP
Boost your immunity!

Fall calls for a strong immune system. The temperature is changing, and it's a busy time of year for most of us. Soup, stew, dahl, and other variations of puréed perfection are great ways to warm the body and protect against illnesses that tend to creep up during this time of year. Just think of soup as a tasty, hearty . . . flu shot!

♥ BEST FRIEND FOOD
Turmeric

Warning: Turmeric will turn your hands, your dishes, and likely your kitchen counters ORANGE. But it's a small price to pay for its wealth of health benefits. Rich in curcumin, turmeric is anti-inflammatory, liver-supporting, digestion-friendly, immune-boosting, and filled with antioxidants. It fights against arthritis, Alzheimer's, and even certain forms of cancer. You may use turmeric in sweet and savory dishes. A tip: Add black pepper to anything with turmeric to enhance your body's absorption of curcumin.

Beauty Bourguignon

This thick stew from the Burgundy region, popularized by Julia Child, is usually made of beef braised in red wine with beef broth, bacon, garlic, onions, and mushrooms. I know what you are thinking: "Sacre bleu!" (yes, you're thinking in French—way to go!) "There is nothing green about this!" But have no fear; you can beef up this classic recipe without bringing home any bacon.

This "Bourguignon" is beauty food at its finest. Beets cleanse the body of toxins, making skin radiant, and they are packed with folate, vitamins A and C, iron, potassium, manganese, and fiber to beautify the body from the inside out. Root vegetables are grounding, healing, "meaty," and starchy, making them perfect for cold-weather cuisine. The stew also features a bouquet garni (a bundle of herbs tied together with a string), veggies, broth, a thick, "meaty" texture, and even a deep red color resembling wine. Let's call it BourguiYUM!

**MAKES 1 HEARTY SERVING OR
2 SMALLER SERVINGS**

BOUQUET GARNI:

1 OR 2 THYME SPRIGS

1 OR 2 BAY LEAVES

A HANDFUL OF FRESH PARSLEY

1 ROSEMARY SPRIG

A FEW SAGE LEAVES

1 MEDIUM RED BEET

1 LEEK

1 TABLESPOON OLIVE OIL

1 GARLIC CLOVE, PEELED AND MINCED

½ RED ONION, PEELED AND CHOPPED

♥ 1 CARROT, SLICED

1 CELERY STALK, CUT INTO ¼-INCH (.5 CM) SLICES

SALT AND PEPPER TO TASTE

¼ TEASPOON HERBES DE PROVENCE BLEND

¼ CUP MUSHROOMS (YOUR FAVORITE VARIETY; SIMPLE WHITE BUTTON MUSHROOMS ARE PERFECT), WASHED AND THINLY SLICED

½ CUP COOKED LENTILS (SEE PAGE 18) OR DRAINED AND RINSED CANNED LENTILS

1 TOMATO, CHOPPED

1 TABLESPOON ARROWROOT POWDER

A HANDFUL OF CHOPPED FRESH PARSLEY, FOR GARNISH

Tie the bouquet garni herbs together with a string or place them in a small tea sachet.* Wash and peel the beet, then cut into ½-inch (1 cm) cubes. Lightly steam for around 5 minutes, until the beet softens just a bit but still feels too hard to eat.

Cut off the "hairy" end of the leek and the green part of the stem. Wash the remaining white part very well. Cut in half vertically, then cut horizontally into around ½-inch (1 cm) thick slices.

Add the olive oil to a saucepan over low heat. Add the garlic and onion and sauté for 1 to 2 minutes. Add the steamed beet, the leek, carrot, celery, salt, pepper, and herbes de Provence. Cover the vegetables with water and add the bouquet garni. Bring to a boil, then reduce the heat to low, cover, and simmer for around 5 minutes.

Add the mushrooms, lentils, tomato, and arrowroot to the stew and continue to simmer, adding water as necessary so it doesn't stick. Once the beets are fully cooked (fork tender) and the stew is thick and aromatic, ladle into bowls and serve garnished with parsley.

Feel free to wipe your plate clean with crusty *Le Pain Quotidien* gluten-free bread (page 40).

Note: You are free to add some red wine here. If you're on a detox, it's not the best option, but a little bit to enhance the flavor of this dish is a nice treat.

*Tip: The bouquet garni also makes an easy veggie bouillon. Just add around 1 cup (250 ml) of hot water, cover, and simmer over the stove until fragrant. You can store this in the fridge and use all week to make soups, cook grains, or simply sip before a meal.

French Lentil Salad with Beets and Spiced Vinaigrette

We all love summer salads, but when autumn comes, we need more filling foods, oui? Enter . . . the lentil! This salad offers a great balance between the richness of the lentils, the lightness of the arugula, and the sweetness of the beets and raisins. It's great for a transitional lunch as the seasons change and is wonderful eaten warm or cold.

SERVES 2

FOR THE SPICY VINAIGRETTE:

2 TABLESPOONS MUSTARD VINAIGRETTE (PAGE 10)

2 TEASPOONS WALNUT OIL (OPTIONAL)

A PINCH OF AS MANY OF THESE AS YOU HAVE IN YOUR KITCHEN: CARDAMOM, CUMIN, CORIANDER, TURMERIC, GINGER, CINNAMON, CLOVES, NUTMEG, CAYENNE PEPPER, BLACK PEPPER

FOR THE SALAD:

1 LARGE BEET

½ CUP (50 G) SMALL CAULIFLOWER FLORETS (OPTIONAL)

♥ 1 TEASPOON LIQUID COCONUT OIL (OPTIONAL, IF USING CAULIFLOWER)

SALT AND PEPPER TO TASTE

2 TABLESPOONS WALNUTS

½ CUP (100 G) DRY LENTILS OR SPROUTED GREEN LENTILS, COOKED (SEE PAGE 18)

2 HANDFULS OF ARUGULA

♥ 1 CARROT, GRATED

2 TABLESPOONS CHOPPED FRESH FLAT PARSLEY

2 TABLESPOONS CHOPPED FRESH HERBS (CILANTRO, BASIL, CHERVIL, MINT . . .)

2 TABLESPOONS RAISINS, SOAKED IN HOT WATER IF HARD

Combine the vinaigrette ingredients in a covered bowl or glass and shake until well mixed.

Peel the beet and chop into small cubes. Steam for 15 to 20 minutes, until fork tender. Drain and rinse.

If using the cauliflower, preheat the oven to 375°F (190°C).

Meanwhile, in a roasting pan, drizzle the cauliflower with the coconut oil and add salt and pepper. Roast for 10 to 15 minutes, until cooked yet still crunchy. Just before removing from the oven, add the walnuts for around 2 to 3 minutes, until toasted (but not burned!). If not using the cauliflower, toast the walnuts in the oven or on the stovetop.

Drain and rinse the lentils and add the lentils to a bowl. Shake up the vinaigrette again and mix it in. Add the arugula, grated carrot, parsley, herbs, raisins, and steamed beets and mix well.

Serve topped with the walnuts and roasted cauliflower (if using).

Make sure to save some of this to eat as leftovers—it's even better after the lentils have soaked up the dressing!

LENTILS
Protein powerhouses

Lentils are some of the wealthiest legumes out there. They're rich in macronutrients: carbohydrates and, *bien sûr*, protein. In fact, lentils are one of the best sources of vegetable protein on the planet. Their vast fortunes of minerals include potassium, phosphorous, calcium, zinc, and magnesium, and their fiber content will keep you full for hours on end. You can inherit their health benefits in many different forms—dress them to the nines in hearty salads or keep them down to earth in simple soups, stews, or spreads. They're definitely a great investment in your health and well-being!

Roll out the red lentils

Red lentils are the sweetest lentil—both in taste and in their relationship with your digestive system. This easy-to-digest variety has a much shorter cooking time than other lentils, doesn't need to be soaked ahead of time, and turns mushy quickly, so it's especially great for soups and stews.

Pancrêpes

Can't decide between a thin French crêpe and its fatter American cousin, le pancake? Try a pancrêpe! Thicker than a crêpe (and thus, much easier to make at home—no special skillet required) but thinner than a pancake, these are the perfect hybrid. Traditionally, in Brittany, sweet crêpes are made with wheat flour and savory crêpes with buckwheat flour, but hey, anything goes in la green cuisine! Buckwheat flour is so nourishing, but it can also weigh you down, so I like the contrast of the lighter, more neutral brown rice flour. If you prefer, use all buckwheat or sub in other flours like sorghum, quinoa, or millet. These work in any season topped with fresh fruit du jour, but they're perfect for a hearty breakfast, brunch, or dinner (why not?) for those bigger autumn appetites!

MAKES 8 PANCAKES (2 TO 4 SERVINGS DEPENDING ON YOUR APPETITE)

♥ 2 TABLESPOONS COCONUT OIL
½ CUP (60 G) BUCKWHEAT FLOUR
½ CUP (60 G) BROWN RICE FLOUR
1 TEASPOON BAKING POWDER
A PINCH OF SALT
1 TABLESPOON MAPLE SYRUP
♥ 1 TABLESPOON LEMON JUICE
♥ 1¼ CUPS (300 ML) ALMOND MILK, HOMEMADE (SEE PAGE 2) OR STORE-BOUGHT, OR MORE TO TASTE

CREAMY SAUCE:

♥ 2 TABLESPOONS COCONUT BUTTER OR CASHEW BUTTER, HOMEMADE (SEE PAGE 14) OR STORE-BOUGHT)
1 TABLESPOON MAPLE SYRUP
1 TABLESPOON WATER

FRUITY SAUCE:

1 CUP (200 G) CHOPPED SEASONAL FRUIT (APPLES, PEARS, CHERRIES, FIGS . . .)
♥ 1 TEASPOON LEMON JUICE
¼ TEASPOON VANILLA POWDER OR EXTRACT
¼ TEASPOON CINNAMON

OPTIONAL TOPPINGS:

1 TABLESPOON OF SWEET BUTTER (PAGE 6)
♥ 1 BANANA, SLICED THINLY
¼ CUP OF SLICED SEASONAL FRUIT
1 TABLESPOON OF TOASTED NUTS OF CHOICE
A PINCH OF CINNAMON

Warm the coconut oil over low heat until liquid. Pour into a dish and set aside.

Blend the buckwheat flour, brown rice flour, baking powder, and salt in a bowl. Add the maple syrup, lemon juice, and almond milk and mix well with a spoon. The consistency should be liquid, but thick. If you prefer thinner pancakes or crêpes, add more almond milk.

Coat a pan with some of the coconut oil and pour in a scoop of the batter, turning the pan so that a perfect circle forms. Alternatively, pour the batter into cookie cutters set in the pan—a great activity to do with kids! (Or adults—I love a good Mickey Mouse–shaped pancake now and then.) Cook for around 2 minutes, until the top starts to bubble, then remove the cutter, if using, flip the pancake with a spatula, and cook until golden brown and cooked through.

Repeat with the rest of the batter. Eat as you go, or keep them warm, arrange in a stack on the plate, and top with sweet butter, your sauce of choice, fruit, nuts, and cinnamon, and dig in!

IF MAKING THE CREAMY SAUCE:

Warm the coconut butter gently over the stove over low heat then add maple syrup and water. Pour over the pancrêpes.

IF MAKING THE FRUITY SAUCE:

You have *deux* options here: (1) Blend all ingredients in a blender until smooth and creamy. (2) Add all ingredients to a small Dutch oven or pot and cook, covered, on low heat for 5 to 10 minutes, until soft. Mash with a fork, then spoon on top of the pancrêpes.

HERE ARE A FEW FILLING OPTIONS FOR SWEET CRÊPES:

NOtella banana NOtella Spread (page 76) and banana slices

Beurre et sucre Coconut oil, coconut sugar, and lemon juice

Confiture au fraises Strawberry Coulis with Goji Berries (page 11)

Amandine Almond butter (see page 14) and seasonal fruit

Miraculous Muesli

I love a piping hot bowl of creamy oatmeal, but it can often be too heavy in the morning. The French love la crème Budwig, a mix of grains, oats, nuts, seeds, and fruit designed to both detoxify the body and replenish it with the nutrients it needs to take on the day. Here's an even greener version, perfect for busy days since it can be prepared the night before, left in the refrigerator, and in the morning—voilà!—breakfast is served! (Well, you do have to actually take it out of the refrigerator, grab a spoon, and set it on the table—butler not included.) This chilled crème is light, refreshing, and nourishing—a bowl of energy without much effort. It's a slumber party in your fridge!

SERVES 1

¼ CUP (40 G) GLUTEN-FREE OATS (OR QUINOA, BUCKWHEAT, OR BROWN RICE FLAKES)

2 TABLESPOONS RAW BUCKWHEAT GROATS

♥ ½ TABLESPOON CRUSHED ALMONDS

½ TABLESPOON CRUSHED WALNUTS

½ TABLESPOON SUNFLOWER SEEDS

½ TABLESPOON PUMPKIN SEEDS

A PINCH OF CINNAMON

1 TABLESPOON RAISINS AND/OR OTHER DRIED FRUIT, DICED (FIGS, APRICOTS . . .)

♥ ½ CUP (125 ML) APPLE JUICE

♥ ½ BANANA

½ APPLE

MULBERRIES, GOLDENBERRIES, GOJI BERRIES, OR A MIX OF ALL OF THE ABOVE (OPTIONAL, FOR A SUPERFOOD BOOST)

♥ ½ CUP (125 ML) ALMOND MILK, HOMEMADE (SEE PAGE 2) OR STORE-BOUGHT

In a bowl, mix the oats, buckwheat, almonds, walnuts, sunflower and pumpkin seeds, cinnamon, and raisins. Pour the apple juice over the mixture and stir again with a spoon. Cover and leave in the refrigerator overnight. (Soaking the nuts, seeds, and dried fruits makes them more digestible, plus the different flavors blend together for a fantastic flavor fusion.)

In the morning, peel and slice the banana, wash and chop the apple into tiny cubes, and add both to the bowl. Add mulberries if using. Pour almond milk over the top.

VARIATIONS:

The apple juice can be replaced with water or *Lait de* Plants (page 1) of choice.

Replace any of the nuts, seeds, and dried fruits with whatever you have on hand.

Top with seasonal fruits instead of or in addition to the banana and apple.

You can also top this with a few spoonfuls of coconut yogurt (page 4).

Apple Tarte Tatin

An apple tarte Tatin fresh from the oven as the weather turns colder is my idea of heaven. According to French legend, the tarte Tatin was invented by the Tatin sisters who accidentally put an apple tart into the oven upside down. They served the pie anyway, and it has become a sacred part of French national heritage (not to mention a wonderful metaphor for overcoming adversity).

Here, instead of baking the tarte "upside down," I add the filling at the very last moment. My gluten-free, butter-free version would probably have the Tatin sisters turning in their graves, but as they say, "an apple tart a day . . ." I may be flouting tradition right and left, but there is one golden (delicious) rule for eating tarte Tatin that I enforce: It must be served and eaten warm!

MAKES 1 LARGE TART (6 TO 8 SLICES)

FOR THE CRUST:

½ CUP (60 G) CHICKPEA FLOUR

♥ ¼ CUP (30 G) ALMOND FLOUR, HOMEMADE (PAGE 14) OR STORE-BOUGHT

2 TABLESPOONS ARROWROOT STARCH

1 TEASPOON CINNAMON

A PINCH OF SALT

♥ 3 TABLESPOONS LIQUID COCONUT OIL

3 TABLESPOONS WATER

FOR THE FILLING:

♥ 4 APPLES

♥ 1 TABLESPOON COCONUT OIL

2 TEASPOONS ARROWROOT STARCH

1 TEASPOON CINNAMON

♥ 1 TEASPOON GRATED FRESH GINGER OR ½ TEASPOON GROUND GINGER (OR TO TASTE)

1 TEASPOON VANILLA POWDER OR EXTRACT

♥ 1 TABLESPOON LEMON JUICE

1 TABLESPOON COCONUT BUTTER (OPTIONAL)

1 SERVING OF CARAMEL SAUCE (PAGE 11)

Preheat the oven to 350°F (180°C). Add the chickpea flour, almond flour, arrowroot starch, cinnamon, and salt to a large bowl and mix together. Add the coconut oil and water and mix well—don't be afraid to use your hands!—until it becomes a sticky dough. Wrap in plastic wrap, place in the refrigerator, and chill for around 30 minutes. (You are invited to do the same!)

Remove the dough from the refrigerator and spread it into a large tart pan, cake pan, or baking dish (around 13 x 9 inches/33 x 23 cm). Pierce the bottom with a fork in several places (to prevent it from bubbling up, even if you yourself are bubbling over with excitement). Cook the crust in the oven for around 15 minutes, until lightly browned but not burned!

In the meantime, make the filling: Peel and chop the apples (I suggest peeling half of them and leaving some unpeeled, for a nice balance of nutrition and texture). Heat the coconut oil in a small pot over medium-low heat, add the apples, and sauté for around 1 minute. Add the arrowroot starch, cinnamon, ginger, vanilla, and lemon juice, then add water to cover the apples by about ½ inch (1 cm). Cover the pot and simmer until the apples soften, around 10 to 15 minutes. Add the coconut butter (if using), and use a fork to crush the apples with a fork until thick and chunky. Pour it over the baked tart crust. Pour the caramel sauce on top.

Le final touch: Top with coconut yogurt (page 4), Crème Anglaise (page 11), or "Split"-Second Banana Ice Cream (page 114).

BeautiFuel Brownies

Let's just get the truth out there right away: These brownies are a sweet, fat-filled indulgence. That said, the sugars are all natural, the fat comes from some of the healthiest fat sources around, and this "indulgence" comes with a long list of healthy consequences. Oh, the omega-3s (walnuts)! The protein (pecans)! The vitamin E (avocado and almonds)! The potassium (dates)! The magnesium (cacao)! Plus, they are easy to digest and anti-inflammatory (cinnamon)! These are even healthy enough for breakfast, since the protein, natural sugars, and caffeinated cacao will fuel your busy day ahead. And, oui oui, they taste like heaven, too. In sum, brownies that make you beautiful, energetic, and happy. You can thank me later. (I accept cash, check, or a large portion of these brownies.)

MAKES AROUND 12 MINI BROWNIE BITES

¾ CUP (100 G) WALNUTS

♥ ½ CUP (50 G) ALMONDS

½ CUP (100 G) DATES, SOAKED AND PITTED

1 TEASPOON VANILLA POWDER OR EXTRACT

1 TEASPOON CINNAMON

♥ ¼ CUP (50 G) CACAO POWDER

A PINCH OF SALT

2 TABLESPOONS PECANS

FOR THE FROSTING:

♥ 1 BANANA

♥ 1 AVOCADO

♥ 1 TEASPOON COCONUT OIL

♥ 1 TABLESPOON CACAO POWDER

A PINCH OF SALT

1 TABLESPOON MESQUITE POWDER (OPTIONAL)

TOPPING:

2 TABLESPOONS PECAN PIECES

In a nut grinder or food processor, grind the walnuts and almonds into a fine flour. Don't grind for too long or it will turn into nut butter (NOT a bad thing, just not quite right for this particular recipe). Add the dates, vanilla, cinnamon, cacao, and salt. Blend into a homogenous dough. Crush the pecans into small pieces and add them to the dough. Form the dough into a ball with your hands then press into a large square pan so that the pan is coated and the brownie mixture is around 1 to 2 inches (2.5 to 5 cm) high.

Refrigerate while you make the frosting. Peel the banana and peel and pit the avocado, then cut both into small pieces. Combine them with the coconut oil, cacao, salt, and mesquite powder (if using) in a blender and blend until smooth.

Remove the pan from the refrigerator and spread the frosting evenly on top of the brownie. Cut into 2- to 3-inch (5 to 7.5 cm) squares. Top with the pecan pieces, and try not to eat the entire tray in one sitting.

VARIATIONS:

Zesty brownies: Add the juice of half an orange and the juice of half a lemon to the dough before mixing. Top the frosted bites with lemon zest and orange zest.

Fruity brownies: Instead of frosting, pour Strawberry Coulis with Goji Berries (page 11) over the brownies.

Crazy brownies: Add cacao nibs, coconut flakes, and goji berries to the dough.

Gorgeous Gâteaux

Marie Antoinette never actually said "Let them eat cake," but these gorgeous gâteaux are fit for a queen. Filled with superfoods like chia seeds, quinoa, lemon, and almond milk, they'll surely revolutionize your baking!

FOR 6 TO 8 GÂTEAUX

♥ ¼ CUP (40 G) ALMONDS

♥ 1 TABLESPOON CHIA SEEDS

3 TABLESPOONS WATER

♥ ½ CUP (60 G) QUINOA FLOUR

¼ CUP (30 G) BROWN RICE FLOUR

¼ CUP (25 G) QUINOA FLAKES OR GLUTEN-FREE OATS

♥ ¼ CUP (30 G) SHREDDED COCONUT

1 TABLESPOON ARROWROOT STARCH

1 TEASPOON BAKING POWDER

½ TEASPOON SALT

½ TEASPOON CINNAMON

1 TEASPOON VANILLA POWDER OR EXTRACT

♥ 1 TEASPOON GROUND GINGER

♥ 1 RIPE BANANA

½ CUP (125 ML) ALMOND MILK, HOMEMADE (SEE PAGE 2) OR STORE-BOUGHT, OR MORE IF NEEDED

¼ CUP (60 ML) LIQUID COCONUT OIL, PLUS MORE FOR PAN

2 TABLESPOONS MAPLE SYRUP

♥ 1 TABLESPOON LEMON JUICE

1 TEASPOON LEMON ZEST

½ CUP (100 G) CHOPPED FRUIT OF CHOICE (SEE IDEAS BELOW)

½ CUP (50 G) NUTS AND SEEDS OF CHOICE (SEE IDEAS BELOW)

Preheat the oven to 350°F (180°C).

Grind the almonds into a fine powder in a food processor. Set aside 1 to 2 tablespoons and add the rest to a big bowl.

Combine the chia seeds and water in a small bowl and leave on the counter to gel into a "chia egg."

Add the quinoa flour, brown rice flour, quinoa flakes, coconut, arrowroot, baking powder, salt, cinnamon, vanilla, and ginger to the big bowl with the almond flour. Mix well.

In another bowl, mash the banana with a fork. Add the almond milk, coconut oil, maple syrup, lemon juice, and lemon zest and mix well. Add the chia egg and mix again.

Pour the liquid ingredients into the flour mixture and stir with a spoon. The dough should be firm, but not too hard—you can add more almond milk as needed. Add the chopped fruit and nuts and seeds (reserving some for the garnish) and mix again.

Grease six to eight cups of a muffin pan with coconut oil. Divide the muffin dough among the cups, filling each around three-quarters full. Top with the almond powder and a few nuts and seeds.

Bake for 15 to 20 minutes, until slightly browned on top. You'll know they're done when your entire kitchen smells like a bakery and a toothpick or fork inserted into one comes out clean.

Let cool for a few minutes (have some patience!), then dig in.

DRESS UP YOUR GATEAUX IN:

Strawberries + sunflower seeds

Strawberries + matcha powder + goji berries

Blueberries + walnuts

Raspberries + coconut frosting (Melt coconut butter in a small saucepan until soft and smooth. Mix with vanilla powder or extract and some maple syrup. Pour over muffins. Let cool.)

Chocolate (add ¼ cup/50 g cacao powder to the dry mixture) + chocolate mousse icing (blend 1 peeled banana, 1 pitted and peeled avocado, 1 soaked, peeled, and pitted Medjool date, ¼ teaspoon cinnamon, ¼ teaspoon vanilla powder or extract, 1 teaspoon mesquite powder, 1 teaspoon carob powder, and 2 tablespoons cacao powder in a blender or food processor until smooth and creamy) + cacao-nib garnish

Cashew frosting (½ cup/50 g soaked cashews, 2 soaked and pitted Medjool dates, 2 tablespoons coconut flakes, 1 tablespoon lemon juice, and ¼ cup water blended in a blender until smooth and creamy)

Granolove Bars

In France, the government requires food advertisements to warn, "For your health, don't snack in between meals." I say non to this advice! Snacking is très bon, as long as the snacks in question are healthy. These granolove bars are great as a quick breakfast on the go or an anytime snack. They're packed with carbohydrates, protein, fiber, vitamins, and minerals.

MAKES AROUND 1 DOZEN SMALL BARS

♥ 2 TABLESPOONS CHIA SEEDS

6 TABLESPOONS WATER

2 CUPS (200 G) GLUTEN-FREE OATS (OR BUCKWHEAT, QUINOA, AND/OR RICE FLAKES)

½ CUP (150 G) DRIED FRUIT OF CHOICE (RAISINS, APRICOTS, FIGS . . .)

♥ ¼ CUP (50 G) ALMONDS AND/OR WALNUTS

2 TABLESPOONS SESAME SEEDS

2 TABLESPOONS PUMPKIN SEEDS

¼ CUP (50 G) SUNFLOWER SEEDS

♥ ¼ CUP (50 G) SHREDDED COCONUT

1 TEASPOON CINNAMON

¼ TEASPOON VANILLA POWDER OR EXTRACT

2 TABLESPOONS GROUND FLAXSEEDS (OPTIONAL)

♥ 2 BANANAS

3 TABLESPOONS MAPLE SYRUP

¼ CUP (60 ML) LIQUID COCONUT OIL

A PINCH OF SALT

Preheat the oven to 350°F (180°C). Combine the chia seeds and water and set aside for around 10 minutes to form a gel.

In a large bowl, mix together the oats, dried fruit, nuts, seeds, coconut, cinnamon, vanilla, and flaxseeds (if using). Peel the banana and break into pieces. Add to another bowl and mash with a fork, then add the maple syrup, chia gel, coconut oil, and salt. Mix with a fork until homogenous and smooth, or combine in a blender. Pour over the oat mixture and stir together with a spoon.

With a spatula, transfer the dough to a rimmed baking pan and spread to cover the pan (the granola mixture should be around ½ inch/1 cm thick). Bake for 20 to 25 minutes, until the edges are brown. Remove the pan from the oven and let cool. Cut into rectangular bars or small squares. Refrigerate for several days or freeze them.

To take with you on the go, throw into an eco-friendly sandwich bag or place in a small glass or BPA-free plastic container. You can also wrap in parchment paper and tie with a ribbon for a pretty presentation or gift for a busy friend or family member.

SUNFLOWER SEEDS
Smart and sexy

Sunflower seeds are rich in protein, vitamins (B1, B5, E . . .), and folate, and the minerals they contain (copper, magnesium, phosphorous, selenium, and tryptophan) have positive effects on anxiety and depression. Their choline also boosts brain function.

Chocolate Bonbons

These chocolate bonbons (the French word for candy) are like chic peanut butter cups: creamy almond butter dressed up in a robe of rich chocolate. Elegant but easy to make, this is la gourmandise *at its finest!*

MAKES 4 TO 6 BONBONS

♥ 3 TABLESPOONS ALMOND BUTTER, HOMEMADE (SEE PAGE 14) OR STORE-BOUGHT

¼ TEASPOON VANILLA POWDER OR EXTRACT

A PINCH OF SALT

♥ 2 TABLESPOONS COCONUT OIL

1 TABLESPOON MAPLE SYRUP

♥ 2 TABLESPOONS CACAO POWDER

Line 4 to 6 cups of a muffin pan with paper liners. Mix the almond butter with the vanilla and salt.

Heat the coconut oil for a few seconds in a small pan over low heat until liquid.

In a bowl, mix the oil, maple syrup, and cacao powder with a spoon until thick.

Pour around ½ inch (1 cm) of the cacao mixture into the muffin liners. Freeze for at least 5 minutes to harden. Remove and place a spoonful of the almond butter filling on top of the chocolate. Pour more chocolate sauce over the top to cover it (if it has hardened, just warm over low heat to liquefy). Place the muffin tin back into the freezer for around 15 minutes, until the chocolate hardens. Take the cups out of the liners and enjoy!

A FEW IDEAS FOR GOURMET BONBONS:

Add a slice of banana or strawberry or a whole (pitted) cherry or raspberry on top of the almond butter before covering with more cacao mixture.

Add some maca powder to the almond butter filling for an aphrodisiac and energizing candy.

Blend the almond butter with 2 soaked, peeled, and pitted dates and a teaspoonful of mesquite, carob, or lucuma powder for a "caramel" center.

Winter

My playlist to love (and be loved, and love yourself!) in winter

Higher Love JAMES VINCENT MCMORROW

Miracle MATISYAHU

Skinny Love BIRDY

XO JOHN MAYER

Love Yourself AYO

Love Someone JASON MRAZ

I Will Wait MUMFORD & SONS

December COLLECTIVE SOUL

Crazy Love VAN MORRISON

Marry Me TRAIN

Always BON JOVI

Give Love MC YOGI

Je ne Veux Qu'elle MARC LAVOINE

Try COLBIE CAILLAT

Brave SARA BAREILLES

In the mood for winter

Winter is "vata" season according to Ayurveda. Vata means cold, dry, and unstable, so we need to balance this with all that is warm and hydrating and try to give our daily lives—and meals!—as much of a rhythm as possible. Root vegetables, particularly ubiquitous during this time of year, are made for this: They are the roots that keep us down to earth and grounded despite the wind and cold of winter.

In winter, we need to eat warming foods: that is, foods cooked at higher temperatures, but also spices and ingredients that literally turn up the heat inside of our bodies.

During vata season, heavier and even more oily or fatty foods (we're talking plant-based fats here, folks!) can bring comfort to body and mind. Salty foods, like seaweed, detoxify the body and strengthen the blood. Blended foods are great in the wintertime to help the body really absorb nutrients.

Winter is a time to rest, reflect, and save our energy, which is usually running pretty low. We need to sleep well and reduce stress as much as possible (I know, I know—easier said than done!). Our bodies need to rest, but we also can't alienate ourselves from the world. Think of this time as "socially charged hibernation." During these dark, cold days, it's even more important than usual to surround ourselves with friends and loved ones to share warmth. (Plus, laughter is the best core workout ever, didn't you know?)

During this season, there are fewer fresh fruits and vegetables available at the market, but this doesn't mean your meals need to be boring! Au contraire! With just a few spices and the ideas in this chapter, you can make your meals smile (and you, too!). And since winter is also holiday time, you'll find some festive recipes to add a bit of green to your holiday hoopla.

Time to cocoon

In winter, it's cold. It's dark. We all just want to stay in our warm comfortable beds and hibernate. Animals do it, so why can't we? In fact, we do! In winter, we're less active, our body temperatures drop, our metabolisms slow down, and we have less energy. This is all totally normal and natural. It's just the body adapting to the seasons; in winter, everything slows down.

Cocooner (pronounced coo-coo-nay) is one of my favorite French words. It literally means "to cocoon" or to cozy up, cuddle up, stay indoors, and relax.

Vive la comfort food!

Let me guess—as soon as you ring in the new year, you're already thinking about making up for the excesses of that long and sumptuous holiday period. Big mistake! We're heading into the dead of winter; this is *not* the time to start eating "light" and feeling cold and hungry all day long. Your body needs meals that are rich in nutrition! The kitchen is a great place to heat things up when the temps drop outside.

Coconut oil

OK, I'm staging an intervention. Are you sitting down? It's time we finally talk about your fat phobia. We've alluded to it before when talking about avocados, nuts, and other green foods, but let's just do this once and for all.

F--?? OMG! The F-word! I'm going to die!

Calm down, please. So where were we? Coconut oil is a saturated fat that—

FAT? SATURATED? It's the end of the world!

Let me continue . . . the body needs saturated fats to function properly. Coconut oil is rich in lauric acid (also found in breast milk!), a saturated fatty acid that balances metabolism.

OK, tell me more . . .

In addition, coconut oil is a wonderful source of potassium, magnesium, iron, phosphorous, copper, zinc, and vitamins A and E. Coconut oil is great for the immune system since its essential fats protect against bacteria, viruses, and yeast.

Coconut oil is one of the best cooking oils since it can reach high temperatures without losing its health benefits. It doesn't go rancid easily, and its chemical structure doesn't change with heat.

So have I assuaged your fears of fat? (*Fatscinating, isn't it?*) If not, it's OK: These things take time. We've been so indoctrinated with fat-phobic media and brand campaigns that we have to rewire our brains and our bellies to embrace this concept. Your new friendship with fat begins today! Let's all do lunch.

Just one warning: Choose your coconut oil carefully. Look for "extra virgin" or "cold pressed" on the label. The oil should have a coconutty scent, not a neutral one.

Seasonal produce

FRUIT

Clementines

Grapefruit

Oranges

Pears

VEGGIES

Brussels sprouts

Cabbage

Cauliflower

Leeks

Mushrooms

Onions

Parsnips

Shallots

Spinach

Squash

Turnips

Good mood yoga

by Tara Stiles

Tara Stiles is a yoga teacher—or yoga guide, as this anti-guru prefers to describe herself—who is changing the world one smile at a time. This "rebel" yogini's message is to "break the rules" and bring a positive energy to all that you do. It's impossible to leave one of Tara's classes without a huge smile on your face. Like healthy foods, yoga in all of its forms makes us happy. Just moving our bodies, breathing in and out, and "turning off" our brains (and our phones!) for a short amount of time have incomparable effects on our mood. In fact, studies have proven that yoga can increase the levels of GABA (AKA the neurotransmitter gamma-aminobutyric acid) in our brains, low levels of which have been linked to depression. For yoga poses to make us smile, I asked the most smiley yoga teacher I know, Tara Stiles! Here is her advice for a happy mind and a happy body (even during a very, very cold winter)!

Note: Text for postures compiled from Tara Stiles's blog and Yoga Cures by Tara Stiles, courtesy of Harmony, 2012. tarastiles.com

When it comes to nourishing and taking care of ourselves, how we feel is more important than what we do. How we feel about ourselves drives our thoughts and actions. How we feel decides not only what we eat, but how our bodies and minds are able to absorb what we take in. We can eat "perfectly" and still get sick. Often this has to do with how we feel, and how that feeling evolves in the ecosystem of who we are. With regular easygoing yoga and meditation practice, we can practice following how we feel. We can practice following our intuition. We can practice loving ourselves. It's a radical concept in nourishment and diet. Self love isn't about eating whatever we want and blindly affirming our value. Self love is about respecting the gift it is to be uniquely our self, in this body, in this mind, carried by this spirit. When we respect all that we are we can begin to balance out unhealthy feelings that drive us to dim who we are. When we respect all that we are, we not only begin to make better choices, but also begin to feel fantastic about who we are and invest energy in cultivating who we are for our highest intention.

Practice how you feel.
Practice paying attention to you.
Practice following your intuition.
Enjoy the ride of connecting with the awesome power that is you.

When you are connected to that awesome power you will make the best choices to nourish that power.

—xo, Tara

1. DANCER

Shift your weight into your right leg. Bend your left knee and grab the inside of your left calf with your left hand. Gently press your foot into your hand to open your back. Reach your right arm straight up. Stay here for five long, deep breaths. Try the other side.

1

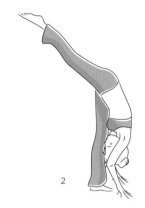

2. STANDING SPLIT

Bring both hands to the floor and touch your fingertips to the ground right under your shoulders. Allow the left leg and hip to open and release, as you lift it up behind you. Walk your fingertips back so they are in line with your toes. Release your head and neck toward the standing leg. Take three long, deep breaths, favoring the exhales a bit more than the inhales. Repeat on the other side. Feel free to fall if you need to here!

3. TREE POSE

Stand tall and comfortably with your feet parallel and a few inches apart. Shift your weight into your left leg. Bend your right knee in to your chest and hug your shin with your hands. Grab hold of your right ankle with your right hand and press the bottom of your right foot into your left inner thigh. Keep pressure going both ways, from your thigh into your foot and your foot into your thigh, just like a magnet stuck to a fridge. Either stay here with your hand holding your ankle for balance or reach your arms straight up. Stay here for five long, deep breaths. Try the same thing on your other side.

4. WARRIOR 3

Hug your left shin in toward your chest, then extend it straight back behind you and bend forward so your leg is parallel to the ground. Flex your left foot and point the toes down. Bend forward and bring your fingertips to the ground to stabilize yourself. Reach your arms out in front of you so your body is in a straight line from your fingertips all the way down your back and out through your left heel. Stay here for three long, deep breaths. Bend both knees slightly and again hug your left shin into your chest and place your left foot next to your right to come back to standing.

5. HAPPY BABY

Lie down on your back. Draw your knees into your chest. Grab the outside of your feet with your hands so the bottoms of your feet point straight up. Gently pull your knees down toward the ground outside your torso using the strength of your arms. If it feels good, rock carefully from side to side to open your back and hips even more. Stay here for ten long, deep breaths.

Cinderella Soup

Once upon a time . . . I created this Cinderella soup. Bibbidi-bobbidi-boo, prepare to witness a simple pumpkin turn into a magnificent winter meal. With just the wave of a magic wand, dinner is served! You'll have to chop up some vegetables and boil some water, but otherwise this soup pretty much makes itself. And you'll live happily ever after, I promise.

This recipe is great with my favorite petite pumpkin, le potimarron (red kuri squash), but it works well with any orange-fleshed squash (think butternut, kabocha, carnival . . .). Make a big batch to share with friends and family (even evil stepsisters) or store in the fridge for an easy, warming meal anytime.

MAKES 4 SMALL APPETIZER SERVINGS OR 2 LARGER BOWLS

1 SMALL COOKING PUMPKIN OR WINTER SQUASH OF CHOICE, PEELED AND DICED (AROUND 1½ CUPS/150 G)

♥ 1 SMALL SWEET POTATO, DICED (AROUND ½ CUP/100 G)

♥ 2 LARGE CARROTS

1 RED ONION

2 GARLIC CLOVES

♥ 2 TABLESPOONS COCONUT OIL

♥ ¼ TEASPOON GRATED FRESH OR GROUND GINGER

♥ ½ TEASPOON TURMERIC (FRESH IF YOU CAN FIND IT!)

SALT AND PEPPER TO TASTE

½ CUP (100 ML) *LAIT DE* COCONUT (PAGE 2) OR BPA-FREE CANNED COCONUT MILK (OPTIONAL, FOR AN EVEN CREAMIER CONSISTENCY)

Peel and chop the pumpkin, sweet potato, carrots, and onion into small pieces. Follow my tips on cutting winter squash on page 141 so you don't cut your fingers off! Peel and chop the garlic (you'll be blending it anyway).

Add the coconut oil to a large pot, then add the onion and garlic and sauté for around 1 minute. Add the fresh ginger (if using fresh). Add the squash, sweet potato, carrots, ground ginger (if not using fresh), turmeric, salt, and pepper. Sauté for another 2 to 3 minutes, then add enough water to cover the vegetables by around ½ inch (1 cm). Cover the pot and cook over medium-high heat until the water comes to a boil. Reduce the heat and simmer for 15 to 20 minutes, until the vegetables soften.

Transfer to a blender or puree with an immersion blender until smooth and creamy. If desired, add the coconut milk gradually until you find a consistency you like.

FOR A SPICIER VERSION

Add ¼ teaspoon cumin, ¼ teaspoon coriander, and ½ teaspoon cinnamon with the turmeric.

FOR A SWEETER VERSION

Replace the turmeric with 1 teaspoon vanilla powder or extract.

PUMPKIN
A magical, fairytale vegetable

Pumpkin contains carbohydrates, vitamins, minerals, and fiber. Thanks to its pro-vitamin A (AKA beta-carotene, which supports the eyes), pumpkin allows us to see the world clearly! It's also a great source of B vitamins, vitamin C, D, and E, calcium, magnesium, iron, potassium, phosphorous, silica, sodium, *lots* of fiber, and numerous other nutrients.

After tasting this magical soup, you'll have all the strength necessary to live your own fairytale. Plus, it makes your skin glow, again thanks to beta-carotene, so you can expect Prince Charming to ride over on a white horse. (And he will definitely be impressed with your cooking skills.)

Soupe Chou-fleur: Cauliflower Soup

Not sure what to do with that big cauliflower head you just brought home that is bigger than your head? Make a big batch of this soup. (Or recycle it! Serve it not one, but deux *ways.) Raw or cooked, hot or cold, cauliflower soup is a winter wonderfood!*

MAKES AROUND 6 SMALL APPETIZER SERVINGS OR 4 MAINS

1 LARGE HEAD OF CAULIFLOWER

1 LEEK

♥ 1 APPLE

1 RED ONION

2 GARLIC CLOVES

♥ 1 TABLESPOON COCONUT OIL

¼ CUP (75 ML) TAHINI

3 TABLESPOONS OLIVE OIL

1 TO 2 TABLESPOONS NUTRITIONAL YEAST (OPTIONAL)

SALT

WHITE PEPPER

Wash the cauliflower and cut into pieces (they can be any size, they're going to be blended anyway!). Clean the leek well and cut off the green parts. Cut the white section in half, then into ¼-inch (.5 cm) slices. Peel then chop the apple into small pieces. Peel and chop or mince the onion and garlic.

Melt the coconut oil in a pot over the stove over medium heat, then add the cauliflower, apple, leek, onion, and garlic, and sauté for a few minutes. Add just enough water to cover the ingredients by around 1 inch (2.5 cm). Bring to a boil, then lower the heat, cover, and simmer for 5 to 10 minutes, until the cauliflower is tender. Take out a few cauliflower pieces and set aside to add at the end if desired. Turn off the heat and pour out half of the liquid into a bowl or glass. Add the tahini, olive oil, and nutritional yeast (if using) to the pot. Blend the soup with an immersion blender or in a high-speed blender until smooth and creamy, adding the set-aside liquid as needed to obtain the soup consistency you prefer. Add any reserved cauliflower pieces and salt and white pepper to taste.

FOR A RAW SOUPE CHOU-FLEUR, COMBINE FLORETS FROM ½ HEAD OF CAULIFLOWER; ½ PITTED, PEELED, AND CUBED AVOCADO; JUICE OF 1 LEMON; 1 TABLESPOON MISO PASTE; ¼ TEASPOON CHOPPED FRESH OR GROUND TURMERIC; ¼ TEASPOON CHOPPED FRESH OR GROUND GINGER; 2 TEASPOONS COCONUT AMINOS OR TAMARI; 1 TABLESPOON CHOPPED PARSLEY; AND 1 CUP (250 ML) WATER IN A HIGH-SPEED BLENDER UNTIL SMOOTH AND CREAMY, ADDING MORE LIQUID AS NEEDED TO OBTAIN YOUR DESIRED CONSISTENCY. ADD SALT AND PEPPER TO TASTE.

CAULIFLOWER
Your winter flu shot!

Cauliflower, or in French *le chou-fleur* (literally "cabbage flower"), is rich in vitamin C, so important in winter to fight against colds, flu, and other viruses.

Cauliflower has a high water content, which is great in winter since we pay less attention to hydrating ourselves without those thirst cravings prevalent in the warmer weather. Cauliflower is full of fiber and very anti-inflammatory and can help to prevent lung, ovarian, and kidney cancers.

Warm Beet and Butternut Salad

If you think salad has to be raw, you're butternuts! Raw veggies are filled with enzymes that aid digestion, but come on, it's winter! I'm freezing and want something that will heat up my body, don't you? Enter . . . the warm salad! A salad may seem like a revolutionary idea in winter, but try it and let's get this "grass roots" movement started! Are you with me?

SERVES 1

1 SMALL BEET

½ CUP (60 G) CHOPPED BUTTERNUT SQUASH (OR SWEET POTATO OR WINTER SQUASH OF CHOICE; SEE PAGE 141 FOR CHOPPING TIPS)

♥ 1 TABLESPOON COCONUT OIL (LIQUID OR SOLID—IT WILL MELT IN THE OVEN ANYWAY!)

SALT AND PEPPER TO TASTE

1 TABLESPOON HAZELNUTS

2 TABLESPOONS MUSTARD VINAIGRETTE (PAGE 10)

1 GENEROUS CUP SALAD GREENS (ARUGULA, ROMAINE, MESCLUN . . .)

1 HANDFUL OF BABY SPINACH OR BABY KALE (TAKE YOUR PICK AT THE GREENS NURSERY!)

1 TABLESPOON CHOPPED FRESH PARSLEY

1 TABLESPOON POMEGRANATE SEEDS (OPTIONAL)

Preheat the oven to 350°F (180°C).

Wash the beet well. Cut it into cubes a little smaller than the squash pieces (around ¼ to ½ inch/.5 to 1 cm wide). Add the beet and butternut chunks, coconut oil, salt, and pepper to a bowl and mix well until the veggies are coated.

Spread onto a baking sheet and cook for around 20 minutes, turn the veggies, and cook for about 10 minutes longer, until the veggies are fork tender. If the squash is done before the beets, feel free to take the squash out of the oven while you allow the beets to continue to cook.

Toast your hazelnuts for a few minutes in the oven, then grind them in a food processor or smash with the back of a spoon (come on, muscles, you can do it!).

In a bowl, mix all of the vinaigrette ingredients well. Add the salad greens and mix with your hands.

Place the dressed salad greens onto a plate, reserving the extra dressing left in the bowl. Top with the baby spinach, and add the roasted veggies. (The spinach will soften and wilt—it's just relaxing and getting ready for the great meal ahead!)

Before serving, drizzle a little more dressing over the top and add the toasted hazelnuts, parsley, pomegranate seeds (if using), salt, and pepper.

Brussels Sprouts à la Pomme

Brussels sprouts have a terrible reputation. Eating these mini green balls from the cabbage family has become a form of punishment for kids everywhere . . . and sometimes adults. But avoiding these nutrient powerhouses is such a shame, since when cooked properly, they are crispy and scrumptious! Serving them à la pomme *("with apple") is even better.*

SERVES 1

1 CUP (200 G) RAW BRUSSELS SPROUTS

♥ 1 SMALL APPLE (PREFERABLY A SWEET, FIRM, RED VARIETY SUCH AS GALA, BRAEBURN, FUJI, OR JONAGOLD)

♥ 2 TEASPOONS COCONUT OIL

SALT AND PEPPER TO TASTE

FOR THE SAUCE:

½ GARLIC CLOVE

♥ 1 TABLESPOON LEMON JUICE

2 TEASPOONS DIJON MUSTARD

1 TEASPOON APPLE CIDER VINEGAR

⅛ TEASPOON CURRY POWDER

♥ A TINY PIECE OF GINGER (TO TASTE)

1 TABLESPOON OLIVE OIL

Preheat the oven to 350°F (180°C).

Cut off the tips of the stems of the brussels sprouts. Remove the outer leaves if browned. Peel and core the apple then cut it into small ½-inch (1 cm) chunks.

In a bowl, mix the brussels sprouts, half of the apple chunks, and the coconut oil, salt, and pepper. Spread on a baking sheet and bake for around 20 minutes, until the brussels sprouts are fork tender, but still crispy. If they start to get mushy or smell foul, TAKE THEM OUT OF THE OVEN!

Meanwhile, to make the sauce, peel and chop the garlic. Add the remaining apple chunks to a blender with the garlic and the rest of the sauce ingredients and blend until smooth and creamy.

When the brussels sprouts are done, remove them from the oven and add to a bowl or plate. Pour the sauce on top. *Voilà!* Enjoy your trip to Brussels (sprouts)!

BRUSSELS SPROUTS
Don't be scared!

Brussels sprouts are rich in folate, which reinforces the cardiovascular system and reduces the risk of birth defects in expectant mothers. Brussels sprouts contain 90 percent water, and they are low in calories but filled with carbohydrates, fiber, and protein (not to mention vitamin C!). Just make sure not to overcook them or they will turn bitter and mushy. *Le* yuck!

Totally Wild Stuffed Squash

Want to hear something wild? Wild rice is not, in fact, rice. It's the seed of an entirely different type of grass. It has a naturally nutty flavor and fibrous, almost rubbery (in a good way, I promise!) texture. It's excellent served with other more tender grains—think: brown rice, quinoa, or millet—for a nice contrast of texture and flavor. Wild rice is a great base for salads, but it's also terrific as a hearty stuffing for winter squash. So go wild!

SERVES 1

I SMALL WINTER SQUASH (CARNIVAL, ACORN, DELICATA, SWEET DUMPLING, KABOCHA…)

¼ CUP (30 G) COOKED WILD RICE (SEE TIP)

½ CUP (30 G) COOKED BROWN RICE (SEE TIP)

1 HANDFUL OF SPINACH

1 TABLESPOON CHOPPED FRESH PARSLEY, PLUS MORE FOR GARNISH

¼ TEASPOON CHOPPED FRESH ROSEMARY

1 LARGE SAGE LEAF, CHOPPED

¼ TEASPOON FRESH THYME LEAVES

♥ 1 TABLESPOON COCONUT OIL

1 TABLESPOON WALNUTS

SALT AND PEPPER TO TASTE

1 TEASPOON WALNUT OIL

Preheat the oven to 350°F (180°C).

Grab your squash. Give it a nice bath. Then, off with its head! No seriously, cut the stem and about 1 inch (2.5 cm) of the top off of the squash (to do this injury-free, see my instructions on page 141). Remove the seeds inside with a spoon. (Note: Save these, rinse them, then roast them—they're yummy and nutritious!)

Place the squash on a nonstick or lightly greased (with coconut oil) baking sheet, cut side down. Bake for 25 to 30 minutes, until the squash "meat" is very soft.

Mix together the wild rice, brown rice, spinach, parsley, rosemary, sage, thyme, coconut oil, and walnuts. Stuff the baked squash with the rice mixture, then return it to the oven for another 10 minutes or so (facing up, of course!). Add salt and pepper to taste. Serve hot topped with a drizzle of walnut oil and parsley.

I hope this dish makes your heart sing, wild thing.

Tip: Use leftover wild and brown rice, or cook according to the directions on page 18, either separately or together. The brown rice should be soft and tender, and the wild rice a bit chewy, but not too rubbery, so cook until the wild rice is done—it's OK if the brown rice is a bit mushier.

WILD RICE

Wild rice thing, you make my insides sing!

Cultivated mostly in North America but sold throughout the world, wild rice is packed with protein and dietary fiber, even more so than brown rice. It contains phosphorous, magnesium, niacin (AKA vitamin B3, very important for blood circulation and the digestive and nervous systems), manganese, copper, and folate.

Roasted Winter Vegetables, Five Ways

Does going to the farmers market in winter depress you? Have you exhausted your yearly quota of leeks and squash or broken the world record for cabbage consumption? Instead of staring dreamily at photos of fresh raspberries or perfect peas, get creative and give those winter veggies a makeover! Here are five "oven-to-table" ways to bathe those "boring" veggies in a sea of flavor. (Note: Winter vegetables may look ugly, but don't judge by appearances!)

AROUND 1½ CUPS (200 G) OF RAW VEGGIES IN ½-INCH (1 CM) CUBES (WINTER SQUASH, BROCCOLI, SWEET POTATO, CARROTS, BEETS, PARSNIPS, JERUSALEM ARTICHOKES, CELERY ROOT, BRUSSELS SPROUTS, SALSIFY, FENNEL, CAULIFLOWER . . . AND MORE!)

SALT AND PEPPER TO TASTE

♥ COCONUT OIL

JERUSALEM ARTICHOKES
Soaking in the sunchokes

Jerusalem artichokes, AKA sunchokes, AKA earth apples, AKA sunroots, go by many names, including the French name *topinambour*. This overlooked food is far from *topinam*boring!

Jerusalem artichokes are among a number of "forgotten" vegetables that have come back in style in recent years. You've probably come across them at the market but snubbed them, am I right? I'll be honest, they're ugly—they look a bit like fresh ginger gone rotten—but they are one of the heartiest veggies around and a great replacement for potatoes in many recipes. These *petites* roots help lower blood pressure, don't cause blood sugar to spike, and boost intestinal health since they are filled with inulin, a prebiotic that feeds beneficial bacteria in the gut. They are also high in potassium, protein, and iron—they really are sun-thing special, aren't they? (They can make you gassy if you eat too many, so exercise moderation.)

THE BASIC TECHNIQUE

Preheat the oven to 350°F (180°C).

Add the vegetables to an oven-safe dish and top with salt, pepper, and coconut oil. If your coconut oil is solid, dollop a couple small spoonfuls onto the veggies and place in the oven for a minute or so, until the oil melts. Mix until the veggies are well coated, then place back in the oven.

Bake for 30 to 45 minutes, until the veggies are cooked. Note: You may want to add the tougher root veggies first, then around halfway through the cooking, add other veggies, like broccoli, brussels sprouts, or cauliflower.

1. MAPLE-MUSTARD VEGGIES

Whisk together 1 teaspoon Dijon mustard, 1 teaspoon maple syrup, 1 tablespoon olive oil, and 1 teaspoon apple cider vinegar. Pour over the warm vegetables when they come out of the oven.

2. SWEET 'N' SAUCY VEGGIES

In a blender, combine 2 tablespoons almond butter, 1 teaspoon miso paste, 1 peeled garlic clove, 1 teaspoon maple syrup, 1 tablespoon lime juice, a pinch of black pepper, a pinch of cayenne pepper, and ¼ cup (50 ml) coconut or almond milk. Pour over the warm vegetables when they come out of the oven.

3. HAPPY HERBED VEGGIES

Before you roast the veggies, add ⅛ teaspoon chopped fresh or dried thyme, ⅛ teaspoon chopped fresh or dried rosemary, and a few chopped sage leaves.

4. CURRIED VEGGIES

Before you roast the veggies, add ¼ teaspoon curry powder.

5. CINNAMON-SPICED VEGGIES

Before you roast the veggies, add ¼ teaspoon cinnamon.

La Haute Kaleture Salad

This is cruciferous-chic at its finest. Kale isn't so great naked, but when dressed up in fancy flavors, it is quite simply the stuff green dreams are made of. Sauerkraut adds a probiotic boost and a salty flare; dulse also adds a naturally salty flavor and protein, vitamins, and minerals to boot. The avocado and tahini make this creamy and satisfying, and the kale, cabbage, sprouts, and seeds add crunch. Fresh from the runway to your plate. Kale Lagerfeld would surely approve.

SERVES 1

♥ 1 CARROT
1 GENEROUS HANDFUL OF KALE
2 TABLESPOONS TAHINI HOLLANDAISE (PAGE 8)
¼ CUP (50 G) THINLY SLICED RED CABBAGE
A HANDFUL OF MESCLUN OR SALAD GREENS OF CHOICE
♥ ½ AVOCADO, PITTED, PEELED, AND THINLY SLICED
♥ 2 TABLESPOONS DULSE (CHOPPED FRESH, OR DRIED FLAKES)
1 TEASPOON CHOPPED FRESH CHIVES
1 TABLESPOON SUNFLOWER SEEDS, TOASTED
2 TABLESPOONS SAUERKRAUT
1 TABLESPOON SPROUTS OR MICROGREENS (OPTIONAL)

Wash or peel then grate the carrot.

Add the kale to a large bowl. Pour half of the Tahini Hollandaise on top and massage the kale well until "relaxed." Add the cabbage and massage again. Add the mesclun, carrot, and the remaining dressing and mix together well.

Add to a bowl or plate. Top with the avocado, dulse, chives, sunflower seeds, sauerkraut, and sprouts (if using).

Serve this salad with miso soup to aid digestion, boost immunity, and warm the entire body.

Warm Lentil Salad

And—voilà—another warming winter salad idea for a light lunch even on a cold day. This salad is great served with gluten-free toast (page 40) spread with faux-mage (page 5).

SERVES 1

♥ 1 LARGE CARROT
2 TEASPOONS OLIVE OIL
SALT AND PEPPER TO TASTE
1 TABLESPOON SUNFLOWER SEEDS
A HANDFUL OF ARUGULA
A HANDFUL OF MÂCHE OR OTHER GREENS
♥ ½ AVOCADO
1 TABLESPOON MUSTARD VINAIGRETTE (PAGE 10)
½ CUP (30 G) COOKED LENTILS (SEE PAGE 18) OR DRAINED AND RINSED CANNED LENTILS
A HANDFUL OF CHOPPED FRESH HERBS
1 TABLESPOON SAUERKRAUT (OPTIONAL)

Preheat the oven to 400°F (200°C). Wash or peel the carrot and slice into long, skinny, french fry–shaped pieces. Toss the carrot pieces in the olive oil, salt, and pepper and spread on a baking sheet. Roast for around 10 minutes, until cooked but still a bit crunchy. Add the sunflower seeds and continue to roast for 2 to 3 minutes, until the seeds are slightly browned and toasted. Remove from the oven.

Add the arugula and mâche to a large salad bowl. Pit, peel, and dice the avocado into small pieces. Toss with the greens, vinaigrette, and lentils. Add to a bowl or plate and top with the roasted carrots. Garnish with the fresh herbs and sauerkraut (if using).

The Greens Who Stole Christmas

Joyeux Noel! I know, I know—the holidays are typically the hardest time of the year for those looking to eat healthy. Whatever holiday you are or aren't celebrating, 'tis the season for overeating! ('Tis also the season for time with family, which can bring up so many emotions and affect the way we eat.) No wonder Santa had some trouble squeezing through that chimney—holiday foods are very indulgent.

Remember: Joy is the healthiest ingredient of all, so enjoy the company of your loved ones, and maybe even the not-very-green treats they'll shower you with. Plus, with just a bit of imagination and without sacrificing pleasure, you can add green to the holiday table. Voilà: three party recipes that are nutritious and delicious—a holiday miracle!

Amaranth Caviar

Something *isn't* fishy about this caviar. Yes, it's fish-egg-free! (But just as fancy.) Amaranth is a lesser-known gluten-free grain with a unique texture. It is a great source of calcium, iron, fiber, and plant protein, including essential amino acids lysine and methionine. When cooked, it is dense and gelatinous, and its tiny grains plump up to form small clear balls that look eerily like caviar. Like the *real* delicacy, this version is *very* (naturally!) salty thanks to the dulse, olives, and capers, and quite dense, so just a little bit goes a long way. This swanky spread is the perfect aperitif to kick off any holiday gathering. Its dark black color reinforces the illusion of this luxury food. Impress your guests!

MAKES 1 SMALL BOWL

♥ ½ CUP (50 G PACKED) DRIED DULSE (OR ¼ CUP/25 G DULSE FLAKES)
½ CUP (40 G) DRY AMARANTH
1½ CUPS (375 ML) WATER
2 TABLESPOONS OLIVE OIL
2 TABLESPOONS CHOPPED BLACK OLIVES
1 TABLESPOON CAPERS
♥ 1 TABLESPOON LEMON JUICE
1 TABLESPOON CHOPPED FRESH PARSLEY

Add the dulse to a bowl of room-temperature water while you prep the other ingredients. (If using flakes, do not soak them.)

Add the amaranth to a small pot with the water. Bring to a boil, then cover and simmer over low heat for 15 to 20 minutes, until all of the water is absorbed. Transfer the amaranth to a bowl and let cool for around 10 to 15 minutes.

Meanwhile, rinse the dulse. Add the olive oil, olives, dulse, capers, and lemon juice to a blender and blend until smooth. Pour this sauce over the cooled amaranth and mix together with a fork. Garnish with fresh parsley.

Serve on toast, crackers, or rice cakes.

Faux Gras

Foie gras may seem upscale, but how it's made is not. This plant-based "foie gras" doesn't involve fattening up a duck ... or the person eating it, for that matter.

MAKES 1 LOAF (2 TO 3 SERVINGS)
½ CUP (50 G) MUSHROOMS
½ RED ONION
1 GARLIC CLOVE
2 TABLESPOONS OLIVE OIL
1 CUP (200 G) COOKED FRENCH LENTILS (SEE PAGE 18)
¼ CUP (50 G) WALNUTS
♥ 1 TABLESPOON LEMON JUICE
♥ 1 TEASPOON COCONUT AMINOS OR TAMARI
1 TEASPOON FRESH THYME LEAVES
1 TABLESPOON CHOPPED FRESH PARSLEY
1 TEASPOON CHOPPED FRESH ROSEMARY

Wash the mushrooms, peel and chop the onion, and peel and mince the garlic.

Add the olive oil to a Dutch oven or pot over low heat and add the onion and garlic. Sauté for a couple of minutes, until the onions become translucent, then add the mushrooms and sauté for another 5 to 10 minutes, until the mushrooms are soft. Combine the mushroom mixture, lentils, and all other ingredients in a food processor and process until homogenous. Transfer to a loaf pan or glass container and refrigerate for a few hours, until firm yet spreadable.

Slice into thick slabs and serve on plates with a side salad and some toast or crackers.

EscarGREEN

I still remember my first time. It was with my French boyfriend. It all happened so quickly. It was such a strange sensation ... that first bite of escargot. While the rubbery, slimy French snails may not have been for me, I loved the sauce they were swimming in! Here, I've replaced the snails with mushrooms, and as in the traditional version, it's all about the sensational—yet simple—sauce.

SERVES 2
1 CUP (500 G) *CHAMPIGNONS DE PARIS* (WHITE BUTTON MUSHROOMS)
2 TABLESPOONS OLIVE OIL
2 GARLIC CLOVES
♥ 1 TABLESPOON LEMON JUICE
1 TEASPOON CAPERS
¼ TEASPOON FRESH THYME LEAVES
1 TABLESPOON CHOPPED FRESH PARSLEY

Preheat the oven to 400°F (200°C).

Wash the mushrooms and remove and discard the stems. Toss the caps in 1 tablespoon of the olive oil, spread on a baking sheet, and bake for 15 to 20 minutes with the gills side down.

Peel and mince the garlic. Add the remaining tablespoon of oil to a pan over low heat. Add the garlic and cook for 1 to 2 minutes. Blend in a blender with the lemon juice, capers, and thyme until it forms a homogenous sauce.

Remove the mushrooms from the oven and pour the sauce over them. Return to the oven for another 5 minutes so that the mushrooms soak in the sauce. Serve garnished with the parsley.

Warming Winter Wonderbowls

Oh, the weather outside is frightful, but the fiber is so delightful. On a cold winter morning, there is nothing better than a piping hot bowl of oats or other grains, velvety plant-based milk, and sweet toppings. Once you get the basic technique down, you can swap in your favorite grains or nut milks and decorate with . . . anything you want! You can even make it ahead and just warm it over the stove in the morning or take some on the road for a busy day. So let it snow, let it snow, let it snow outside while you warm yourself up from the inside.

Happy Hazelnut Quinoa Bowl

Quinoa is a complex carb that will give you sustained energy, instead of a jolt with a crash later on. It's also rich in magnesium, so it can help relax blood vessels and ease stress-related migraines. Packed with protein, vitamins, and minerals, plus a *natural* sweetness, this is happiness guaranteed in a warm, creamy bowl. Feel free to use any nut milk you like here, but hazelnut makes for a nice change.

SERVES 1

♥ ¼ CUP (30 G) DRY QUINOA

1 CUP (250 ML) HAZELNUT MILK, HOMEMADE (SEE PAGE 2) OR STORE-BOUGHT

¼ TEASPOON CINNAMON

¼ TEASPOON VANILLA POWDER OR EXTRACT

2 DRIED APRICOTS OR FIGS, CHOPPED INTO TINY CUBES

1 TABLESPOON CRUSHED HAZELNUTS

♥ 1 BANANA

Add the quinoa to a small saucepan. Pour ½ cup (125 ml) of the hazelnut milk over the quinoa and add the cinnamon and vanilla. Bring to a boil, then reduce the heat, cover, and simmer for 10 to 15 minutes, until the liquid is absorbed. Add the dried fruit to the quinoa. Turn off the heat and let sit, covered, for a few more minutes while you toast the hazelnuts (in the oven or over the stove). Slice the banana. In another saucepan, heat the remaining ½ cup (125 ml) of hazelnut milk over low heat until warm. Pour the quinoa mixture into a bowl. Top with the banana and hazelnuts. Pour the warmed hazelnut milk over the top.

You can make this the night before. After cooking the quinoa, let it cool and leave in the refrigerator, either with or without the banana, hazelnuts, and dried fruit. In the morning, add to a saucepan with the remaining hazelnut milk, cover, and simmer until warm. Add a spoonful of almond butter or hazelnut butter (see page 14) for an extra protein boost!

Oat là là Bowl

This breakfast is for anyone with a big appetite in the morning. The oats will keep you full for hours, plus they're a good-mood food, rich in the tryptophan that feeds our favorite feel-good chemical serotonin, and their soluble fiber stabilizes blood sugar levels. Sudden drops in blood sugar levels cause fatigue, depression, and mood swings, so it's important to keep them under control. This warming, comforting, and oh-so-sweet bowl of goodness will put a smile on your face even on a cold, dark, wintry morning!

SERVES 1

⅓ CUP (30 G) GLUTEN-FREE OATS (OR QUINOA, BUCKWHEAT, OR BROWN RICE FLAKES)

⅛ TEASPOON VANILLA POWDER OR EXTRACT

⅛ TEASPOON CINNAMON

A PINCH OF NUTMEG

A PINCH OF CARDAMOM

A PINCH OF CLOVES

1 CUP (250 ML) *LAIT DE* NUTS (PAGE 2) OR STORE-BOUGHT NUT MILK OF CHOICE—GO NUTS!

1 TABLESPOON RAISINS

1 TABLESPOON WALNUTS

OPTIONAL TOPPINGS:

♥ SLICED BANANA, FRESH FRUIT, MAPLE SYRUP, COCONUT FLAKES . . .

Add the oats, vanilla, cinnamon, nutmeg, cardamom, cloves, and ⅔ cup of the nut milk to a small saucepan and bring to a gentle boil. Reduce the heat to low, cover, and simmer for 5 to 10 minutes, until the oats absorb the liquid and the mixture becomes creamy. Add the raisins and mix together with a spoon. Cover and let sit for 1 to 2 minutes while you heat the remaining ⅓ cup milk in another saucepan over low heat until warmed. Toast the walnuts in the oven or over the stove. Add the oatmeal to a bowl. Top with the toasted walnuts and warmed milk. Add toppings of choice.

Creamy Coconut Cardamom Snow Bowl

Pear and cardamom are such a wonderful flavor pairing. If desired, you can use leftover buckwheat or soak raw buckwheat overnight, rinse, then blend with the other ingredients over very low heat for just a few minutes.

SERVES 1

¼ CUP (45 G) RAW BUCKWHEAT GROATS

♥ 1 CUP (200 ML) *LAIT DE* COCONUT (PAGE 2) OR BPA-FREE CANNED FULL-FAT COCONUT MILK*

⅛ TEASPOON VANILLA POWDER OR EXTRACT

⅛ TEASPOON CINNAMON

⅛ TEASPOON CARDAMOM

½ PEAR

♥ 1 BANANA (OPTIONAL)

1 TABLESPOON COCONUT FLAKES

Add the buckwheat, coconut milk, vanilla, cinnamon, and cardamom to a small saucepan and bring to a gentle boil. Reduce the heat to low, cover, and simmer 5 to 10 minutes, until the liquid has been absorbed. Meanwhile, cut the pear into small cubes and slice the banana (if using). Pour the buckwheat into a bowl and top with the pear, banana slices, and coconut flakes.

*If your coconut milk is very thick, try ½ cup water (125 ml) and ½ cup (100 ml) coconut milk.

Zit-Zapper Magic Oat Cream

Oats absorb oil from the surface of the skin, making them great for acne-prone skin. Lemon juice's astringent properties also make it great for pushing oils out of the skin. It kills bacteria and reduces redness. If you have very dry skin, skip the lemon since it can dry you out even more.

3 TABLESPOONS OATS
♥ 1 LEMON

In a food processor, process the oats into a powder. Squeeze the juice out of the lemon and add to the oat powder. Mix with a spoon until it forms a "dough." Apply the dough to pimples and allow it to sit for around 15 minutes. Rinse! (Yes, that's zit!)

Soap Oat-pera

There's nothing dramatic about this simple exfolioating cream. Skin tends to dry up in winter, so this will exfoliate and hydrate! (Feel free to eat the leftovers!)

¼ CUP (25 G) GLUTEN-FREE OATS
½ CUP (125 ML) WATER
♥ 1 TABLESPOON COCONUT SUGAR

Add the oats and water to a small saucepan and bring to a gentle boil. Reduce the heat to low, cover, and simmer until the oats have absorbed the water. Add the coconut sugar, stir, check that it's not too hot, then spread over your face. Rub well to exfoliate, then rinse well.

Stylish Snowballs

These energy balls are a great treat to make anytime, but especially when you're home on a snow day! They are healthy, protein-packed, and fiber-filled. The kids can add their favorite colorful superfoods, nuts, berries, or flavorings . . . and so can you! These are full of natural sugars to get you ready to go outside and roll around in the snow.

Go!

FOR 6 TO 8 BALLS

♥ ¼ CUP (80 G) SHREDDED COCONUT

10 DATES, SOAKED AND PITTED

♥ 1 CUP (50 G) ALMONDS, WALNUTS, OR PECANS

¼ TEASPOON VANILLA POWDER OR EXTRACT

1 TABLESPOON MAPLE SYRUP (OPTIONAL)

Set aside 1 tablespoon of the coconut. Mix the rest of the ingredients in a food processor into a firm dough. Form the dough into little balls with your hands. Roll the truffles around in the remaining coconut flakes (AKA the "snow") until coated. Refrigerate for around 30 minutes to harden. Eat anytime!

FOR EXTRA-SPECIAL SNOWBALLS:

Add 2 tablespoons cacao powder to the mixture before processing, then mix 2 tablespoons cacao nibs in by hand before you form into balls.

Add spirulina powder before processing for a green variation!

Add spices (cinnamon, nutmeg, cardamom, cloves, ginger . . .) for spicy snowballs!

You can also easily turn these into lollipops. Just pierce the balls with a toothpick, straw, or thin wooden stick before you place them into the refrigerator, and *voilà*: Your candy is ready!

TODAY'S SPECIAL

Sablés ("Butter" Cookies)

Sablés *are French butter cookies from Normandy. My version has a buttery flavor from the coconut oil and a crumbly texture, and they're so rich in protein thanks to the almond butter and flour. I highly recommend dipping these in a (warmed) glass of "Totally Nuts" milk (page 2) or any* Lait de Nuts *(page 2). You can crumble them up atop coconut yogurt (page 4), fruit, or applesauce, or even spread some Caramel Sauce (page 11) or Crème Anglaise (page 11) between two cookies to make sandwich cookies.*

♥ 1 CUP (110 G) ALMOND FLOUR, HOMEMADE (SEE PAGE 14) OR STORE-BOUGHT

½ TEASPOON CINNAMON

¼ TEASPOON VANILLA POWDER OR EXTRACT

½ TEASPOON BAKING SODA

¼ TEASPOON SALT

♥ 1 TABLESPOON CACAO POWDER (OPTIONAL, FOR CHOCOLATE COOKIES)

♥ 2 TABLESPOONS COCONUT OIL

♥ ¼ CUP ALMOND BUTTER, HOMEMADE (SEE PAGE 14) OR STORE-BOUGHT

1 TABLESPOON MAPLE SYRUP

1 HANDFUL OF PECANS OR WALNUTS, CRUSHED

2 TABLESPOONS HIGH-QUALITY DARK CHOCOLATE CHIPS OR PIECES (OPTIONAL)

Preheat the oven to 350°F (180°C). Melt the coconut oil until it becomes liquid.

Add the almond flour, cinnamon, vanilla, baking soda, salt, and cacao to a big bowl and mix together well. Add the coconut oil, almond butter, and maple syrup. Mix in a food processor until it forms a dough, then add the nuts and chocolate chips (if using).

Form the dough into small balls with your hands then press each one onto a baking sheet lined with parchment paper and bake for around 20 minutes, until golden brown. Let them cool for a few minutes so they aren't too crumbly and fall apart. (Yes, you can do it! Sip your warm nut milk slowly while you wait!) Dip your cookie into the milk. Close your eyes. You're six years old again—isn't this fun?

Le Chocolat Chaud (Hot Chocolate)

I grew up drinking sugary, watery instant hot chocolate complete with inflatable marshmallows. It wasn't until I went to Paris that I realized hot chocolate should actually be just that: Hot. Chocolate. This molten, rich, thick, smooth, intense sip of heaven is true cocoa ecstasy. Make sure to relax and sip it slowly so that you can taste the potent flavor with your entire body and enjoy a cacaorgasmic experience that also happens to be guilt-free.

SERVES 1 CHOCOHOLIC (OR TWO KIDS OR TWO NORMAL PEOPLE)

1 CUP (250 ML) BRAZIL NUT MILK (HOMEMADE—SEE PAGE 2—OR STORE-BOUGHT) OR NUT MILK OF CHOICE

1 TEASPOON MESQUITE POWDER

♥ 1 TABLESPOON COCONUT BUTTER (OR COCONUT OIL)

♥ 1 GENEROUS TABLESPOON CACAO POWDER

¼ TEASPOON CINNAMON

¼ TEASPOON VANILLA POWDER OR EXTRACT

A PINCH OF SALT

A PINCH OF CAYENNE PEPPER (OPTIONAL, FOR THE BRAVE!)

2 SQUARES OF YOUR FAVORITE DARK OR RAW CHOCOLATE BAR (OPTIONAL, FOR CHOCOHOLICS ONLY)

Blend the nut milk, mesquite, coconut butter, cacao, cinnamon, vanilla, and salt in a blender until smooth. Add the cayenne if you're feeling adventurous. Pour the mixture into a small saucepan, cover, and heat gently over low heat until warmed. Add the chocolate bar (if using) and continue to simmer until the chocolate is melted and the mixture is rich and velvety. Pour into a mug.

Tips: Add more chocolate if you want it to be thicker (and don't have any plans to sleep in the imminent future) or more milk for a lighter, more liquid texture.

For haute chocolat with a "marshmallow" froth, make homemade nut milk according to the instructions on page 2, and pour it into a tall glass or jar. The froth will migrate to the top, and you can scoop it up to add to your hot chocolate.

Macaccino!

This macanificent milkshake is a wonderful way to balance hormones, which can often be out of whack in the cold, dark winter months. It's so invigorating, but also warming and uplifting. Have this in the morning instead of coffee for all-day energy!

SERVES 1

1 CUP (250 ML) BRAZIL NUT MILK, HOMEMADE (SEE PAGE 2) OR STORE-BOUGHT

1 TEASPOON MESQUITE POWDER

½ TEASPOON MACA POWDER*

¼ TEASPOON CINNAMON

♥ ½ TEASPOON FRESH GINGER OR GROUND GINGER (OR TO TASTE)

¼ TEASPOON VANILLA POWDER OR EXTRACT

*Go slowly with maca. If you are already a macaddict, feel free to add as much as you'd like here, but if you're just starting out, try ⅛ to ¼ teaspoon and work your way up. I recommend the gelatinized form of maca—it's much easier to digest and more potent. Maca is often sold in raw form in the United States, but that's not how it's traditionally eaten in Peru.

Blend all ingredients in a high-speed blender. Pour into a tall glass or glass jar. The froth from the milk will migrate naturally to the top of the glass or jar. Use a spoon to scoop up the frothy, creamy layer and set it aside. Add the rest to a small saucepan, cover, and heat until warm. Pour into a mug, coffee cup, or teacup and top with the froth.

For a quick boost of energy any time of day, add just ½ to 1 teaspoon maca powder to your smoothie or snack, or even to oil for a sweet salad dressing.

Maca is an energy powerhouse, but not faux energy like coffee—we're talking energy that will last all day long—and all night long, if you know what I mean. Don't know what I mean? Well, here we go: Maca is a libido-boosting superfood that will get you in the mood for love. So whether you choose to eat it cold or warm it up, things will definitely be heating up!

Matchai Tea Latté

Continents converge in this delicious drink that blends Ayurvedic spices with traditional Japanese matcha tea. This is a great alternative to coffee—it will wake up your body and your taste buds in the morning and nourish you at the same time!

SERVES 1

♥ 1 CUP (250 ML) ALMOND MILK, HOMEMADE (SEE PAGE 2) OR STORE-BOUGHT
1 TABLESPOON COCONUT BUTTER (OR COCONUT OIL)
½ TEASPOON MATCHA POWDER
¼ TEASPOON CINNAMON
A PINCH OF CARDAMOM
A PINCH OF NUTMEG
A PINCH OF CLOVES
♥ ¼ TEASPOON GROUND GINGER OR MINCED FRESH GINGER (OR TO TASTE)
¼ TEASPOON VANILLA POWDER OR EXTRACT

Blend all ingredients in a blender or shaker. Warm slowly over the stove in a small pot. If the matcha starts to clump up, you can add the mixture back to the blender and blend until smooth or mix quickly with a whisk or spoon.

MATCHA TEA
Energy in green powder form

Matcha is such an amazing source of energy, the kind of energy that lasts for an extended period of time, unlike the caffeine rush à la coffee. Ancient samurai warriors drank this tea before combat, but it's also a great weapon against stress since it is rich in L-theanine, an amino acid that gives a sensation of calm and aids with concentration.

Matcha is rich in antioxidants and also in catechins, which fight against free radicals and protect against cancer. Matcha boosts the metabolism and can either aid weight loss by helping to burn calories or help give an appetite to those with digestion problems. Yes, it's a matcha made in heaven!

Turmerilkshake

This anti-inflammatory drink is my favorite before-bedtime healing beverage or gentle wake-up on a cold morning (see a photo with Avocado Tartines on page 43). The gorgeous orange spice swirled with fluffy white nut milk crème is a sight for sore eyes, and the ginger, cinnamon, and turmeric are the best remedy for a sore body or belly.

SERVES 1

♥ 1 CUP (250 ML) ALMOND MILK, HOMEMADE (SEE PAGE 2) OR STORE-BOUGHT
¼ TEASPOON CINNAMON
♥ ¼ TEASPOON TURMERIC, PLUS MORE FOR GARNISH
♥ ¼ TEASPOON GROUND GINGER (OR MORE IF YOU LIKE IT SPICY OR HAVE A COLD/FLU!)
♥ 1 TABLESPOON COCONUT BUTTER (OR COCONUT OIL)

Blend all ingredients in a high-speed blender until smooth and creamy. Allow it to sit for 1 to 2 minutes, until the foam floats to the top. With a spoon, scoop out 1 to 2 tablespoons of the froth and set aside. Add the rest of the mixture to a small saucepan and warm gently over the stove. Just before serving, top with the froth and another sprinkle or *deux* of turmeric powder and mix just once with a spoon. This is milkshake art at its finest.

A Few of My Favorite Green Things

The quality of the products that we put inside and onto our bodies is always important, but especially in green cuisine, where food is medicine. *Voilà*: a list of my favorite products to stock your pantry. Most can be found in stores or ordered online. These are the products I typically use in the recipes, so if you are using different products, you may need to adapt the recipes accordingly. Here are my favorite products and brands, but I like to interchange! (You like your favorite pair of jeans, but you don't wear them every day, do you? Mix things up!) I'm always discovering new green things I love every day, so make sure to stay connected on my site lafleurparisny.com for *le* scoop!

MATCHA:
Got Matcha | gotmatcha.com

TAHINI AND NUT BUTTERS:
Dastony | dastony.com

NUTS (RAW AND SPROUTED):
Living Nutz | livingnutz.com

MUNG BEAN (AND OTHER BEAN-BASED) NOODLES:
Explore Asian | explore-asian.com

MISO:
South River Miso (I use the white chickpea miso in most recipes) | southrivermiso.com

HEMP SEEDS:
Happy Hemp | happy-hemp.com

CHIA SEEDS:
The Chia Co. (I use white chia in most recipes) | thechiaco.com.au

GRAINS/LEGUMES AND SPROUTED GRAINS/LEGUMES (SPROUTED QUINOA, GREEN LENTILS, BROWN RICE, AND MORE):
Tru Roots | truroots.com

SUPERFOODS (MULBERRIES, GOLDENBERRIES, GOJI BERRIES, CACAO, MACA, AND MORE!):
Navitas Naturals | navitasnaturals.com

VANILLA POWDER, MESQUITE POWDER, AND OTHER SUPER SUPERFOODS:
Wilderness Poets | wildernesspoets.com

COCONUT OIL, MATCHA POWDER, GULA JAVA COCONUT SUGAR, SPICE BLENDS, OIL BLENDS AND MORE!:
Aman Prana | www.noble-house.tk

ESSENTIAL OILS:
Young Living | youngliving.org

SPICES:
Simply Organic or Frontier Co-op | simplyorganic.com | frontiercoop.com

COCONUT OIL, COCONUT MANNA, AND HEMP AND CHIA PRODUCTS:
Nutiva | nutiva.com

PROTEIN POWDER:
Sprout Living or Epic Protein | sproutliving.com

COCONUT WATER:
Harmless Harvest | harmlessharvest.com

TRÈS CHIC WHOLE-LEAF TEAS, CERAMIC TEA ACCESSORIES AND PAPER GOODS:
Paper and Tea | paperandtea.com

TEAS AND HERBAL BLENDS:
Lov Organic, Organic India, Yogi Tea, and Traditional Medicinals | us.lov-organic.com | organicindia.com | yogiproducts.com | traditionalmedicinals.com

COCONUT AMINOS:
Coconut Secret | coconutsecret.com

COCONUT MEAT (AND WATER):
Exotic Superfoods | exoticsuperfoods.com

APPLE CIDER VINEGAR (AND OTHER RAW, HIGH- QUALITY PRODUCTS FOR COOKING AND SEASONING):
Bragg's | bragg.com

GLUTEN-FREE OATS, GRAINS, AND BAKING PRODUCTS:
Bob's Red Mill | bobsredmill.com

MACA POWDER (AND CAMU POWDER):
Whole World Botanicals | wholeworldbotanicals.com

CHOCOLATES:
Fine & Raw (& green & chic!) | fineandraw.com

Très Green, Très Clean, Très Chic Cheat Sheet

Bien sûr, I always recommend homemade versions of everything, but there's not always time, I know! Here are a few already-made, but Rebecca-approved products!

ANCIENT GRAIN GRANOLA, COOKIE AND PANCAKE MIXES, AND HOT CEREAL:
Purely Elizabeth | purelyelizabeth.com

COCONUT YOGURT:
Anita's coconut yogurt | anitas.co

GLUTEN-FREE BREADS (RICE-MILLET AND SPROUTED FOR LIFE GF ARE MY FAVORITES):
Food For Life | foodforlife.com

GREENS POWDERS:
Aloha (use code Greenchic for a 10% discount) | aloha.com

Healthy Kitchen

LE HAUT DE GAMME OF GREEN LIVING! IN-COUNTER STEAMER, INDUCTION AND ELECTRIC COOKTOPS, CAST-ROASTER GRIDDLE, COMBI-STEAM OVENS, TEPPAN YAKI GRIDDLE, AND THE FINEST REFRIGERATORS IN THE WORLD:
Gaggenau | gaggenau.com

THE BLENDER OF ALL BLENDERS—YOUR NEW BEST FRIEND AS YOU EMBRACE A HEALTHY LIFESTYLE:
Vitamix | vitamix.com

APPLIANCES (FOOD PROCESSOR, TOASTER, SLOW COOKER, AND MORE!):
KitchenAid | kitchenaid.com

JUICER:
Breville | brevilleusa.com

PORTABLE WATER FILTER:
Soma | drinksoma.com
Whirlpool EveryDrop | everydropwater.com

INCREDIBLE (AND SUSTAINABLE!) COOKING AND EATING TOOLS:
Eating Tools | eatingtools.com

Voilà: some spots in Paris and NYC that have my *très* green, *très* clean and *très* chic stamp of approval.

Eat and Drink

UNITED STATES:

The Fat Radish, New York, NY | thefatradishnyc.com
Pure Food and Wine, New York, NY | oneluckyduck.com/pages/pure-food-and-wine
Angelica Kitchen, New York, NY | angelicakitchen.com
The Butcher's Daughter, New York, NY | thebutchersdaughter.com
Blue Hill NYC/Stone Barns Farm, New York, NY | bluehillfarm.com
Sun In Bloom, New York, NY | suninbloom.com
Candle Café and Candle 79, New York, NY | candlecafe.com | candle79.com
Hu Kitchen, New York, NY | hukitchen.com
Jennifer's Way, New York, NY | jennifersway.org
M.A.K.E., Santa Monica, CA | matthewkenneycuisine.com/hospitality/m-a-k-e-santa-monica/
La Cabana, The Four Seasons, Los Angeles, CA (vegan options!) | fourseasons.com/losangeles/
Café Gratitude, Los Angeles, CA (vegan) | cafegratitude.com
Sweetgreen, multiple locations, USA | sweetgreen.com
Le Pain Quotidien, multiple locations, USA/France | lepainquotidien.com

PARIS, FRANCE:

Chambelland bakery (incredible vegan, gluten-free bread!) | chambelland.com
L'Arpège (French capital of vegetables) | alain-passard.com
Alain Ducasse at Le Plaza Athenée (vegan upon request—so many grains and vegetables!) | alain-ducasse.com/en/restaurant/alain-ducasse-au-plaza-athénée
Café de Flore (for people-watching and Mariage Frères tea) | cafedeflore.fr
Ze Kitchen Galerie (vegan upon request) | zekitchengalerie.fr

The Merci Canteen (vegan friendly) | merci-merci.com

Café Pinson (vegan!) | cafepinson.fr

Rose Bakery (vegan-friendly)

Pousse-Pousse (vegan and raw options) | poussepousse.eu

Café Charlot (people-watching and organic tea) | cafecharlotparis.com

Bob's Kitchen/Juice Bar/Cold Press/Bake Shop (vegan-friendly and friendly in general) | bobsjuicebar.com

Sol Semilla (vegan and packed with superfoods!) | sol-semilla.fr

OTHER GREEN-FRIENDLY SPOTS:

La Palme d'Or Cannes, France (vegan upon request) | cannesmartinez.grand.hyatt.com/en/hotel/dining/la-palme-dor.html

Es Saadi Gardens and Resort, Marrakesh, Morocco (paradise for mind and body in one of the most beautiful cities in the world, complete with an all-organic slow food restaurant with their own vegetable garden!) | essaadi.com

Green, Clean, Chic To-Go

UNITED STATES:

Sakara Life: A healthy, organic (and vegan and gluten-free!) meal delivery service on the East Coast | Sakaralife.com

Lulitonix, NYC: Blends with (health!) benefits | lulitonix.com

Heartbeet Juicery, New York, NY | heartbeetjuicery.com

Juice Press, New York, NY | juicepress.com

FRANCE:

Nubio (cold-pressed juice) | nubio.fr

Bojus (cold-pressed juice) | bojus.fr

Move

Strala Yoga, New York, NY | stralayoga.com

Elena Brower, New York, NY | elenabrower.com

Le Klay, Paris, France | klay.fr

Marc Holzman | marcholzman.com

Tout ça Pour ça/Mika de Brito and Sidonie Silliart | toutca-pourca

Rasa Yoga, Paris, France | rasa-yogarivegauche.com

Equinox, New York, NY | equinox.com

Beyoga, Paris, France | beyoga.fr

Big Apple Yoga, Paris, France | bigappleyogafrance.com

Atelier Marais, Paris, France | atelier-marais.fr

Yoga Montclair, Montclair, NJ | yogamontclair.com

Yoga on a boat on the Seine with Cassandra Kish, Paris, France | vidyaayogaparis.com

Take Care of You

The "calm mind" massage at the Mandarin Oriental, NYC | mandarinoriental.com/newyork/

A manicure/pedicure at Ten Over Ten salon, NYC | tenoverten.com

A manicure /pedicure by Kure Bazaar in Paris | kurebazaar.com

Grocery Shop

NEW YORK:

Union Square Greenmarket: Shout out to my market faves: Two Guys from Woodbridge (best microgreens on the planet), Windfall Farms, Tweefontein Herb Farm (fantastic all-purpose spice blend "Herbes de Tweefontein"), Hawthorne Valley (the sexiest sauerkraut) | grownyc.org/greenmarket/manhattan-union-square-m

Forager's | foragerscitygrocer.com

Westerly Natural Market | westerlynaturalmarket.com

Integral Yoga Natural Foods | integralyoganaturalfoods.com

Whole Foods | wholefoodsmarket.com

Life Thyme Market | lifethymemarket.com

PARIS:

Marché Raspail Organic market (Sundays): Shout out to my market faves: Hermione and her homegrown herbs, KALE galore thanks to the *végolutionary* thekaleproject.com, Epibio épicerie, C'bio, Au Coin Nature . . .

Marché Batignolles (Saturdays)

Biocoop, particularly Welcome Bio | biocoop.fr | welcomebio.fr

La Rûche qui Dit Oui (CSA) | laruchequiditoui.fr

ONLINE ANYWHERE:

oneluckyduck.com

rawguru.com

Happy Places

For some fresh air or an escape from reality.

The Luxembourg Gardens, Paris, France

Pierce Camp Birchmont, Wolfeboro, NH
The Soho House, New York, NY
Le Jardin des Plantes, Paris, France
Les Jardins de Courance, France
La Maison de Dr. Hauschka, Paris, France

Positive Fashion

These brands are the epitome of *le* green chic—they use earth-friendly materials, give back to the world, and/or have a really positive message. Oh, and they happen to be *très* glam!

EKYOG, France | ekyog.com

Anthropologie, USA | anthropologie.com

Satya Jewelry, New York, NY | satyajewelry.com

Merci, Paris, France | merci-merci.com

YUJ Yoga, France | yuj.fr

Madewell, USA | madewell.com

Live the Process, USA | livetheprocess.com

ABC Carpet and Home, New York, NY | abchome.com

Stella McCartney, everywhere | stellamccartney.com

TOMS, everywhere | toms.com

Warby Parker, USA | warbyparker.com

Manduka, USA | manduka.com

Yoga Concept, Paris, France | yogaconcept.com

Troy Cloth and Paper Co., USA | troyclothandpaper.com

V-Keen, USA | v-keen.com

Reminder to live in the present: NOW watch | stealtimeback.com

Beauty from the Outside In:

Dr. Hauschka (all-natural face washes, exfoliators, and crèmes de la crèmes!) | drhauschka.com

Les douces angevines (the secret to Marion Cotillard's glowing skin and my little secret from France, too) | lesdoucesangevines.com

Kure Bazaar ("the good nail philosophy"—85% natural polishes in vibrant colors) | kurebazaar.com

Tata Harper (Farm-to-skin fabulousness fresh from Vermont!) | tataharperskincare.com

Uslu Airlines (less toxic nail polish in fabulous colors) | usluairlines.com

Osmia Organics (soaps, serums, and glosses all made by hand and with love in Colorado) | osmiaorganics.com

Lotus Wei: These pure flower essences transform mood and mind through acupuncture meridians. Flower therapy at its finest. | lotuswei.com

RMS Beauty (the only makeup that will ever touch my skin—*le* best) | rmsbeauty.com

SW Basics of BK (beauty from Brooklyn!) | swbasicsofbk.com

Intelligent Nutrients (organic face, body, and hair products are always the smartest choice) | intelligentnutrients.com

Mio Skincare (fit skin for *la vie*—creams, shapers, serums, oils, butters, and more liquid love for that beautiful bod of yours) | mioskincare.com

Shobha (Sugaring is like waxing, but it's gentler on the skin and, at Shobha, contains only sugar, lemon juice, water, and glycerin.) | myshobha.com

Biologique Recherche (The best mediskin for your face and body. Their facials are life-changing and their P50 toner, lotions and serums are revolutionary.) | http://www.biologique-recherche.com

Healthy Resources Online:

For *très* green, *très* clean, *très* chic mamas- and mamans-to-be: Mama Glow | mamaglow.com

For tips on green living: the Environmental Working Group | EWG.org

Green and chic magazine: *Beauty and Well Being* | beautyandwellbeing.com

Wellness for everyone | mindbodygreen.com

The health scene from NYC to LA | wellandgood.com

Lifestyle-chic | thechalkboardmag.com

Merci Beaucoup (Thank You)

"Let us be grateful to the people who make us happy; they are the charming gardeners who make our souls blossom."
—Marcel Proust

Merci beaucoup . . .

. . . to my parents Beryl and Steve Leffler and my cheese-loving sister Erica who have always supported me and who put up with many meat-free, dairy-free, and gluten-free meals during the making of this book. *Je vous aime beaucoup.*

. . . to my grandmother and her grandmother and her grandmother and my grandfather (who owned his own food shop) and his father (a baker!), who, from generation to generation, have shared their love for cooking, scents, and tastes that remind me of my childhood, my own little "Proust Madeleines." They've proven that *l'amour* is indeed the most important ingredient.

. . . to my friends from Paris to NYC and all across the world who always give me the most important ingredient: laughter! And especially those who have been there for me during the more delicious and less delicious times in my life.

. . . to Coralie Miller who put this book bun in the oven from the start and who learned to speak fluent "Rebecca" in the process. I'll always be grateful to you, *chère* Coralie.

. . . to Marabout, particularly Agnès, Hélène, and Laure, for having confidence in me and in this project from the start and for helping me to spread *la végolution* in France.

. . . to Sandra Mahut, the best photographer in the universe, who managed to capture my world through the magical lens of her camera.

. . . to Cara Bedick for bringing this project across the Atlantic.

. . . to The Experiment's Matthew, Dan, Karen Giangreco, and Sarah Schneider, plus Pauline Neuwirth & Co, for turning my little "experiment" with healthy living into a beautiful and delicious American book.

. . . to Molly Cavanaugh for doing a marvelous job editing this book, making sure nothing was "lost in translation," and keeping my punning under control. You've been a joy to work with!

. . . to Professor John Rassias, thanks to whom I left NY for Paris more than ten years ago to follow my dreams and whose vivacious spirit continues to inspire me every day.

. . . to the yogis and yoginis who have brought so much light into my life on so many levels and who have taught me so many things on and off the mat: Elena Brower, Marc Holzman, Tara Stiles, Carol Issa, Anne Vandewalle, Cassandra Kish, Michael Taylor, Humberto Cruz, Anna Gannon, Kati Rediger, Sandrine Bridoux, Heidi Kristoffer, Jes Allen, Omni Kitts Ferrara, Joe Gandarillas, Mika De Brito . . .

. . . to the health professionals who have taught me about the mind-body connection and the importance of living *la vie en* green: Dr. Leo Galland, Dr. Mark Hyman, Ani Phyo, Dr. Marie-Laure Bigot, David Wolfe, Sarah Britton, Gena Hamshaw, Laetitia Cerou . . .

. . . to the chefs, restaurants, and food writers who have kept me well-nourished in France and the USA: Jean-Charles and Rose Carrarini and the Rose Bakery staff, Sébastien Gaudard, Sarma Melngailis, Christian Sinicropi, William Ledeuil, Alain Ducasse, Alain Passard, Elenore Bendel Zahn, Lawrence Aboucaya . . .

. . . to Roger Sorrentino for showing me the art of *la gourmandise* and for sharing his passion for life, culture, and especially food with all Lefflers.

. . . to my fearless recipe testers! Emma Potts, Eve Lynch, Robin Deliso, Clare Gupta, Clémence Moulaert, Elsa Reiss, Rachel Reiss Buckley, Samantha Bassler, L. Francesca de la Torre, and more!

. . . to you, *mes chers* readers, for embarking on this green adventure with me. I hope that this book will, even in a small way, change your life like mine was transformed once I started living *la vie en* green.

. . . to the lemons. Because without them, this book would not exist.

Index

About the Author

Rebecca Leffler is an author, journalist, and consultant who, after a long career in entertainment as France Correspondent for *The Hollywood Reporter* and film critic on the French TV network Canal+, has traded the red carpets of Paris for the green streets of New York. Rebecca hosts "Green, Clean, and Chic" events in New York and Paris on both a public and corporate level and is an expert in branded entertainment and communication for wellness brands.